INTRODUCTION 3

A word to those of you who came in late: Instructions on decoding volumes in this series are given in **Footsore 1** and will not be repeated here. Also, for lessons in snowline-probing and how to learn to stop worrying and love clearcuts, see **Footsore 2**. Space thus is saved for a bit of basic training in beachwalking.

"Good grief!" one exclaims. "Next you'll be teaching us how to breathe. What's to learn about walking beaches?"

Well, to start, you'll play heck trying to walk a beach if there isn't any. And if there is, you can't fully appreciate what you're seeing if you don't know what you're looking at. So, read on.

(But first note: Trips in this volume were originally surveyed in the fall-winter-spring of 1977-78. The situation was rechecked and some changes made in the spring of 1981, and several more in the summer of 1983. Revisions will be made in future editions as required by the ever-trammeling hand of man. If you wish to assist by bringing blunders to the surveyor's attention, please address your denunciations c/o The Mountaineers. Never be kind to guidebook writers—it only encourages them.)

WHAT THAT OLD GLACIER DID

Four *glaciations* by the Juan de Fuca and Puget Lobes of the Cordilleran Ice Sheet, which in the Pleistocene Epoch invaded from Canada, have been identified in Western Washington lowlands. First were the Orting and Stuck Glaciations, of unknown dates (but less than 2-3 million years ago); their handiwork has been obscured by successors. The Salmon Springs Glaciation culminated prior to 38,000 years ago with a maximum reach 15-20 miles south of Olympia. After the Olympia Interglaciation came the Fraser Glaciation, with two *stades* (intervals of advance). Between 15,000 and 13,500 years ago, during the first, the Vashon Stade, Seattle was under 4000 feet of ice. (Maximum ice depth in the Bellingham area was about 7000 feet; Olympia, about 1200 feet; the terminus, 100 feet.) The glacier pushed beyond the Nisqually River but stayed only briefly in its southernmost extension and Vashon drifts thus are scanty there. The Everson Interstade was succeeded by the Sumas Stade of 11,000 years ago; this time the Canadian ice barely got over the border.

Only in several areas does hard rock outcrop on **Footsore** shores, which mainly are of *glacial drift,* a term inclusive of all materials transported by the ice. An *erratic* is a boulder that rode the glacier until ultimately dumped. *Till* is an unsorted mixture of particles of every size from clay to boulders; the concrete-like "hardpan" characteristically erodes into vertical walls. Most drift has been sorted by meltwater, *sand* and *gravel* deposited by water of lesser or greater velocity in river beds and deltas, *clay* settling out in lakes from ice-milled rockmilk. In places there is *loess*, sandy deposits that appear to have been laid down by water but in fact came from winds blowing over barren wastes of glacial outwash plains.

Fraser-Vashon drift, the most abundant from the Seattle vicinity north, is unconsolidated and new-looking where it dates from the time of glacial retreat, more compacted from the time of advance, having been overridden by the ice

3

sheet. Whether a layman can readily distinguish the older Vashon drifts from the Salmon Springs is debatable. However, he will frequently observe old-looking drift, more compacted (by weight of later ice) or even folded or faulted, often somewhat cemented by yellow-orange iron oxides, getting along toward becoming mudstones, shales, sandstones, and conglomerates; cliffs of this "nearly rock" may be quite tall and vertical.

The walker also sees beds of matted leaves and twigs, usually somewhat oxidized toward a carbon black but containing branches and logs, cedar bark and fir cones, that appear to have come from the woods mere months ago.

A surveyor of the mountain front cannot comprehend the terrain ("island" peaks, riverless valleys) without knowing there once was a Really Big River, maybe two or three times the volume of today's Columbia, the sum of all the mountain rivers thwarted from direct seaward courses by the northern wall of ice stretching across the Puget Trough from Olympics to Cascades. Forced southward along the ice margin, Really Big eventually attained the ocean via the valley of today's Chehalis.

Similarly, a surveyor of inland-sea beaches must realize that the glacier caused ups and downs of the water surface and thus the shore location. First, the ice wall from range to range dammed freshwater Lake Russell, which to empty south to the Chehalis River had to fill to a height substantially above modern Puget Sound. The trained eye thus discerns, at various levels above today's beaches representing various levels of the old lake, the flats of old bay floors/lakebeds, the steeps of wave-cut cliffs.

Then, when the ice front retreated north and let the salt flow in, there wasn't as much water as now, much of the world's supply being locked up in continental glaciers. As these melted, sealevel rose some 200 (or 300?) feet from the Pleistocene minimum, reaching today's approximate level about 6000 years ago. Above the beachwalker are one or more fossil shores; below, unseen under the water, is a drowned shore. Old valleys also have been drowned; arms of the sea invade inland as *estuaries*. The rivers, however, fight back, dumping loads of sediment that invade the sea as *deltas*.

Finally, in some places the land, released from its burden of ice, has risen in recent eons, enough for old beaches to be elevated several feet or many above today's beaches.

HOW BEACHES GET HOW THEY ARE

The *coast* is an indefinite strip landward from shore. The *shore* is the narrow zone between low-tide shoreline and high-tide shoreline. The *shoreline* is the intersection of water and land.

The chief agents in eroding the shore are wind-generated *waves* that carve *wave-cut cliffs* whose debris forms *beaches* of cobbles, gravel, and sand. Waves that strike the shore obliquely have a component of motion along the shore; the resulting *longshore currents* transport materials, depositing some on beaches, using some to build *spits* and *bars*. In any locality the orientation of spits and bars is determined by the direction of the dominant longshore current, a resultant of the dominant winds and the orientation of the shore. (*Tidal currents* go back and forth and accomplish relatively little constructive.)

As waves erode inland the beach widens. The retreating cliff leaves behind a *wave-cut bench,* a platform of rock (or, in most of our area, drift) usually

4

FOOTSORE 3

Walks & Hikes Around Puget Sound

By Harvey Manning/Photos by Bob & Ira Spring
Maps by Gary Rands/The Mountaineers • Seattle

*Stillaguamish River • Skagit River • Puget Sound
Trail – Everett to Bellingham • The Northern
Isles • North Kitsap and Olympic Peninsulas*

The Mountaineers: Organized 1906 "to explore, study, preserve and enjoy the natural beauty of the Northwest."

Copyright © 1978, 1981, 1983 by Harvey Manning
All rights reserved

Published by The Mountaineers,
715 Pike Street, Seattle, Washington 98101

Published simultaneously in Canada by
Douglas & McIntyre, Ltd., 1615 Venables St.,
Vancouver, British Columbia V5L 2H1

Manufactured in the United States of America
First edition, October 1978; revised May 1981, September 1983

Library of Congress Catalog Card No. 77-23727
ISBN 0-916890-65-1

Designed by Marge Mueller
Cover photo: City of La Conner and Swinomish Channel with
Mt. Baker in distance, taken from highway bridge to Fidalgo
Island. This view is a worthwhile sidetrip from the
McGlinn Island walk.

Deception Pass from Bowman Bay trail

covered with sand and gravel that gradually are moved seaward by the *undertow* and dumped in deep water, forming a *wave-built terrace,* at whose outer edge is the dropoff that wading children are warned against.

Driftwood at Cavelero Beach County Park

Width of the bench and terrace and thus the beach they constitute depends partly on how long the waves have been at it; the inland sea isn't old enough for much erosion of hard-rock shores and that's why there's so little beachwalking in such places as the San Juan Islands and the west side of Hood Canal.

Beach width also depends on vigor of the waves, which depends on strength of the wind. Weather shores (in our area, mainly south and west) tend to have the wider beaches, lee shores (north and east) the narrower; in fiordlike estuaries the wave action on all shores may be so feeble the beach is mere inches wide. Beaches of protected shores with meek waves are uncleanly green: trees typically lean horizontally far over and close to the beach; fallen logs are not churned around and abraded to splinters or floated away, they just lie placidly where they fall, growing seaweed and barnacles. Walking such beaches, narrow and perhaps steep, cobbles and gravel weed-slimy, can be a misery of slithering and brushfighting and log-crawling and pulling seaweed out of your hair.

Not all shores have beaches. Rock cliffs may plunge directly into deep water. Delta *saltmarshes* may merge with bay-bottom *tideflats;* some of these vast low-tide expanses of sand or mud, also found in shallow bays perhaps rimmed by skinny beaches, can be walked (gucky, ooky, best done in hip-length rubber boots, slowly) a long way from shore, far out in birdland.

As wave-cut bench plus wave-built terrace grow, the widening beach may become *"complete."* Above regularly-washed sands and gravels a *driftwood line* of logs is thrown up by big storms and remains untouched by ordinary high tides, perhaps jostled once or twice a decade. Behind the driftwood is a sand ridge rising above the high-tide shoreline, a *dune line* of particles blown from sun-dried beach. Though usually not resembling the classic marching dunes of deserts, being mostly vegetation-anchored, the sand ridge encloses a shallow *lagoon:* this may be freshwater, fed by a creek or seepage, may dry in summer, may be partly a freshwater marsh; or it may be tidal, connected to the sea by a channel, may be sometimes tideflat, may be partly saltmarsh; normally a lagoon holds a raft of old, bleached driftwood cast up by big storms.

A longshore current picks up material when it hits the shore, drops material when it runs out in deep water and loses momentum. When a current manages to fill an offshore area, creating a shallows, breaking waves then build an *offshore bar* that may be raised above the normal high-tide line by storm tides and ultimately connected to the shore, enclosing a lagoon — another route to a complete beach.

Longshore currents work to straighten out shores, by this process: When the shore bulges abruptly out or curves abruptly in, the currents tend to keep going straight, soon losing momentum in deep water and dropping loads. Thus *spits* are built. When one terminates in open water, it forms a *point.* When it connects mainland to an island, the latter becomes a *tombolo.* When a spit reaches across an indentation and intersects the shore, it closes off a lagoon — still another route to a complete beach. When a spit pushes across the mouth of a bay and nearly or completely closes it off, it's called a *baymouth bar* — here are the great big lagoons, marshes, dredged boat basins, fancy yacht-and-mansion subdivisions, ecological disasters.

WHY THE TIDE WAITS NOT

Understanding the mechanism of tides is not essential to beachwalking; caused by the moon (most important) and sun (very helpful), they are shaped by some 250 factors only digestible by a computer. But the habits of tides are easily observed — and jolly well had better be if a walker doesn't care to become an involuntary surfer or cliff-clamberer.

Of the several types that occur around the world, our inland sea has a *mixed tide,* with two high-low cycles in a period of approximately 24 hours and 50 minutes (so, each day the tides are about 50 minutes later than the day before); alternate highs are nearly equal and lows very unequal, or vice versa.

A tide is not, as commonly imagined, a ridge of water dogging the moon around the globe, but an up-and-down, thus in-and-out, motion in a tide basin, in our case the Pacific Ocean. The tide enters and leaves the inland sea mainly through the Strait of Juan de Fuca, to a minor extent through the Strait of Georgia. The tides thus are earlier near the ocean. The tide table for Seattle, published in the daily newspapers along with moon phases, is the reference for **Footsore** walkers; to correct for other areas, subtract 30 minutes for Dungeness Spit, 20 minutes for Quimper Peninsula and Whidbey Island's west coast, 10 minutes for Everett; add 6 minutes for Tacoma, 35 minutes for Steilacoom.

The difference on the open ocean between *high water,* the highest level of a tide cycle, and *low water,* the lowest, is much less than on the inland sea, where narrowing shores constrict the tidal current and "pile up" the water. At the mouth of Admiralty Inlet the *mean tide range* (the year's mean of the vertical differences between daily high and low waters) is a meager 4 feet; at Olympia it's a whopping 10.5 feet. At Seattle the daily tide range builds to around 16 feet in June and January, in May and October-November dwindles to as little as 1.7 feet.

Highs and lows vary a lot, depending on the mix of those 250 factors. In a recent year, Seattle's highest forecast highs (14 feet) came in December-January (and slightly less in June-July), the lowest high (7.4) in May (nearly matched in fall). The lowest lows (-3.3) were in June and January, the highest lows (7.2) in December-January-February. As can be seen, some highs are virtually the same as some lows. At Seattle, during a month the highs may vary up or down 4 feet or more, the lows 8 feet or more.

The greatest difference between high and low comes on a *spring tide,* which has nothing to do with the season but occurs twice every month, near new moon and full moon, when sun, moon, and earth are in line. The tide range at Seattle is then as much as 16 feet (a whole lot). The least difference is in a *neap tide,* near the first and last quarters of the moon, when the heavenly bodies are farthest out of line. The tide range at Seattle is then less than 2 feet (hardly anything).

Okay, those are the numbers. Which affect a beachwalk?

First is the *height of the high water.* Since that's how beaches are made, at the highest highs the waves are pummeling the cliff and anybody who gets in the way. Generally, then, when the high forecast for Seattle is 13 or 14 feet, there is going to be dang little beach anywhere on the inland sea. (Note: The forecast tides published in tide tables are the *astronomical tides* created by moon and sun and etc. The actual tides usually are to some extent *meteorological tides,* responding to differences in atmospheric pressure and force of winds and perhaps to a glut of water from flooding rivers; in *"sunshine tides"* with high atmospheric pressure, levels are under the forecast; in *storm tides* the levels may be several feet over the forecast, surprising the heck out of beachdwellers and delta farmers and marina operators and ferryboat captains.) With a forecast of 10 or 11 feet, and good weather, considerable stretches of beach will be easy-open at the high — but will be skinny and have many obstacles, such as bulkheads and fallen trees and pieces of slid-down bluff. With a forecast high of 9 feet or less, most beaches will be mostly negotiable, though some obstacles may remain until the tide ebbs to 7 or 6 feet or less. Except on feeble-wave beaches, at that level the main obstacles may be human constructions.

Second is the *height of the low water.* Feeble-wave beaches are best walked at quite a low level to avoid a brushfight; however, an adjoining exposed mudflat can be a boot-sucking snare and delusion. (Note: The

Beach at Camano Island State Park

mudflat immediately adjoining the beach commonly is a soupy quickmud, while outside that narrow belt the mud/sand is wet and sticky but solid and easy-walking.) Strong-wave beaches may be most effortlessly walked on the wide, firm sands of a wave-built terrace exposed at a very low tide, much easier going than a sloping gravel beach.

Third is the *time of the high water*. In a neap tide the high may be so low there's nothing to worry about. In a spring tide, look out — some of those so-and-so's flood scarily fast and practically climb the cliffs. When it is suspected the beach may be wiped out by the day's high, the better part of valor is to schedule the trip for an outgoing tide. If the high is around 8-10 in the morning, a person can set out then or soon after, and though perhaps forced to clamber the bank a little or crawl over logs or wait a while at obstacles, can journey relaxed and comfortable in the knowledge the beach will grow steadily wider until late afternoon and won't shrink to uncomfortable skinniness until evening; the return will be a cinch. Walking on an incoming tide can be nervous business but is not irrational if the high is low, if the beach will be left well before the high, or if an escape is available leading to a decent overland return.

What do you do if there's no daytime neap or afternoon low? Head for the all-tides-walkable "complete beaches" of benches-terraces, baymouth bars, spits. Or hie yourself to a delta dike or a handy shoreside railroad trail.

WHERE TO FIND A BEACH FOR YOUR FEET

Thanks to easily-eroded glacial drift, most of the inland sea is beach-shored. And thanks to the hiker's pal, that lovely and nearly-omnipresent drift cliff, hundreds of miles of beach are "wild" — that is, the landowners of record are kept at a respectful distance from the water by walls of till and gravel and sand or, even better, clay that is ever on the move, dragging down trees and bushes and houses.

A bluff of 200 feet and more usually is just about a perfect guardian; houses may be atop but probably can't be seen and the residents rarely toil to and from the water. With lower bluffs the owners, though still normally out of sight on high, safely back from the unstable brink, maintain contact with the beach. Studying their means of doing so adds interest to a stroll. There are spiffy electric cablecars, cog railways, tramways, and inclined elevators; two-and-four-storey-tall timber stairways, masterpieces of engineering and carpentry; well-maintained, railing-protected, switchbacking trails; toboggan-slide mud-chute paths; decrepit old staircases missing critical pieces and ending in air, the bottoms torn apart by storm waves; spooky ladders fit only for daring young fools; and even — heaven help us! — rope ladders dangled down overhangs. As the bluff lowers, houses approach the water, but even a bank of a mere dozen feet may shelter the stealthy beachwalker from picture-window eyes. It's when the bluff dwindles to naught that civilization uncomfortably crowds the waves. Near Puget Sound City, few indeed are the unbuilt-on spits and benches, and often bulkheads extend the flats along the bases of bluffs; these are the beach-invading villains that compel an inland detour, a bulkhead scramble, a wade, or a wait for low tide.

If a walker can somehow get on a wild beach he's home free, often for miles. As with kayaking, it's the "put-in" that's the problem. (Unlike a kayaker, a walker isn't too concerned about the "take-out"; infrequently will residents muster with cutlasses to repel boarders.)

What's a good put-in? First, there must be someplace to park. However, this needn't be near the beach — after all, if you're going to be walking a few miles, another ¼ or ½ mile is no sweat. Second, there must be access from road to beach without climbing a fence or walking through somebody's garden or otherwise being a boor.

Contrary to the opinion of the masses, public parks are not necessarily good put-ins; in heavily-populated areas, on summer Sundays the neighbors may be up to here with crowds swarming off the ends of public beaches, they may shout a lot, and gripe to park rangers, and call the police. The same applies, though to a lesser extent, to public street-ends and public boat-launches.

Sometimes a put-in can be made where there is no public access. Examples are a private community boat-launch or swimming beach and a subdivision with as-yet-vacant beach lots. The key to using these is to park a goodly distance — if necessary, ½ mile or more — away. A major agony of beach communities is slobby, thoughtless invaders leaving cars any old place, blocking driveways, clogging narrow streets. If the car is placed considerately and distant, an alien often can walk a private community road to a private boat-launch and onto a private beach with no greeting from the locals but hospitable smiles — if even aware of the alien's presence, they'll usually assume he's some resident's guest.

In the best legal opinion, there is no such thing as a fully "private" beach— every beach is open to *walking*, if done quickly and quietly (no picnicking, clamming, or garbaging). However, for purposes of this book any walking on a privately-owned beach (which means most of the inland sea) is treated as "trespassing." Trespassing never should be attempted except where tolerated. And where is that? Well, in walking hundreds of miles of inland-sea beaches the surveyor rarely was challenged. The reason, aside from niceness of beach residents and a sympathy for humble strangers who like beaches and don't own any, is that were "No Trespassing" to be strictly enforced, not even locals could walk far, each property-owner condemned to forever pace only his petty plot. (In many a beach community there is, in fact, a curmudgeon whose single purpose in a curdled life is to keep neighbors' feet off his sand.)

There definitely is a "toleration season." It cannot be precisely defined, differs from place to place, and must be sensed on the spot, but the elements are clear enough: Toleration is least on a sunny summer Sunday, near major population centers, on heavily built-up beaches; it's greatest in bad weather,

Bonaparte's gull

on weekdays, in winter, at a goodly distance from the masses, on mostly-wild beaches.

During put-in and take-out, and also while passing a row of water-close homes in the course of walking an otherwise-wild beach, a person must adhere faithfully to the Trespassing Code: travel not in mobs but in small groups, the smaller the better; leave the dogs home and also the kiddies if they can't be taught to stifle childish shrieks; be quiet; leave no trash and commit no offenses against sanitation; dig no clams and pick no oysters and gather no souvenirs; build no fires; do not picnic near homes; walk by houses quickly; do not stop to stare at the houses, the boats, the flowers, the sunbathers; walk as far from houses as the waves allow; under no circumstances walk through a yard, even if the tide is high and you must otherwise wade or turn back; if challenged, humbly apologize, politely explain your innocent purpose, and if permission to proceed is denied, go find another beach — there are plenty around.

Yes, beach people are mostly nice. And yes, respectful, discreet trespassers are accepted lots of places the loud-mouthed rowdies aren't. Still, the sanest, kindest, most generous and hospitable of beach folks will turn surly if too much imposed upon. Any private beach has a "carrying capacity" for trespassers; if the capacity is exceeded, the beach will be "destroyed" — closed to all alien walkers in all seasons. Therefore, should you come to a planned put-in and observe others already trespassing, switch to another put-in, another beach. Spread out, don't gang up.

ACKNOWLEDGMENTS 3

As with **1** and **2**, the origins of **3** lie, first, in the lore amassed by thousands of Mountaineers snooping around woods and rivers and beaches for 70-odd years and, second, in the pioneering volume by Janice Krenmayr, **Footloose Around Puget Sound.**

Information was supplied by a number of friendly people in government: Mt. Baker-Snoqualmie National Forest, Don R. Campbell and W. C. Fessel, Jr.; Washington State Parks, William A. Bush, Ralph Mast, Ken Hergeman, John R. Schaffer, and a bunch of nice folks whose names I didn't catch; Department of Natural Resources, Terry Patton; Department of Game, John G. Garrett; Snohomish County Parks, William T. Belshaw, Cory Prentice, and Glen Turner. Data were freely lifted from Dee Molenaar's pictorial landform map of the state of Washington, invaluable for overall orientation. A world of unsuspected wonders was revealed by Les Tracy, ranger of the Fire Mountain Scout Reservation. Ed and John Pollock can be publicly thanked for loyal service as native guides in the Skagit Valley; however, most locals met along the way and taking pity on a lost stranger must be anonymous here, since jotting down their names would've made them nervous.

Of special help in the 1981 recheck were Bob Rose, chairman of the Anacortes Forest Land Advisory Committee; Larry Kay, Washington State Parks; Reed Jarvis, National Park Service; Louis Reed; and folks in State Parks and the Forest Service whose names I didn't catch.

H.M.

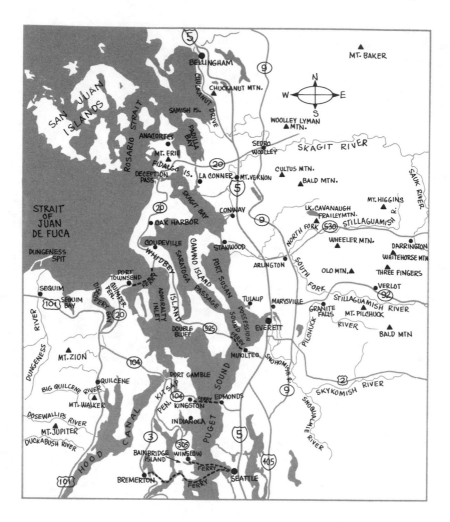

CONTENTS 3

Stillaguamish River near Blue Stilly Park

STILLAGUAMISH RIVER

Drive north from Puget Sound City and the first river entirely beyond urbia-suburbia, and the first north of the Nisqually to meet tidewater in pastoral rather than industrial mode, is the Stillaguamish. Each year hundreds of thousands of folks do indeed drive north and burn millions of gallons of gas flinging vehicles around the Mountain Loop Highway, the most alpinely scenic in the state, and burn tons of rubber pounding lugs and sneakers on famous trails. Indeed, the Verlot-Pilchuck entry to the Mountain Loop is a de facto Cascade Gateway Recreation Area, lacking little but bus service to be a perfect prototype.

Yet only a rather small portion of the province receives proper attention from pedestrians. Not to knock the ever-popular highland gardens, walkers weary of snow piled deep until far into summer ought to try the springtime rambling in sunny tree farms, and the all-year tramping in green glooms of wild-jungled canyons.

In reality two rivers unrelated until issuing from the mountain front, the Stillaguamish has cow-watching and barn-admiring in fields of delta and floodplain, green tunnels in old second-growth, wide-horizon big-sky clearcuts of private and public tree farms, and (gloryosky!) preserved wilderness in Mt. Baker-Snoqualmie National Forest. Of all the river basins close to Puget Sound City, it offers the greatest variety within **Footsore's** stipulated 2-hour round-trip drive.

To introduce the subprovinces, first is the flood plain of the united river from the delta to Arlington, route of the proposed Bays-to-Glaciers Trail whose two branches would proceed up the North Fork to Darrington and on, and up the South Fork to the old Monte Cristo Railroad and on.

Scarcely under-appreciated is the Pilchuck subprovince, whose summit trail and cirque lakes are throngod. Neglected, however, is a full half of the mountain, the south slopes above the Pilchuck River (the River not the Creek; "pilchuck" is Chinook jargon for "red water," or as we call it, "mountain tea," and there's a lot of it around). The question is: why has no government agency been smart enough to reopen the south-slope summit trail, free of white slop months before the north-side trail is suitable for gentlefolk?

Between the forks, westward from the proposed Whitehorse-Three Fingers-Boulder River Wilderness, a subrange of the Cascades thrusts far out in lowlands. Pristine wilderness of the Boulder River contrasts with shelterwood patchcutting by the Forest Service on Green and Meadow, which contrasts with down-to-the-last-bush scalping of Olo, Blue, and Wheeler by Scott Paper Company on its Stillaguamish Tree Farm; this latter jurisdiction not only provides splendid tree-free views but because of the locked-gate policy pretty well excludes razzers, and there's a mercy. West is another contrast, the abrupt edge of the mountains formed by 1770-foot Ebey Hill and 2240-foot Jordan Mountain, whose 1000-foot cliffs plunge directly to pastures; not surveyed for this volume because they presently offer only woods walks, of which there's a plenty hereabouts, these peaks will become famous when Second Wave clearcutting opens up the views.

Between the North Fork and the Skagit River is another peninsula of mountains pushed far out toward saltwater. Stimson-Washington-Frailey, an "island" of peaks cut off by the weird valley occupied by Deer Creek, Lake

Cavanaugh, and Pilchuck Creek (the Creek not the River), is an outstanding opportunity for a city-close, mountain-edge, all-year trail system; horrifying to report, rumor has it the DNR sees this as an opportunity for yet another of its infamous "ATV Parks." North of Weird Valley, the Cultus Mountains feature snowline-probing and highland-roaming and scenery-staring in the vast clearcuts of DNR and Georgia-Pacific tree farms and timber mines.

A hiker shouldn't spend all his time appreciating only the birds and beasts, flowers and trees. The glacial geology of the Stillaguamish is some of the craziest around. To comprehend the landscape, one must visualize the ice overtopping peaks as high as 4000 feet, pushing from the lowlands up such valleys as those of Lake Cavanaugh and Jim Creek, and up the Stillaguamish North Fork nearly to Whitehorse, and up the South Fork far past Pilchuck, dumping all that gravel and clay and till. The observer also must visualize the Big River, carrying as much water as today's Columbia, fed by all the streams of the North Cascades, united in flowing around the ice margin, dodging this way and that, trying to find a way to Aberdeen.

USGS maps: Stanwood, Arlington West, Arlington East, Lake Stevens, Granite Falls, Silverton, Clear Lake, Oso, Fortson, Darrington

Stillaguamish River Upstream To The Forks (Map — page 18, 20)

Once the Sound-To-Mountains Trail (see **Footsore 1**) has firmly set the pattern, then will be time to establish the Bays-To-Glaciers Trail. For the delta segment on shores of Port Susan and Skagit Bays, see the Puget Sound Trail. For the two branches extending iceward from Arlington, see North Fork Stillaguamish River and Monte Cristo Railroad. For what can be done now to sample the inbetween section, read on.

Stanwood to Silvana (Map — page 18)
The 2-mile-wide floodplain features meanders and sloughs and oxbows, cows in green pastures, handsome old farmhouses and barns. The rustic scene is traversed by an excellent trail marked by two parallel steel rails.

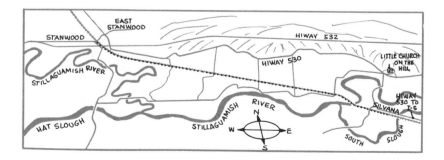

Little White Church on the Hill

Leave I-5 on Exit 208 and drive Highway 530 west to Silvana, elevation 29 feet; park and hit the tracks west. Or, continue driving (pausing to visit the famous Little White Church on the Hill) to Stanwood, elevation 7 feet; park and hit the tracks east. For shorter walks, a half-dozen country lanes off 530 cross the tracks.

Except when the infrequent train passes, the dominant sounds out there in the middle of the plain are birds singing in creek tanglewoods, cows mooing, plows plowing, grass growing.

Round trip up to 11 miles, allow up to 7 hours
High point 29 feet, minor elevation gain
All year

The Island (Map — page 20)

A water-side path on pasture edges and river bars readily could be established the 8 river miles from Silvana to Arlington, but at present the route is cluttered by barbed-wire fences and brush. However, easements purchased by the State Game Department make possible an easy, fairly lengthy walk that samples the section known as The Island, enclosed between the present river channel on the north side of the floodplain and an old one, now occupied by Portage Creek, on the south side.

From Exit 208 on I-5 drive Highway 530 west ¾ mile and turn north on Gulhaugen Road 1¼ miles to the end by the river (beside Exit 208), elevation 40 feet.

The path begins in willow woods, drops to a gravel bar, climbs to a pasture edge. Occasional fences (to keep cows in, not people out) are simply stepped over. On the bluff across the river is a wildwood from which bears emerge to go fishing. According to a camper met by the surveyor, the place is infested by sasquatches, red eyes burning in the black night, nostrils steaming, B.O. sending dogs into hysterics. The broad, green-brown river sweeps along between steep bluff and farmers' riprap, dividing around an island of cottonwoods.

In 1 long mile is private (public camping) Blue Stilly Park and a second Game Department access (from Highway 530 via Strotz Road, ½ mile east of Exit 208). Gravel bars and pastures lead around a bend a final ½ mile to a mean-it fence marking the end of easement.

Round trip 3 miles, allow 1½ hours
High point 40 feet, no elevation gain

The Forks (Map — page 20)

The magnificent sandbar is thronged in season with kiddies building castles, bigger folks swimming in the deep, brown-green, silt-murky pools, and by fishermen.

Drive Highway 9 north in Arlington to the town edge and Haller Bridge Park, elevation 60 feet.

At medium-low water the big bar is walkable downstream ¾ mile. The Dike Road can be walked another 1 mile to the boggling-huge Norwest gravel mine.

In low-enough water one can mosey up the South Fork a ways, and also cross the river and poke around a bit on the North Fork. River forks are geographically significant and ever-amusing.

Round trip 2-4 miles, allow 1½-2½ hours
High point 60 feet, no elevation gain

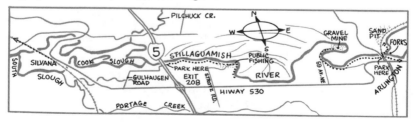

East Arlington Park (Map — page 21)

Among lowland rivers of the region the South Fork Stillaguamish is surpassed for wild excitement only by the famous Green River Gorge. A terrific trail there will or ought to be, someday, the entire great 15 miles from Arlington to Granite Falls, tying to the Monte Cristo Railroad (which see). To see how terrific, sample the excellent stretch in this 200-acre Snohomish County Park.

Drive Highway 530 east (Darrington-ward) ½ mile from the Arlington town-edge bridge and turn right on Jordan Road. In 1 more mile turn right again, again on Jordan Road. In 2¼ more miles cross Jim Creek; just beyond on the right is a parking area-trailhead. However, for the suggested introductory trip, drive on. In ¼ mile is a sign, "East Arlington Regional Park," and the farm-house and barn converted to ranger's headquarters; here is another parking area and trailhead, but drive on, ½ mile more, to another park sign. Here turn right. The park has four levels — four alluvial terraces representing four river eras. From the highway on the topmost level, 209 feet, the entry road drops to a terrace with an old orchard and then drops to a broad field which is crossed to the riverbank, this being the last step down, to the water. Here, ½ mile from the highway, park, elevation 100 feet.

As of 1978 the park is undeveloped, plans being mulled. The one-time farm probably will be made a working farm again so urban children may experience sights and sounds and aromas of the rural past. But there also will be walking to be done, as there is now.

For the introduction, go downstream first, at pasture's edge, home of once and future cows, into alder-cottonwood forest on an undrivable road that ends in ½ mile on a river bar across from a 200-foot wall of glacial clay and till. A fishermen's path proceeds another ½ mile, nearly to Jim Creek; where the terrace pinches out, a rude path ascends to the next level and a good trail linking the other two previously-mentioned trailheads.

Now go upstream, close by the river in the narrowing pasture, ½ mile to the terrace end and park boundary. It's all wild, just trees and water and birds. A path continues and might be walkable another 2 miles or so. Or might not.

If, after this introduction, further exercise is desired, the route of the future perimeter trail can be approximated by following farm lanes and game traces. And by no means ignore the gravel bars.

Introductory round trip 3 miles, allow 2 hours
High point 100 feet, no elevation gain
All year

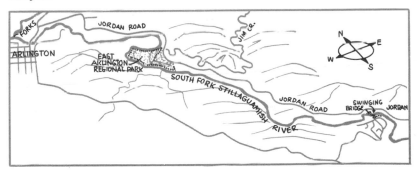

Waterfall on way to Pilchuck Vista

While in the vicinity, don't overlook another prize offered by Snohomish County Parks. Continue upriver on Jordan Road a scant 3 miles to Jordan (a grocery store). Park in the space provided and cross the Jordan Bridge, a swinging footbridge built in 1977 to replace the rotted-out historic structure. The span gives a bouncing walk (don't run) and fine river views; a path leads to a picnic-type gravel bar.

Pilchuck Vista (Map — page 23)

When the summit trail on the north side of Nanga Pilchuck is up to your hiking shorts in snow, as is normally the case until late July, why fight it? Come to the sunny south side of the mountain, where the undrivable old logging road melts out in April, perhaps even March, and climbs to views across the Pilchuck River valley to the Skykomish and on south to Seattle, and out west to Granite Falls and Everett and Port Susan Bay and Whidbey Island, and much more too.

From Highway 2 at Monroe drive north on Woods Creek Road (part of the way signed Yeager Road) 11 miles to a Y where the left goes to Snohomish. Turn right, and in a couple hundred feet right again, following signs for Lake Roesiger Park. Continue 4 miles to the north end of the lake and at the junction there proceed straight. In 2¼ more miles, a long 17 from Monroe, gravel road SL-P-SP-500 makes a reverse turn right. (This spot also can be reached by driving the Monroe highway south 5 miles from Granite Falls; see Littler Pilchuck.) The (unsigned) "Sultan Basin Road," as some maps mysteriously call it, follows the Pilchuck River upstream. At 4 miles from the blacktop is a Y, 706 feet; go left, uphill, climbing very steeply from the river, on SL-SP-510. In 1½ miles is a Y; make the reverse turn right, climbing even more steeply. In a scant ½ mile, a total 6 miles from the highway, is a Y. Park here, elevation 1600 feet.

The newer road (SL-P-519) climbing left is to on-going logging; the older,

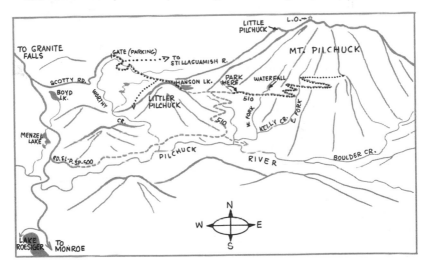

narrow road contouring right, SL-P-SP-510, is the hiking route. Until such time as it is improved for more logging, it will be impassable to four-wheelers at no great distance from the Y; the very low beer-can count indicates razzers, too, are rare.

The way ascends eastward across steep slopes of Pilchuck. In a scant ½ mile is the first joy — the 60-foot waterfall, in a narrow slot, of West Fork Kelly Creek, a cool corner on a warm day, stirring thoughts of showerbaths. Windows in the second-growth open to valley and lowland vistas. In 1 mile more, at 2150 feet, just past a road-obliterating blowout, is dandy East Fork Kelly Creek; a logging spur crosses, but a hundred feet short of the stream, switchback west into a bit of nice virgin forest, recross the blowout, switchback east and west and east again, emerging from greenery into a poorly-restocked clearcut of the early 1950s and the start of wide views. At 2750 feet the road crosses East Fork Kelly Creek, brawling down granite boulders, and climbs to another creek; just before it, switchback west; views become nearly continuous. At 3200 feet is the final switchback, under a granite wall. Going east from here, the way crosses a small marsh flat below a basinlet and ascends to an end on a promontory, 3525 feet, 4½ miles from the car. Climb a few yards up the clearcut to a knoll, marveling at how little the shrubby trees have grown in a quarter-century. This ain't farming, this was a cellulose mine.

From Knoll 3550, close to the uppermost limit of the clearcut, above the gulch of loud Boulder Creek, admire the panorama. Virgin forests rise steeply to the 5324-foot summit; from near here a trail used to go to the top, and ought to be reopened. Below is the Pilchuck River. Across is the amazing plateau where sits Echo Lake, and beyond are Woods Creek valley, Skykomish valley, Monroe, High Rock Hills, Big Haystack, Seattle. Leftward are Pilchuck headwaters and, across the unseen Sultan River, Blue. Rightward are Lake Roesiger, Lake Stevens, farms and hamlets, Everett pulpmills, the Olympics.

Round trip 9 miles, allow 6 hours
High point 3550 feet, elevation gain 2000 feet
April-November

Littler Pilchuck (Map — page 23)

On the absolute westernmost edge of the Cascades, snuggled at the foot of Pilchuck's subsummit, Little Pilchuck, boldly stands the jaunty footstool peaklet of "Littler Pilchuck." Prominent from miles around, it'll become a far-famed all-year viewpoint once some benevolent logger trims obnoxious greenery from the summit. But don't wait. There's plenty to see now from clearcut slopes — pulpmill plumes of Everett, shining waters of Possession Sound. And the stroll has many other nice things, including marsh-meadow-shored Hanson Lake.

Drive Highway 92 to the east edge of Granite Falls. At the stoplight there, turn right on Alder. In three blocks turn left on the backroad highway to Monroe. At a Y in 2 miles, go left on Scotty Road. In 1½ miles pavement ends at a sign, "Scott Paper Stillaguamish Tree Farm." In 2 more miles is a gate. Park here, elevation 720 feet. (Even if the gate is open, do not drive on —

some non-benevolent logger may lock your car in. But don't complain about Scott's gate policy; the exclusion of public vehicles is what makes this a nice quiet footroad, the peace broken only by an occasional logging truck.)

At the Y just beyond the gate go right, across the wide lake-meadow valley of Worthy Creek. On the far side go right. Climb in big second-growth by a noble waterfall, cross and recross and recross Worthy Creek, and emerge into big skies of the tiny-tree plateau. Ahead leaps up the imposing bulk of Pilchuck. Also leaping up, less ambitiously, is 2350-foot Littler Pilchuck.

At all the many junctions stick with the obvious main road, steering toward Littler. At 3 miles from the gate the way reaches its base and a Y. For the view, take the sideroad right, rounding the slopes ¾ mile to a deadend at 1500 feet. See northward to Jordan and Blue and Olo and Green, see west to Everett, the Snohomish estuary, Hat Island, Whidbey Island. From here, or perhaps from Hanson Lake, along about 1980 there ought to be an easy route to the summit of Littler, which by then surely will be scalped.

From the Y the main road proceeds a long ½ mile to Hanson Lake, 1400 feet, with ducks and meadows and a fringe of 5-foot cedars and hemlocks and spruce. Very pretty. A striking contrast to the slope of Pilchuck, which is being denuded expeditiously.

Round trip (viewpoint and lake) 9 miles, allow 6 hours
High point 1500 feet, elevation gain 800 feet
All year

There's a lot more exploring to do on sideroads up the Pilchuck scarp, to an overlook of Lake Julia, and elsewhere. And for an entirely different trip, after crossing the meadow-lake valley bottom of Worthy Creek, take the left fork. From it, spurs lead to other peaklet viewpoints. It is also possible, if not entirely pleasant, to descend precipitously (but perhaps safely) into the Wilderness Gorge of the Stillaguamish and look across to the Monte Cristo Railroad.

Monte Cristo Railroad (Map — page 25, 29)

Even without the railroad the South Fork Stillaguamish upstream from Granite Falls would rank as a chief treasure of the region, the white water of

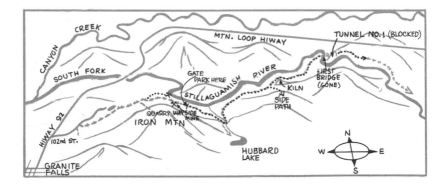

Tunnel No. 6 on the old Monte Cristo Railroad

the wild river churning through the green gorge at the edge of the lowlands, close to Puget Sound City, open to walking the whole year.

But there is (or was) the Everett and Monte Cristo Railway (or, Hartford and Eastern Railroad), a monument to the most colossal mining idiocy in the history of the Northwest. To bring out the gold and silver and other goodies, the railway was built through canyon and forest, reaching Granite Falls in October 1892 and Monte Cristo in August 1893. That winter floods tore out the grade, as other floods did other winters. Rebuilt in 1902, the line was operated with a gasoline-engine car (the "Galloping Goose") through the 1920s, largely for tourist excursions. A flood in 1930 ended that, and in 1936 the track was dismantled, and in 1942 an auto road was completed to Monte Cristo, occupying most of the grade from Verlot upvalley.

However, the 12 miles of rail grade from Granite Falls to Verlot have been pretty much left alone. Artifacts of the awesome engineering feat compete for attention with scenery of the gorge. This is truly Class A material, and may Snohomish County Parks or State Parks preserve it. Even now, with only Divine Providence and Scott Paper Co. as guardians, the route has become a famous prowling ground for history buffs and wildland fans.

Wayside Mine to First Bridge (Map — page 25)

A green-lawn path through wildland forest beside a wild river. Middens from railroad crews. A towering lime kiln and accompanying limestone mine. At the end, stonework and twisted iron of the fallen bridge.

Follow Highway 92 through Granite Falls. From the stoplight on the east edge of town drive north ½ mile and turn right on 102 Street, signed "Gun Club." At the Y in ⅓ mile, go right on the lesser road — the start of the remaining railroad grade. Proceed ¾ mile, by a shingle mill, to a junction where the major road swings uphill right to a quarry and a lesser one drops left to a gravel pit and the least (your way) goes in between.

(As a sidetrip, walk the road left to the gravel pit and on down ¼ mile to the river and an open-mouth mine, worked within the past few years by Ram Mines Inc. Nice spot for a picnic.)

The middle road, which is the old rail grade rebuilt in 1977 as a logging road, is drivable another ½ mile along the precipice to the Wayside Mine and a bit farther to a gate, elevation 380 feet; space for several cars at the gate and several more at the mine. From the gate the new road swings into the valley of Hubbard Creek and ascends to Hubbard Lake and Second-Wave clearcuts. At ⅓ mile from Wayside Mine spot a path down to the creek and across to the trail, maintained by local Scouts.

The lane winds along the gorge in ferns and moss and waterfalls, by garden walls of metamorphic rock, through maples and hemlocks. Rusted saws and kitchenwear, broken glass and rotten lumber, speak of workers on the railroad. A hundred feet below, the river tumbles through giant boulders. A clearcut up above has kindly refrained from invading the wild gorge but has dropped some crawl-over logs onto the grade.

At about 1¼ miles from Hubbard Creek, in the gulch of a lesser creek, the trail forks. The right goes up to a clearcut; drop left. Soon beyond, behold! A tower of great blocks of rock, 25 feet high. Here was cooked the limestone from which was made the lime from which was made the cement from which was

Lime kiln buried in a jungle like a lost Mayan temple

made the railroad. Past the kiln a path climbs to a deep trench in the hillside, the limestone mine.

In another ⅔ mile the grade (overgrown and mucky and obstructed by logs from the clearcut) cuts through a ridge to the bridge site. A very rude path skids 100 feet down by the concrete pier to the river, gray-green water boiling in white rapids around mossy boulders. Across the river is the other pier — and the collapsed mouth of Tunnel No. 1, longest of the bunch, 1500 feet from end to end.

Round trip 5 miles, allow 3 hours
High point 550 feet, elevation gain 250 feet
All year

First Bridge to Tunnel No. 3 (Map — page 29)

From First Bridge upstream 2½ miles to (blocked) Tunnel No. 3 the benefactor Scouts have not as yet improved a trail. Explorers here must be sturdy and indefatigable. Much of a rainy, drippy-brush, salmonberry-slashing, slippery-muck day the surveyor suffered pain, frustration, and humiliation here. He has no guidance to offer. However, new clearcuts have eased the way.

Tunnel No. 3 to Old Robe (Map — page 29)

Here is everybody's favorite tour, the long-famed classic. Tunnels and masonry most vividly preserve memories of the railroad. And the reason for the tunnels is that here the river is its most exciting, a white turmoil in a slot gorge of black cliffs and green jungles. In miles the walk is short, but the archeological riches make for a long day. Scott Paper has logged above with care to leave the wild gorge undisturbed.

Drive Highway 92 east from Granite Falls 7 miles to where the Canyon Creek-Green Mountain Road turns off left. Park on the wide highway shoulder, elevation 1000 feet.

David Ripperger, Eagle Scout of Troop 43, has erected a handsome large brick-and-log sign, "Old Robe Historic Trail," to mark the trailhead. The trail crosses the clearcut and descends a forested hillside to an alluvial terrace, at ¼ mile intersecting a woods road. Turn right and follow the road as it drops to a lower terrace, makes a U-turn upvalley, then a U-turn downvalley. (Here the old rail grade is joined. A grownover lane goes upvalley a short bit to a sidechannel of the river. In low water a person might wade to a causeway — but to little purpose, since Robe Valley starts here and the 1 mile upstream to the site of the Rotary Bridge is built up and PRIVATE KEEP OUT.)

At 1 mile from the highway the woods road ends on the riverbank and the trail proceeds downstream along the edge of a wide, marshy alder bottom. In ⅓ mile the bottom ends and the grade slices into the canyon wall. (Here a sidetrail climbs to rotten boards, a chimney, and a trail to a logging road, an alternate approach from the highway.)

Now the fun! Somewhat subdued above, the river enters a gorge and turns crazy white. Here began the engineering feats, the blasting and concreting, the hole-digging and wall-building. At ¼ mile from the alder bottom is Tunnel No. 6, a spooky cavern 30 feet high and about as wide, 300 feet long, littered with old timbers, ties still set in rock slots.

Returning to daylight, a walker finds the river a tumult of white cataracts, the grade narrow, the gorge wild, the ghosts pushy. A bit farther is Tunnel No. 5,

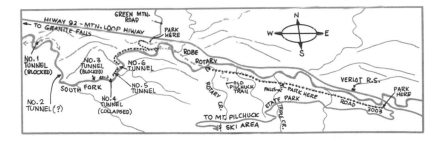

Water cascading down on the Monte Cristo Railroad

100 feet long, the downstream mouth partly blocked. The grade enters a deep cut blocked by a heap of debris (Tunnel No. 4, collapsed) over which the path clambers. Then comes a single concrete span arched over a rock chute plunging to the river, and a decent place to halt, at 800 feet, ½ mile from Tunnel No. 6. The chute demands a couple steps most folks won't care to dare. And anyhow, a few yards on is Tunnel No. 3, blocked, no way through and the exposed trail over the top of the ridge not something to discuss in polite society.

Round trip 4½ miles, allow 5 hours
High point 1000 feet, elevation gain 400 feet

Rotary Bridge to Verlot (Map — page 29)

Across the river from the highway the grade parallels the stream in great green woods, passes beaver marshes and waterfalls, and joy would reign supreme — except that 2 miles of the way are a narrow but well-maintained road. Still, when the road quits there remains a superb stretch of wheelfree walking, so tangled at the end, indeed, as to become virtually free of feet.

Drive Highway 92 to the east end of Verlot and turn right on the Pilchuck State Park Road. Almost immediately turn right again on the Monte Cristo Grade Road. For the longest possible walk, park here, elevation 999 feet.

When crowds of machines aren't razzing and putt-putting by, the road is a grand stroll, close by the river, past a fine waterfall of a nameless creek, a noble rock wall, the stub of the old bridge over to Verlot Campground. Then edging inland, the way goes through silvery alders by a marshy pond fed by waterfalls of Heather Creek. More gorgeous forest, another beavery pond, and at 2 miles, where a sideroad leads right to private lots by the river, the road abruptly narrows. If you've been driving, quit now, elevation 900 feet.

In a few steps is Triple Creek, the bridge a mass of collapsed timbers but the crossing generally a simple hippetty-hop involving naught worse than wet ankles.

(Before crossing, admire the waterfall. Then take the trail uphill 200 feet to an even more admirable falls. Amid intense green of the mossy big-tree underworld, the whiteness of the 40-foot falls dazzles.)

Machetes wielded by Scouts have trenched the salmonberry thickets ½ mile beyond Triple Creek. There the way returns to the river, then thrusts into a great swamp (beavers at work) where are heard the falls of nearby Hawthorn Creek. But as of 1978 (and 1981) the machetes had quit and so did the surveyor.

May the benefactors return with cold steel to finish the slaughter of the brambles. In the scant 1 mile downstream from the swamp will then be added these items of interest: Hawthorn Creek; the short sideroad uphill to what was in 1940 the start of the trail to the summit of Pilchuck; Rotary Creek; the site of the railroad bridge to old Rotary.

Round trip 1 or 3 or 7 miles, allow 1-5 hours
High point 999 feet, minor elevation gain
All year

Heather Lake (Map — page 33)

The trees are the superstars here, the lake merely an extra added attraction — prettiest, indeed, when you can't see it, all covered with snow beneath cirque cliffs dribbling (or thundering) avalanches. Bright are the blossoms of summer but dumfounding in all seasons are the giants of the forest primeval. The trail is popular with snowline-probers, starting as it does from the all-year road to the Pilchuck ski area. What with ice-skaters in early winter, families coming with kids for winter and spring romping, there's probably no weekend of the year that hikers don't visit the lake, so the route generally is boot-beaten and evident. But to repeat, if snow grows too deep or slippery, forget the lake — the trees are what it's all about anyhow.

A shoulder of Mt. Pilchuck overlooking Heather Lake

Drive Highway 92 to the east edge of Verlot and turn right on Pilchuck State Park Road. At 1¼ miles is a large parking area for the Heather Lake trail. The road to this point is open all winter — except when Nature closes it with snow, trees or floods. Elevation, 1350 feet.

The hiker-only (peace!) path follows a logging road of the late 1940s up through tall second-growth. Nearing Heather Creek, in views down to the valley and across to Green and Olo and Three Fingers, the trail quits the old road and switchbacks steeply upward, leaving trees 30 years old for those centuries ancient, leaving the young forest for a system that is, aside from the ages of individual members, 10,000 years old. What a change in mood! The young forest is claustrophobic dense-lush. The old forest is an open, airy, green-light chamber under the canopy of high-arching branches. Confronted by cedars 7 feet in diameter, one feels the urge to drop to the knees. (Considering the price of cedar, while there it would do no harm to murmur a prayer for their preservation.)

The cathedral of solemn cedars and hemlocks continues upward to the lip of the cirque, where the way flattens amid subalpine trees. Commonly the snowline is met here. Proceed, if desired, to the shore. Watch the skaters. Or the avalanches. Or the flying snowballs. Or the water ouzels. Or whatever is happening. Clamber onto a shoreside boulder for lunch. Circle the shore, in proper season sniffing the pretty flowers.

Round trip 4 miles, allow 3 hours
High point 2450 feet, elevation gain 1100 feet
June-November (for the forest, March-December)

Mount Pilchuck (Map — page 33)

From Chuckanut Mountain to the Bald Hills, up and down the length of the Cascade front, the **Footsore** series spotlights dozens of mountain-edge viewpoints. However, undisputed monarch of them all is Nanga Pilchuck. Pushing an abrupt and imposing vertical mile above farms and villages, jutting so far out in lowlands that from the top you can practically see fish jump in saltwater bays, it provides a panorama beyond praise. Towers of downtown Seattle, pulpmill plumes of Everett and Port Townsend, oil-refinery plumes of Anacortes. Puget Sound and Possession Sound and Strait of Juan de Fuca and Skagit Bay. Olympic Mountains and San Juan Islands and Vancouver Island. Volcanoes from Baker to Glacier to Rainier. Near and far, a couple or several thousand Cascade peaks. There's too much for one trip, you must keep returning, again and again.

Drive Highway 92 to the east edge of Verlot and turn right on the Mt. Pilchuck State Park Road. From November 1 to April 1 the road is gated at the Heather Lake trailhead, and open beyond only to non-motorized use — no snow-mobiles, no motorcycles, peace, it's wonderful. Other times of year, drive as far as you can — usually 7 miles to Rotary Creek and just beyond to the new trailhead, elevation 3100 feet.

When the trail started down by the Stillaguamish River (see Monte Cristo Railroad) this area, 5 trail miles from the road, was called Cedar Flats and was

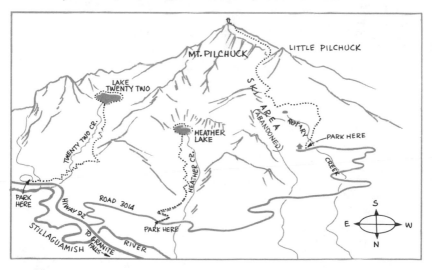

the standard camp for summit climbers. Logging in the late 1940s and early 1950s obliterated the lower trail, until then among the most popular hikes in the state. Much of the upper portion was devastated to develop a portion of 1975-acre Mt. Pilchuck State Park as a fifth-rate ski area that was closed in the late 1970s.

Skirting desolation, the trail ascends in splendid virgin forest, passing glades bright with flowers in season, bushes blue with berries in season. At the cliffy base of Little Pilchuck the way sidehills to the site of the upper lift terminal at 4300 feet. Then, leaving all this seventh-rate nonsense behind and below, the path enters a garden of ice-polished-and-scratched granite slabs, heather and alpine shrubs, flowers and creeks. And the view north grows. At 4600 feet the Little Pilchuck saddle is topped. And now the view south begins. Climbing steeply along granite walls of the final peak, the trail swings around on south slopes into clumps of storm-sculptured mountain hemlocks, then switchbacks and scrambles to the granite-jumble summit, where short ladders lead to the old fire lookout, 5324 feet.

The cabin offers some shelter from the oft-freezing blasts but no solace for the giddy, hanging as it does above the northern precipice. If the ocean of air doesn't make you dizzy, the 360-degree view very well may, what with swinging the head around and around.

Round trip 4 miles, allow 4 hours
High point 5324 feet, elevation gain 2300 feet
July-October

Lake Twenty Two (Map — page 33)

A daughter of the surveyor was much impressed, at a certain age, by white-foaming torrents plunging down cliffs — as she called them, "wow-fows." The climb to Lake Twenty Two ends in a cirque where waters ripple and cliffs beetle, and that's all very pretty. But this really is a walk to exclaim at the wowfows. And the wow trees. Set aside in 1947 to permit comparison of virgin systems with managed (logged) ones, the 790-acre Lake Twenty Two Research Natural Area is among the most-visited, most-loved wilderness forests in the Cascades. (No camping, no fires, walk softly.)

Drive Highway 92 east 1 mile from the Mt. Pilchuck Road and turn right to the trailhead parking area, elevation 1100 feet.

The trail begins in an arboretum of giant trees and tiny flowers, gently ascending the forest slope downvalley ⅓ mile to a junction with the old trail. The loitering ends here, the way now is straight up the hill. Tree-gawking continues, the crown canopy of 3-foot hemlocks and 9-foot cedars high above the steep slopes of moss and ferns. In ¾ mile, at 1400 feet, is a bridge over Twentytwo Creek and the first of the wonderful falls; particularly on hot summer days, many walkers never proceed past the green pools and chill spray. But a bit farther is a sidepath to a truly sensational falls, and soon another. Now the way leaves the creek and ascends an avalanche slope with views over the valley to Green, Liberty, and the tip of Three Fingers, and up the valley to Big Four. Also in sight are clay banks — silt deposited in the lake

Mt. Rainier from near summit of Mt. Pilchuck

Twentytwo Creek from trail to lake

dammed by the Puget Glacier, from which the Big River flowed over the divide east of Pilchuck (see Twin Falls Lake).

Switchbacking over the top of the avalanche slope and a rockslide, the trail reenters big-tree forest, crosses any number of sipping creeks, passes another terrific falls, and at last flattens in a little valley to the lakeshore. A solemn spot, avalanche snow lingering most of most summers beneath the cirque headwall. But if snow prevents reaching it, as it well may in spring at the avalanche slope, the trip is still a huge success at the third wowfow. Or second. Or first.

Round trip 5 miles, allow 4 hours
High point 2450 feet, elevation gain 1400 feet
June-November (to the wowfows, March)

Bear Lake and Pinnacle Lake (Map — page 37)

Excellent old lichen-decorated trees, valley views, a forest lake minutes from the car, and a subalpine lake a good sweat distant.

Drive Highway 92 east 5 miles from the Verlot Ranger Station and just before Schweitzer Creek turn right on road 3015, signed "Bear Lake Trail 6" and "Bald Mountain Trail." Avoid obviously lesser spurs and stay on the main road, climbing to views over the Stillaguamish valley to Three Fingers. At 2¾ miles is a junction. Road 3015 goes ahead to Boardman Lake. Turn right on 3015B, signed "Bald Mountain Trail" and "Bear Lake Trail 3." In 1½ miles is a Y, the uphill left signed "Bald Mountain Trail." Go right on a contour, cross Black Creek, dodge spurs, and in 1½ more miles cross Bear Creek to the trailhead parking area, elevation 2650 feet

The graveled turnpike trail (hikers only — peace, it's wonderful!) ascends in hemlock-cedar forest a short bit to a Y. The right fork offers in passing a broad view down to the valley and the source of the Stillaguamish River's murkiness, a bank of blue clay (deposited in a lake dammed by the Puget Glacier). A few feet onward is forest-ringed Bear Lake, 2775 feet.

Back at the Y, the left fork soon loses the fancy gravel and becomes a staircase of roots and rocks switchbacking up and up to a ridge crest. From there the way swings into the valley of Black Creek, passes little ponds in little subalpine gardens, and drops a bit to the shores of Pinnacle Lake, 2 miles, 3800 feet.

Presumably a pinnacle is in the vicinity? Cliffs, at least, and in season there surely are pretty flowers, and the trees are pleasing. What else? Golly knows, maybe bears. All the surveyor can testify to is a bowl of milk, a homogeneous blur of fog and snow, some of the latter so flat it doubtless was the lake. But that sort of scene is nothing to sneeze at, not with pointy-top trees in Japanese-etching silhouette, and a varied thrush trilling.

Round trip 4 miles, allow 3 hours
High point 3800 feet, elevation gain 1300 feet
May-November

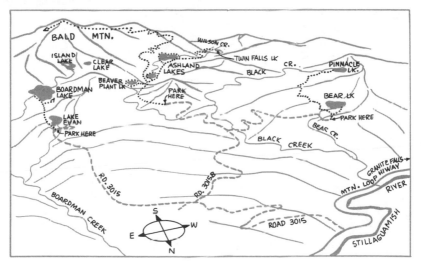

Swimming in the icy waters of Bear Lake

Ashland Lakes and Twin Falls Lake (Map — page 37)

Behind the ice dam of the Puget Glacier a huge lake filled, fed by the Skagit and Suiattle and Sauk and Stillaguamish Rivers. The level rose to overtop the ridge east of Pilchuck and the Big River flowed over the granite spine, waterfalling to join the Skykomish River. Ice and Big River have been gone these 15,000 years but the waterfalls remain, though now only Wilson Creek tumbles down the granite walls. Between upper and lower falls is the pothole of tiny Twin Falls Lake, which might be called "Plunge Basin Lake," or "Falls-In-Falls-Out Lake." This final feature of the trip is the show-stopper, but for shorter hikes or early in spring there are three delightful subalpine meadow-marsh lakes on the way.

Drive as if for Bear Lake (which see) to the Y at 4¼ miles. Go left, uphill, on the lesser road signed "Bald Mountain Trail." Avoid deadend logging spurs. In ¼ mile is a Y; go right. In another ¾ mile, shortly after crossing the East Fork of Black Creek, is a Y; park here or go left, steeply, roughly uphill, in a clearcut of the mid-1960s, a short bit to the parking area and trailhead, a scant 5½ miles from the highway. Elevation, 2700 feet.

Note the broad valley westward, below Pilchuck. Here, where Black Creek now flows, the Big River crossed the ridge. At the far end of the trough is Twin Falls Lake; the trail, however, takes a roundabout route via Ashland Lakes.

The trail begins on an old cat road but soon enters virgin forest of lichen-hung hemlocks and big old half-alive cedars. Built by the state Department of Natural Resources in 1972-75, the trail is novel, interesting, and a bit controversial. A few call it costly and obtrusive; most call it meadow-preserving, mud-avoiding, wheel-excluding, and environmentally sensitive. Much of the length consists of plank walks, parts are puncheon, others are cedar-round "stepping blocks," and still others are granite staircases. Fun.

In ¾ mile a sidetrail drops left to Beaver Plant Lake, 2880 feet, a shallow meadow-bog-pond ringed by plank walks, permitting a circling of the shores without stomping them to black muck. Campsites here.

At the far end of the lake is a Y in the puncheon. The left is to Bald Mountain (which see); go right. In a short bit is another Y, the two paths (the right is shortest) going around opposite shores of Upper Ashland Lake on plank walks, rejoining at the outlet, 2860 feet. More camps.

Now the trail drops a bit, following the lake outlet, Wilson Creek, switchbacking. In a long ¼ mile a sidetrail goes left, dropping a bit to Lower Ashland Lake, 2700 feet, 2 miles from the trailhead. Another shore-circling loop in meadows and forests. More camps.

The way starts down for real, first crossing Wilson Creek. (Incorrectly shown by the USGS map, this creek actually flows to the waterfalls of the Big River.) Contouring and switchbacking, dodging through granite cliffs, twice via bridges built to avoid having to blast rock, the trail comes in view of the lower waterfall and a vista out the Pilchuck River valley, sidehills to the lip of the lower waterfall, which flows from a pool of foam-flecked weak tea beneath a marvelous granite wall. A few steps more lead to the plunge basin of the upper falls, 2300 feet, 1½ miles from Lower Ashland Lakes, 3½ miles from the trailhead.

Sit by the shore (or on a summer day swim the waters) and admire the upper

Boardwalk on the Ashland Lake trail

waterfall dropping 125 feet down the granite. In mind's eye see, here, the Big River, maybe as big as today's Columbia. Horrors.

For views, visit the privies on a rock outcrop above the camp. Look to the 400-foot falls below the lake and south over the valley of Pilchuck River to the lowlands.

Round trip to Twin Falls Lake 7 miles, allow 5 hours
High point 2900 feet, elevation gain 1000 feet
May-November

Bald Mountain Ridge (Map — page 37)

From a distance it seems a nondescript ridge, probably offering undistinguished walking. But in reality it's a busy trail, always something happening — a lake or pond, 12-foot-diameter cedar snags "nursing" 3-foot-diameter hemlocks, glacier-rounded, ice-scratched granite buttresses bulging from the hillside, and views through splendid forest to Three Fingers, Pilchuck, and Puget Sound lowlands.

Drive to the Bald Mountain trailhead, 2700 feet, and hike 1 long mile to the Y beyond Beaver Plant Lake. (For all this, see Ashland Lakes.)

Turn left and ascend in ancient, huge, decrepit cedars and old large firs and hemlocks, past boulders topped with trees. A sidepath goes to an overlook of Beaver Plant Lake. The way swings around the end of Bald Mountain Ridge, under a noble granite wall that surely will tempt climbers: sirs and mizzes, please content your cragspeoples' hearts with the clean slabs and cracks, do not molest the magnificent moss. The trail drops a bit to a marsh-pond and creek at the wall foot, then climbs to a ridge-end window with a look down to Ashland Lakes and out the Pilchuck River.

In excellent big-hemlock forest the trail climbs steadily to a saddle at 3950 feet, 2 miles from the Beaver Plant Y. Here is a capper to the many small joys so far, a vista over the Stillaguamish to crags of Three Fingers, Liberty, Big Bear, and Whitehorse, and east to rough peaks of the Monte Cristo area. Just below in the trees is Clear Lake.

Three Fingers from Bald Mountain trail

Boardman Lake

If more is desired, continue on the trail ¼ mile and just past some granite cliffs scramble steep woods to the first top of Bald, 4250 feet. Through licheny, crooked hemlocks are wide windows south out the Pilchuck River to low country of the Skykomish, west to Pilchuck, and a repeat of the northward panorama. Below in the forest are Island and Boardman Lakes.

The Bald Mountain trail goes on and on, to the highest summit and down to Sultan Basin; see **101 Hikes in the North Cascades.**

Round trip to 3950-foot saddle 6 miles, allow 5 hours
High point 3950 feet, elevation gain 1300 feet
May-November

Lake Evan and Boardman Lake (Map — page 37)

Of the many lake walks in the vicinity, this is the easiest, a nice afternoon's toddle for a 2-year-old.

Drive as if for Bear Lake (which see) to the junction at 2¾ miles and proceed straight ahead on road 3015. At the Y immediately beyond, go right and ascend through views over the valley of Boardman Creek to Mallardy Ridge and a long way up the sinuous Stillaguamish valley. At about 2¼ miles from the junction the road crosses and recrosses Evan Creek to the trailhead parking area, elevation 2800 feet.

In a few steps the trail (hikers only) passes Lake Evan, 2751 feet, surrounded by hemlock-cedar forest which continues the whole easy 1 mile to the crest of a little ridge and down to Boardman Lake, 2981 feet.

It's a handsome big lake, the shore partly forest, partly rockslides from spurs of Bald Mountain. Waterfalls sound of the creek tumbling from the next-higher cirque, that of Island Lake. A fishermen's rude path is said to lead there in another mile but that wasn't toddled by the surveyor.

Round trip 2 miles, allow 1½ hours
High point 3150 feet, elevation gain 600 feet
May-November

Trout Lake and Olo Mountain (Map — page 43)

Saunter along a wheelfree footroad in lovely woods, by cattail marshes, to a beautiful lake deep in a valley. Or sturdily climb high and see cirques and ski tows on the side of Pilchuck, smoke curling from cabins by the Stillaguamish, the radio towers of the Navy, plumes from Everett pulpmills, and the Mukilteo ferry. Thanks to a Scott Paper Company gate, see it all with no racketing razzers to jar the contemplative spirit. The route is excellent for snowline-probing; it starts by the highway, crosses numerous creeks never prettier than when snowmelt-fat, and at several elevations reaches contenting-view turn-arounds, satisfaction guaranteed.

Drive Highway 92 east from Granite Falls a scant 5 miles to a sign, "Masonic Park." Of the two roads off the highway left, take the first, going a couple

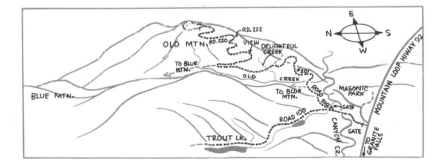

Mud Lake (Trout Lake)

hundred feet to a gate. Most of the year this gate is closed and public wheels of all kinds are banned from the road; at such time park here, elevation 601 feet.

In fishing season, from spring to fall, the gate is open and signed "Trout Lake." Drive the highball-wide logging road as it drops ⅓ mile to Canyon Creek and a Y just beyond the bridge. Park here, elevation 500 feet.

The left, road 100, leads to Trout Lake, or Mud Lake as some maps rudely slander the pretty thing. The gate is open on fishing-season weekends, so don't do the walk then, for gosh sake. But on fishing-season weekdays, or weekends the rest of the year, come enjoy. The trip has special attraction on winter days when the snowline on the highway.

In the first mile the pleasant road crosses the creek, climbs by a clearcut, and levels off beside a cattail marsh (the old Johnson Dean Millpond). The way is then in mossy maple forest, over little streams, to the lake — a true gem, not the least muddy — tucked in the second-growth-forested hills. Continue ¼ mile more to a rocky point which the photographer, who surveyed this trip but is unaccustomed to walking, recommends as a great spot to soak sore feet.

Round trip from second gate 5 miles, allow 3 hours
High point 665 feet, elevation gain 200 feet
All year

Now for the highlands. Even when the highway-side and road 100 gates are open, the right fork at the Canyon Creek Y, road 200, is gated shut, always closed to public wheels. Olo is ever-lonesome.

Go right ¾ mile on road 200, through a frog city, to a Y. The major road left climbs high on Blue Mountain; go right on lesser road 201. In ½ mile is a bridge over lovely Olo Creek and the end of flatwalking. Switchback up and up in second-growth from 1940s logging, by windows over Canyon Creek to the lakebed-flat ridge dividing it from the Stillaguamish River. Topping the moraine ridge, the road starts up a rock-hearted ridge. At 1¾ miles from Olo Creek bridge is a Y, 1400 feet; go left on the lesser road, over a delightful creek, by roadcuts in black metamorphic rock decorated with moss gardens. A series of creeks climaxes in a waterfall down a quarry. Just beyond, 1 mile from Delightful Creek, is a junction with a better road from the Blue Mountain network; switchback right onto this road 220. See the Navy towers on Wheeler.

At 2500 feet, ¾ mile from Quarry Junction, 5 miles from the highway, pow, a view that demands a long halt (and if snow is deepening, a turnaround). To the trip's best view of Pilchuck are added Big Four, Rainier, Issaquah Alps, Everett, and Olympics.

In ¾ mile more, at 2800 feet, is a Y; go left on lesser road 220, cut in outcrops of red jasper, and pass a serpentine quarry. Now short second-growth from the 1960s thinly screens a wide world. Where a sideroad goes left to a 1970s clearcut, climb right to the ridge crest. The summit is close. Good grief but there's a lot of air around, an enormous sky. At 1½ miles from the 2800-foot Y is the last Y. Both forks must be walked.

For the East-South Vista, go right a few yards, until at 3350 feet the road starts down toward on-going logging. Sit on a stump of a recent clearcut and wow away an hour: the near headwaters of Canyon Creek, the finger of Liberty, the brilliant glacier on Three Fingers, and Pilchuck, Si, Tiger. Contrast the total scalping of Olo done by Scott Paper with the Forest Service cutting of small patches on Green, across the valley.

For the West-North Vista, from the Y go left ½ mile to the road-end at 3400 feet, just below the 3451-foot summit, too cluttered with 1977 slash to be worth an effort. Along the road and at the end: Seattle towers beside Elliott Bay, Possession Point on Whidbey Island, Strait of Juan de Fuca, Port Townsend pulpmill plume, Ika and Erie and Constitution in the San Juans, Devils and Cultus, Twin Sisters and Baker. And close by, Blue and massive Wheeler, and between them the six Navy radio antennae stretched over Jim Creek.

Round trip from highway 15 miles, allow 9 hours
High point 3400 feet, elevation gain 3000 feet
March-November

Green Mountain (Map — page 46)

In olden days the big-timber green of Green Mountain contrasted vividly with the granite white of Pilchuck south and the rock brown and glacier white of Three Fingers north. Of course, there then was nothing to see from Green itself but trees. Now, patched by clearcut brown, the two peaks are fabulous platforms for stupendous panoramas. Various lower viewpoints on the early-melting south-slope route make dandy snowline-probing destinations.

Drive Highway 92 east from Granite Falls 7 miles and turn north on road 320, signed "Canyon Creek, Green Mountain." At a Y in 2 miles, 1360 feet, go right on road 318. In 1¾ more miles, at 2000 feet, where road 3032 goes straight, switchback left on 318. In 1½ more miles, at 2500 feet, is the next switchback; somewhat before here begin the view windows designed for snowline-probers. In 1 long mile from this switchback, at 6¼ miles from the highway, is the recommended parking area on a wide shoulder at 2900 feet. From here begin the two separate hikes, on road 318 to East Peak, on spur 318B to West Peak.

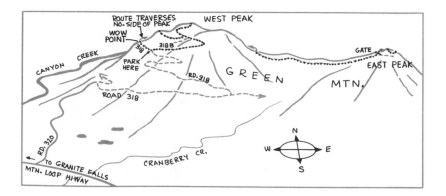

Three Fingers from Green Mountain

East Peak

Let it be plainly understood the walk is on a readily-drivable road where sports razz and even family sedans chug. That's their tough luck. Trying to enjoy scenery from a moving car is like watching a speeded-up movie; it's frustrating and causes hypertension. Pity the poor motorists as you walk, permitted by a foot pace to savor the glories.

A short way from the parking shoulder is Yaw-aw Point, so called for the howls of drivers who fail to make the U-turn around the far west end of Green, goggling as they are at the tremendous view, basically a lower version of that from the West Peak (see below), but including the Issaquah Alps. Climbing east, the road overlooks Canyon Creek to naked Olo and the Navy radio towers on Blue and Wheeler. Alternating between patches of virgin timber left to seed intervening clearcuts of the 1950s, the way rounds a corner to a blasting view of Three Fingers, every detail clear from Goat Flat to the three summits, and of Bullon and Whitehorse. Then appears the rock fang of Liberty. Passing the West Peak and climbing to a saddle, the road follows the crest in views south to Pilchuck ski slopes and granite slabs and the cirques of its northside lakes. At the foot of East Peak is a Y; go left on 318F, gated; everyone has to walk the last ½ mile. At 4 miles is the naked summit, 4100 feet. To previous views are added Monte Cristo peaks, Glacier, Index, and Cultus.

Round trip 8 miles, allow 5 hours
High point 4100 feet, elevation gain 1200 feet
June-November

West Peak
East Peak is pretty well into the Cascades; West Peak hovers over the lowlands.

From the parking shoulder ascend road 318B, climbing east 1 mile, then switchbacking northwest in a 1948 clearcut another ½ mile to a 3450-foot saddle.

Several things can be done from here. One, climb old cat tracks and fight slash to the 3810-foot summit of West Peak, a conquest that will gratify egos of members of the American Subalpine Club but will not edify because the summit clump of virgin forest blocks horizons. Second, ascend rightward from the saddle to a shoulder with a grand view north. Third and best, ascend left from the saddle to the 3550-foot subpeak freshly denuded in 1977, opening the widest single view of all. In the middle of everything, out west beyond the gleam of Lake Stevens, is Everett, steaming away by Port Gardner Bay. Beyond are Whidbey Island, the Port Townsend pulpmill, Olympics. South are the Mukilteo ferry, Seattle, Rainier. North are San Juan Islands and Baker. For golly sake stay for the main show — sunset.

Round trip 3 miles, allow 2 hours
High point 3550 feet, elevation gain 650 feet
May-November

Wheeler Mountain (Map — page 49)

Tired of the everyday world? Want to get away from it all? We offer you — **escape.** Magnificent views, yes, every step (all 42,000 or so of them) of the trip. But more — the creepy suspicion you have walked right out of the world and never will get home again, not in this lifetime.

Drive Highway 92 east from Granite Falls 7 miles and turn north on road 320, signed "Canyon Creek, Green Mountain." In a Y at 2 miles, go left on 320, signed "Canyon Creek 6." It's actually 7 (staggeringly scenic) miles along slopes of Green to the crossing, from which 320 turns west on slopes of Meadow. At 4¾ miles from the crossing is a Y; go left on road 3121, cross Meadow Creek onto slopes of Ditney, and after a final 3¼ miles cross a large nameless creek to a signless Y, 16 or 17 miles from the highway. Park here, elevation 2100 feet.

Walk the left fork, maintained only sporadically and partially, but sometimes drivable the first mile or so; contour and then descend 2 miles to a T at 1691 feet with the Scott road; the road is firmly gated miles and miles away at

Highway 92, except in fishing season (see Trout Lake, page 43). Go right, round a corner, climb and dip, 1½ miles to the crossing of Big Jim Creek at 1950 feet. The route at last touches the base of Wheeler.

At the Y beyond the crossing turn left, downvalley, and climb to a promontory and an extension of the views south to Rainier. The road switchbacks up the ridge spine to a Y at 2720 feet, 1½ miles from Big Jim Creek; go left. (The right climbs to the top of, and all over, 3450-foot East Peak of Wheeler, with views, a plateau of lakelets, and no doubt plenty of fun; West Peak, however, gave the surveyor all the fun he could handle in one day.)

Prominently in view much of the way have been the six wires draped 1½ miles through the air over Jim Creek from towers on Blue and Wheeler. Presumably because of them, when passing creeks the surveyor felt a strong urge to jump in, shouting "Dive! Dive!" Informed of this, a Navy security officer said it was stuff and nonsense; the Jim Creek messages to submarines around the world are, of course, in code. He did warn that hikers illegally snooping too near the towers are liable to burst into flame.

From the Y a contouring 1¼ miles into and up the valley of Little Jim Creek lead to a two-creek gulch on the side of East Peak. Just beyond are the first confusing junctions of the day. At a first Y, go right, uphill. At a second, go left, contouring ¾ mile to the crossing of Little Jim Creek, 2800 feet. A couple minutes upstream, in the headwaters basin, is a surprising little lake, the shores a meadow-marsh skunk-cabbage farm.

Now for the final assault; beyond the creek looms mighty West Peak. Swing around the valley, climbing to a Y; take the left downvalley fork. Excitement impels weary legs as horizons grow in every direction across the rolling, shrub-dotted ridges, uncannily Scottish-moorlike. At 3300 feet, 1 mile from Little Jim, the road completes a sweeping switchback to the right near the ridge crest; at a Y here, go right. A bit beyond is another Y; both forks are mandatory.

First take the right, contouring a scant 1 mile to Whammo Landing, 3400 feet, 9 miles from the car. WHAMMO! This is what you came for: the straight-down view to cows in green pastures, to meandering river and bug-infested

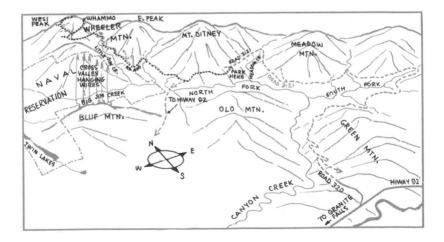

49

Catkins on alder tree

highway; east over skinned-brown East Peak to virgin-green Ditney and white Whitehorse and Three Fingers; a long arc of the North Cascades; the flat strata, faultline, and dipping strata of Higgins; Frailey, Cultus, and Baker. And do not miss the lakebed-flat moraines of the Puget Glacier at the mouth of Boulder River valley. Gosh.

But save some gasps, return to the previous Y, and take the left. In a few feet is another Y; go right, and at the next two Ys also right, and at the next, left. This isn't really confusing because the summit is near and impossible to miss; in ¾ mile from Whammo Landing Junction the way curves around onto the absolute tippy-top of West Peak Wheeler at 3700 feet. Whee. Added to an inferior but still stunning version of the Whammo panorama is the west view: San Juan Islands, Whidbey, Camano, and silver-shining waterways from Skagit Bay to Puget Sound. On the way back, a spur offers a south view: Blue, Olo, Pilchuck, Everett, Issaquah Alps, Seattle.

But in case you hadn't noticed, the sun is sinking in the west and the coyotes are howling and it's time to run for home. Hope you make it.

Round trip 20 miles, allow 12 hours
High point 3700 feet, elevation gain 2800 feet
April-November

North Fork Stillaguamish River Trail (Map — page 52)

Walk from the Puget Sound plain far into the Cascades, partly on banks of wild river in a fine green frenzy of forest, partly in pretty pastoral scenes right out of Old America. Several times a week the trail is traversed by iron horses, but except for these pleasing visitations the lane is quiet, too bumpy for wheels not equipped to run on rails, mostly too distant from auto roads for internal-combustion noise to distract.

As the North Fork of the Bays-To-Glacier Trail, the route may well be much-tramped in future years by backpackers — who even now can find pleasant camps, conveniently spaced. The surveyor made the journey with two one-way walks on separate days, each time thumbing back to his stashed car. The main use, of course, will be for day hikes, Highway 530 providing any number of access points.

Mile 0-4¾: Arlington to Trafton Fishing Hole (one-way walk 4¾ miles)
Arguably the very best part of the whole trail, the more glorious for its nearness to Puget Sound City.

Drive Highway 9 to the north edge of Arlington and park at Haller Bridge Park, elevation 40 feet.

Walk north over the highway bridge, just below the union of the river's two forks, climb the embankment to the railroad grade, and turn left the short bit to the Y of Arlington Junction; go right. After an unprepossessing initial 1 mile past an enormous, motorcycle-infested sand pit, joy begins. For much of a long 2 miles the trail is sliced in hanging-garden walls of rotten sandstone and conglomerate dropping to green pools and white rapids of the wild river, the bird avenue nearly arched over by crowding alders and maples. Wildwoods-

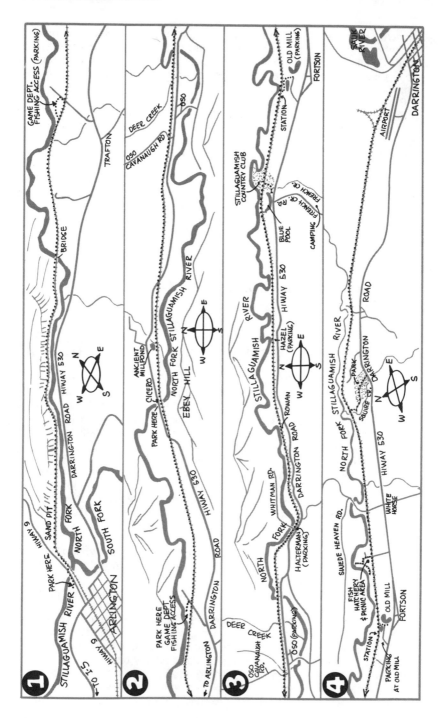

wild water end at a river bridge, a logical turnaround for a short walk (6 miles round trip); picnic on any of several secluded gravel bars-swimming beaches.

Now is introduced the route's second major mode, the pastoral, which henceforth alternates with the wild. Beyond fields abruptly rises the front of the Cascades — Washington, Stimson, and "Little Ridge" north, Ebey Hill south. From here on the cows in pastures and herons in sloughs of cutoff meanders are too frequent to be noted. Splendid old wooden barns (they don't build 'em no more). Graceful old farmhouses with full-length verandas where many a generation has spent summer evenings in "front porch" swings.

Suddenly the river is again beside the tracks; as it diverges leftward, hikers can drop to a streambank woods road for the final ¼ mile to an unsigned Game Department fishing access on a gravel bar of the wild river flowing through wildwoods.

Mile 4¾-7¼: Trafton Fishing Hole to Cicero Bridge (one-way walk 2½ miles)

Of lesser interest, but featuring vast pastures with nice barns.

Drive Highway 530 east ⅓ mile from Trafton Road and turn north on a road which in ½ mile crosses the railroad tracks. Just beyond on the left is the unsigned Game Department public fishing access. Park here, elevation 98 feet.

Wild river is briefly touched, a slough crossed, and the trail heads out for the middle of the broad floodplain fields. Now the route is definitely leaving lowlands, passing between the portal peaks of Stimson and Ebey. The rails cross the highway and parallel it a last ¼ mile to side-by-side highway and railroad bridges at Cicero.

Mile 7¼-10¾: Cicero Bridge to Oso (one-way walk 3 miles)

More visions of America Past, including rotting artifacts of a lumber mill.

Drive Highway 530 east 3½ miles from Trafton and park by or near Cicero Bridge, 125 feet. The gravel bar here is a popular swimming beach.

The trail briefly touches the river here, then swings away past a large slough with mossy concrete footings and old pilings and a collapsing wooden bridge; presumably this was a millpond. Frailey now dominates the view north. Big-tree forest leads to another touch of the river, across which is a hideaway farm with a gorgeous old barn.

Highway 530 is crossed (parking available) to the route's only significant sally into civilization. With the tracks close by the highway, an old millpond is passed, then an operating peckerwood sawmill, and the historic, picturesque Oso School. The trail crosses the paved Oso-Cavanaugh Road and river-size Deer Creek, the bridge embellished with such graffiti as "Welcome to Oso, Partytown USA." Wheeler now dominates the view south, but up the valley can be glimpsed glaciers. Frailey falls to the rear on the north and ramparts of Higgins come in sight ahead.

Mile 10¾-16¾: Oso to Hazel (one-way walk 6 miles)

The dominant mode shifts from the pastoral toward the wild, the alpine. The geology gets great.

Drive Highway 530 to the major metropolis between Arlington and Darrington, quaint old Oso, elevation 200 feet.

Mt. Higgins and Stillaguamish River

The trail passes a shake mill, community chapel, and fire station, and crosses the river. The valley-bottom flat, previously 2 miles wide, narrows to less than 1 mile. The way hits the river and follows it to Halterman, where Whitman Road (parking) is crossed, 2 miles from Oso.

Wheeler walls the valley on the south. But to the north, now, a central feature of the trail dominates: the geology-textbook folding and faulting of Higgins north, horizontal strata divided by a faultline from folded, dipping strata, one of which forms the great naked slab known as the Roller Rink.

The pastures diminish to occasional openings in woods. For a long stretch the tracks are beside or very near the stream, the river wild, the forest noble.

Note hereabouts terminal moraines of the Puget Glacier, identifiable by exposures of gravel in hillocks.

Decrepit shacks of Rowan Station are passed, and then comes the longest highway-side piece, ameliorated at Hazel by a return to the river.

Mile 16¾-20½: Hazel to Fortson Mill (one-way walk 3¾ miles)

Farms yield to woods, farmhouses to stumpranch cabins and summer homes.

Drive Highway 530 east from Oso 6 miles to 310 Street NE (Hazel Road, a section of old highway replaced by a cutoff), which leads to riverside parking, 300 feet.

At every pasture opening in the woods, Higgins grows more impressive. Boulder River is crossed. The trail again follows wild river a long way, passes the long slough called Blue Pool, where fields open on the vista to Whitehorse. In deep woods are fancy cabins of Stillaguamish Country Club, where the tracks cross French Creek. Mingled fields and woods lead to an old train station and millpond.

Mile 20½-27½: Fortson Mill to Darrington (one-way walk 7 miles)

Lots of folks spend the whole day prowling Fortson Mill, surely among the route's top attractions. But also the alpine views climax, and the solitude.

Drive Highway 530 east 10 miles from Oso. Just after passing a powerline swath, turn left on obscurely-signed Fortson Mill Road to a huge paved circle, around which are artifacts of the vanished mill. Turn right at the circle and drive a woods road by the millpond to a parking area at the east end, elevation 400 feet.

Find a road-path by the pond, over its outlet on a plank bridge, down the pond to the tracks near Fortson Station of yore. (However, do not neglect the mill — poke around concrete structures, ax-hewn timbers, rotting pilings, and mysteries; try to figure out what all these vanished structures were for.)

But to proceed east: Highway 530 from now on is distant, making this the longest lonesome stretch of the route. The bad news is that the river is also mostly distant. And pastures become few, meaning forests block the view just as the most impressive part of Whitehorse is passed; this gasper of a mountain thus is better admired from the highway than the trail.

Nevertheless, there is another highlight near Fortson. At a long ½ mile from the station a road from Highway 530 (here ½ mile south) leads to ponds and picnic areas of a public fish hatchery in a bulge of forest enclosed by a river meander. A sidetrip to hatchery and river can fill up what's left of a day after polishing off Fortson Mill.

Whitehorse Mountain

To proceed east: In ½ mile is Swede Heaven Road (crossed ½ mile from Whitehorse Store on Highway 530), giving great views of Higgins and Whitehorse. For an interesting sidetrip, walk north on this road, over the Stillaguamish, to fields and barns and terrific Whitehorse-Higgins views at the old community of Swede Heaven.

In lonesome woods the trail crosses Squire Creek; less than ½ mile upstream via rude paths is Squire Creek County Park. The next big event is a succession of decks of logs and rail spurs off left to mills which are the chief reason the railroad still runs.

The mainline tracks bend south to the Darrington Airport, with stupendous views of Jumbo and overpowering Whitehorse's glaciers, and to beautiful downtown Darrington, elevation 549 feet.

One-way trip 27½ miles
High point 549 feet, elevation gain 500 feet
All year

Boulder River (Map — page 57)

How could so gorgeous a wilderness woodland survive at such low elevation, so near cities and sawmills? A miracle? Sort of. Canyon walls too
expensive to gouge for tracks saved the valley from railroad loggers. Then, as
modern engineers were cranking up to bulldoze roads over the ridges and
haul away the juicy giants, the preservation spirit rode to the rescue. If we all
keep the faith there will be a Boulder River-Whitehorse-Three Fingers Wilderness. And what a treasurehouse! Virgin forest, wild river, white waterfalls on
green-mossy canyon walls.

From Arlington drive Highway 530 east 20½ miles and turn south on French
Creek Road. Pass French Creek Campground and at 3¾ miles from the
highway reach a Y. Park here, elevation 948 feet.

The Boulder River trail takes the right fork, straight ahead on the olden-day
railroad grade, which was briefly opened in 1952 for a gypo logging show and
since has reverted to footpath. In big second-growth the grade contours the
sidehill steeply above the Boulder River, cutting through ferny rock walls. At ¾
mile valley and trail turn sharp left. Here are sidepaths to the frame of a trail
shelter, down (on the 1952 logging road) to camps by the river, and up a short
ridge to terrifying (but poor) looks straight down to Boulder River Falls and out
over the Stillaguamish valley to the strata of Higgins.

Back on the main route, a cliff marks the end of old railroad and start of pure
trail, and the transition from great second-growth to awesome virgin forest. In
½ mile is the site of the now-gone second trail shelter and the still-here central
extravaganza of the trip. Most parties end the hike here, 1¼ miles from the car,
and many camp overnight to enjoy the scene: huge boulders in the river,
sandbars for wading edges of wide green pools, just a bit milky from stone-
grinding of Three Fingers Glacier, and (gasp) the 200-foot vertical wall in-

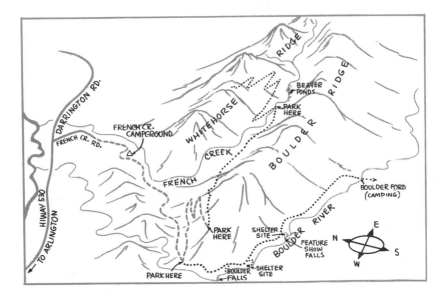

scribed with lacework of white foam. Upstream a bit from this delicacy is the show-stopper — a much larger falls down the same precipice.

Enough, certainly. But there's more. Beyond is still another super falls. And let us now praise the forest, so saturated in this dank valley that trees, and rocks, and loitering hikers are covered with moss. Cedars grow to 8 feet thick and firs nearly that diameter and hemlocks also do themselves proud. Going up and down, passing a series of delicious creeks, in a scant 3 miles more, 4 miles total from the road, the trail reaches Boulder Ford. A footlog crosses the river, but this is the logical turnaround and lunch spot, with just the tiniest windows upvalley to glaciered headwater peaks.

Round trip to ford 8 miles, allow 6 hours
High point 1550 feet, elevation gain 1000 feet
February-December

French Creek and Whitehorse Ridge (Map — page 57)

Broad views over the wide green valley to geology lessons of Higgins. Close looks at glaciers of Whitehorse and Three Fingers. Plus an assortment of creeks and beaver ponds. A single route offers two quite different walks, one lower down for snowline-probing, the other up high for late spring-early summer.

Drive to the Y at the trailhead for the Boulder River (which see), elevation 948 feet. The left fork is the road to French Creek headwaters. For the snowline-prober, park here.

In lush mixed forest the narrow, steep, little-driven, oxcellent footroad switchbacks up Boulder Ridge, by rock walls and waterfalls. At 2 miles, 2100 feet, a bit past the final switchback, wide windows open to tumbled green forests on Puget Glacier moraines, flat pastures of the floodplain, and downvalley to Fralley and Lake Cavanaugh and upvalley to snowy peaks in the Glacier Peak Wilderness. The main show is Higgins, across the valley; on its western half the strata lie horizontal, and east of a fault they dip steeply in an overturned fold. Particularly fascinating is a giant rock slab, at this distance appearing absolutely smooth, ideal for a sensational rollerskate run (to eternity, of course).

If postholing withers ambition, this vista is sufficiently sensational for a lunch spot-turnaround. Essentially the same view recurs as the road ascends the steep sidehill 1½ miles, partly in virgin timber, to a corner at 2450 feet. Here the way turns into French Creek valley, where the white tip of Whitehorse shows over intervening Whitehorse Ridge.

Round trip 4 or 7 miles, allow 4 or 6 hours
High point 2100 or 2450 feet, elevation gain 1200 or 1500 feet
February-December

Nothing says the whole road can't be walked later in the year. However, from late spring on it may be considered ethical to drive 5 miles from the

A tributary cascading into Boulder River

Mt. Higgins from French Creek road

Boulder River trailhead to a vast clearcut of 1961, replanted in 1962, still sporting naught but tiny shrubs amid the weeds, and park at the crossing of French Creek, 2500 feet.

Two hikes appeal. One, short and sweet, is to the beaver ponds. Just before the bridge over the creek, take off on a logging spur. In a scant ½ mile are the dams, several large and many smaller. A bit beyond, the excellent creek emerges from virgin forest.

The big trip is the climb to the crest of Whitehorse Ridge. The road, perhaps drivable 1¼ miles more to Big Blowout Canyon near the valley head, switchbacks from this perfect wheelstop (unless repaired for more logging) in and out of clearcut and virgin forest, crossing creeks and recrossing. White Whitehorse and Three Fingers rise above the green foreground ridge. The road dwindles to a cat track and ends in a landing at 3900 feet.

The views from here are about as good as they get, but to finish the job, pick an easy way the short distance up slash to a 4100-foot saddle in Whitehorse

Ridge. Across the head of French Creek is the junction of this ridge with Boulder Ridge. Beyond is the summit snowfield of Whitehorse, close enough to spot the people (and sometimes the big, shaggy dogs) kicking steps. And crags of Bullon, and rock towers and crevassed glacier of Three Fingers, and Tin Can Gap. And out the slot of Tupso Pass, a bit of lowlands. Look the other way down to the Stillaguamish valley, across to Higgins, north to the tip of Baker.

Round trip 6½ miles, allow 5 hours
High point 4100 feet, elevation gain 1600 feet
May-November

Stimson Hill (Map — page 61)

In the early 1950s, when kindly loggers finished letting daylight in the swamp, this first high rise of the Cascades on the north side of the North Fork valley provided a mind-blasting panorama over lowland plain and saltwater-ways. And so it will again, lo these many decades hence, when Second Wave clearcutting repeats the favor. Until then, though there is one window north-ward from the summit, the chief satisfactions of the ascent will be the peace and quiet in a green tunnel through middling-to-big second-growth; perhaps the most attractive time for the ascent is in winter, as a snowline-prober, enjoying animal tracks.

Drive Highway 9 north 3½ miles from Arlington and turn east on Grandview Road. In 4½ miles turn left on Cedarvale Road and continue 1½ miles to a horseshoe bend and Rock Creek. Park in a wide spot beyond the bridge, elevation 700 feet.

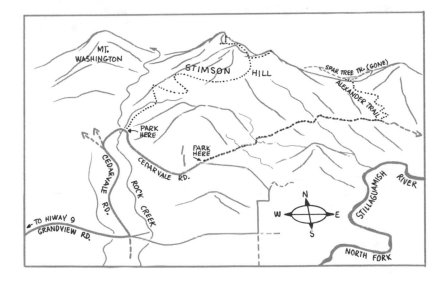

Rock Creek on side of Stimson Hill

Walk up beside a branch of Rock Creek on a track too rough to drive. In a scant ¼ mile the track joins a narrow forest-management road which, because it starts on private property and is there gated, sees few wheels. The pleasant footroad soon crosses the branch of Rock Creek, displaying a gorgeous big mossy boulder draped with ferns. Very steeply the road climbs, switchbacking, in mixed forest. Aside from birds, squirrels, and (in season) flowers and mushrooms and blueberries, the big excitement is a funny little artesian spring in a roadside bedrock wall, the gushing water churning a miniature sand volcano in the tiny pool.

At a scant 3 miles the road flattens to a 2750-foot saddle. A sideroad leads right to a 2807-foot summit from which the loggers had a fabulous view — that even now is only just barely screened out. Tantalizing, maddening.

("If seven gypos with seven saws
Logged here half a day,

Do you suppose," the Walrus said,
"That they could make 'er pay?"
"No chance," said the Carpenter,
"But then we'd see the bay.")
The main road proceeds a scant ½ mile along the ridge, through dense woods, by scattered tall snags and nearly-meadows, to a deadend on the side of the 2850-foot highest summit. Here at the road-end, on a very steep sidehill, is quite a nice window out north to Frailey and the Lake Cavanaugh valley and Cultus country, Baker and all. (So supposes the surveyor, who could hardly see the tip of his nose, so thick was the fog.)

Round trip 7 miles, allow 5 hours
High point 2750 feet, elevation gain 2050 feet
February-December

Alexander Trail (Map — page 61)

Mysteries. Who or what was Alexander? Why and when was a trail of that name built? And why so bloody steep? And why, after striking so bravely upward into great wildland forest, does it abruptly come to naught? Whatever the answers, the trail deserves to be preserved from Second Wave clearcutting and made an entry to the superb lowland-edge, mountain-front trail system that deserves to be built

Drive to the bridge over Rock Creek (see Stimson Hill) and continue on Cedarvale Road 1¼ miles to where Cedarvale bends right, a 1977 logging spur deadends left, and a narrow, 1977-graveled woods road diverges left. This woods road (old logging railroad) is the route; it can be driven more or less uncomfortably some distance but the best place to park is at Cedarvale, elevation 629 feet.

In pleasant mixed forest the way contours the base of Stimson Hill. New spurs go off left and right to clearcuts and the road deteriorates to mudholes and washed-out bridges, becoming a dandy footroad little bothered by wheels. Fine creeks decorate the way. The road drops a couple hundred feet to the base of recent logging and there becomes drivable, from the other direction. No matter. Shortly, at 2 miles from Cedarvale, a large, old wooden sign to the left announces "Alexander Trail, SNF." Another mystery — why such a big, elaborate sign? The whole business smacks of the CCC.

After a short bit on ancient logging grades, at the brink of a gully the trail turns left and becomes for-sure never-anything-but trail. Pause here to wonder at a moss-and-fern-covered boulder big as a two-storey house.

Now address the slope and proceed straight up. In roughly ¾ mile old Alexander gains about 1200 feet, beside the aforementioned gully. Don't worry about motorcycles, not here! Amid large Douglas fir grown up since logging of the 1920s or so are several huge old-growth specimens, "wolf trees" the loggers didn't care to mess with. At 1300 feet, off the trail on the edge of a mossy cliff, is a nice picture window out to green pastures of the Stillaguamish, to Ebey Hill and Arlington. Aside from that the entertainments are mainly those of a chanterelle sort of forest. At ¾ mile, about 1800 feet, the

Alexander Trail

Alexander, in excellent shape despite 40 years of zero maintenance, simply fades away like an old soldier. So, at the little creek here, have lunch and skid back down the hill.

The surveyor had ambitious plans for the day, intending to follow the Alexander to other trails given equal prominence on the USGS map of 1956. Just beyond the fading-out point the Alexander passes through a saddle in Stimson ridge and connects (says the map) to the Spar Tree Trail, which connects to both the Frailey Mountain Truck Trail and the Mt. Washington Trail. However, ambition failed in a sudden onset of midnight blackness with many bright lights and loud noises. Just as well — until doughty machete-armed good-deeders arrive, those trails are pure fiction.

Round trip 5½ miles, allow 5 hours
High point 1800 feet, elevation gain 1600 feet
February-December

Frailey Mountain (Map — page 65)

The summit lookout tower is gone but the looking-out is as fantastic as ever. Below south are green fields of the North Fork Stillaguamish, the right-angles of human geometry contrasting with the sweeping curves of river geometry. Out the valley west are saltwaterways, and east are glaciered towers of Whitehorse and Three Fingers. And below north, in spitting distance, is remote, tucked-away Lake Cavanaugh.

Drive Highway 530 east 8 miles from Arlington and turn north on McGovern Road, which points straight at the old lookout site, recognizable by the notch in the ridgetop forest. In ½ mile, where the road turns east, two driveways go

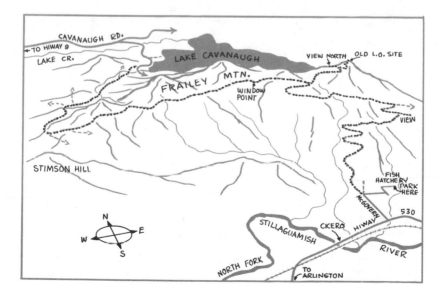

Telephoto from Frailey Mountain of Whitehorse Mountain rising above the Stillaguamish valley

straight. The left of these, signed "private driveway, please close the gates (stock)," is the hiking route. However, there is room on the nearby, skimpy shoulder for only one or two cars; if one or two cars have beat you to it, drive east ½ mile more to park at the Arlington Fish Hatchery, elevation 160 feet. (Do not — repeat, DO NOT — block those driveways or the county road. If hikers bother the residents, that's the end of the hike.)

Back at the left driveway, walk through the private property, respecting the hospitality, turning back if it has been canceled; this is the entry to a forest-management road but the DNR somehow has not yet acquired a public easement.

At present the route is a pleasant footroad, the very low beer-can count indicating minor botheration by wheels. Shortly it bumps into the mountainside and starts up, relentlessly, with some switchbacks, in lush mixed-species second-growth. At 2 miles from the county road the way switchbacks left at 1275 feet.

Note: The Frailey route is an ideal all-winter snowline-prober, starting low, on an early-melting south slope, with big-view turnarounds at various elevations. This switchback is the first such: a grownover spur off the switchback goes in just a few yards to a slide area and a fine view from Arlington to Three Fingers.

Continuing on, in a short bit is another switchback with a grownover spur going east. (This spur was surveyed nearly 1 mile, to where it splits in several branches. Though viewless, it's a pleasant stroll in fine forest, some virgin. Paths connect from the forks to the Oso-Cavanaugh Road, a third approach to Frailey in addition to the two surveyed for this book.)

Continuing on, at 1600 feet, ½ mile from the 1275-foot switchback, is a zounds of a panorama. East are close Whitehorse and Three Fingers and distant Pugh, south across valley farms are Wheeler and Blue and the Navy radio antennae stretched over Jim Creek, and Pilchuck and Rainier, and west are lowlands and water.

The road burrows through tall second-growth, cuts rock walls, climbs, and flattens, the views growing enormous on a steep, airy sidehill, especially west past Stimson to Arlington and Possession Sound and Olympics, south to Issaquah Alps and Seattle. At 1 mile from the 1600-foot zounds is another holy cow of a snowprober-turnaround at 2050 feet.

But continuing on, in ½ mile more, after a westward heading of 2 miles, the road switchbacks east; in ½ mile more is a Y at 2450 feet. The left is to the Other Side of Frailey (which see); go right a few feet to another wow vista, this time with Glacier emerging from behind Whitehorse. Swing into a saddle and climb a last ½ mile from the Y to the summit, 2666 feet, 5 miles from McGovern Road.

Actually, the view from the lookout site is no better than those had before, so the summit isn't worth it for that. However, a couple hundred feet before reaching the top, spot a path left through woods to a cliff-edge. This is worth it. Below is Lake Cavanaugh, in that odd valley that makes Frailey-Stimson-Washington an "island" of peaks cut off from the main Cascades. Hear the dogs bark, the cabin owners chopping wood, whistling while they work. Beyond the odd valley are the weird Cultus Mountains, featuring queer Bald and "Bumpy Ridge," and Haystack, Talc, Iron, and Coal, and Big Deer and Little Deer, and Gee Point, and Higgins.

Round trip 10 miles, allow 8 hours
High point 2666 feet, elevation gain 2500 feet
April-November

Frailey Mountain (The Other Side of) (Map — page 65)

Frailey is a long mountain, for better than 7 miles forming the divide between Stillaguamish and Lake Cavanaugh valleys, and one hike doesn't do it justice. The ascent from the north is similar to that from the south, culminating in the same views (terrific), but there are more ghosts. And in some good future the route may be the entry to a whole system of mountain-edge-wildland trails.

From Highway 9 just north of milepost 44, at the south end of Big Lake, make an acute-angle turn south onto blacktop Cavanaugh Road. Houses and blacktop end at mile 5. About ½ mile past milepost 10 is a Y of northshore and southshore roads; go right, over the lake outlet to the shore, and at 1 mile from the Y, as the main road bends left, spot an old boulder-blocked sideroad to the right. Park here, elevation 1020 feet.

The way begins on the swampy valley floor in second-growth dating from 1920s railroad logging. In several minutes is a small creek, the bridge long gone; rig a plank or get your ankles wet. At ¾ mile the old road is joined from the right by a newer road leading to Second Wave clearcuts in the valley bottom; taking off from the Cavanaugh Road, this gated road all too often is open, and the trip thus may be marred on days the two- and four-wheelers are roaring. Proceeding by marshes and creek-access paths, the road passes two spurs off right to clearcuts. At the second, at 1½ miles, the Frailey road switchbacks left and starts a steady climb.

Ferns drape rock walls. Small creeks splash. Windows open to modest views down to fresh clearcuts and over the Lake Cavanaugh-Pilchuck Creek valley to "Bumpy Ridge" on Cultus and the freaky rock dome of Bald. At 1 mile from the start of the uphill is the Big U-Turn around the west end of Frailey.

About those ghosts. Nowadays it hardly seems possible, but in olden days this was a railroad grade, with standard locomotives and (on the steeper stretches) sidewinders steaming like crazy hauling the big sticks. Bits of rotting trestles remain. A large landing is passed that for one summer a half-century ago was a noisy scene, donkeys steaming, whistlepunks whistling, engines going choo-choo and hiss-hiss. Rusting in the brush is all manner of good junk to kick at and wonder about. Across the valley on Stimson Hill is a gigantic landing, probably in use several years. So massive was the soil disturbance that even now only alder grows there, its reddish-brown (winter) or light green (summer) contrasting with darker green of surrounding second-growth conifers. From the landing radiate alder lines, marking the spider-web pattern of old railway grades and skidways. On this side of Frailey the ghosts compete with the views.

Speaking of views, after screened preliminaries they climax at Window Point, 2250 feet, 3 miles from the Big U-Turn, 5½ miles from the start. All this final way is a lovely stroll by creeks and cliffs on a footroad so narrow and exposed and so prone to washouts in glacial till as to daunt the mass of wheels. The view is to sloughs of the Snohomish River and pulpmills of Everett and all the sights described for the other hike up Frailey. Ships sail the saltwaterways, I-5 roars, Olympics rise serenely, towers of Seattle tower.

To rest is not to conquer. It's 1½ miles from Window Point to the junction with the road from the Stillaguamish and ½ mile more to the summit, 2666 feet.

The USGS map surveyed in the 1940s shows trails to Stimson Hill and Mt. Washington — the Alexander Trail (which see), Spar Tree Trail, and Mt. Washington Trail. The surveyor followed cat tracks gouged by a cedar-miner of the mid-1970s, and then grownover railroad grades, and spent hours wandering nowhere, in the heart of solitude. More ghosts — old loggers' camps, rusty kitchen middens. But no trails. The situation cries out for stout-hearted adventurers with sharp machetes. When they've reopened the trail to

Telephoto of Three Fingers from Window Point on Frailey Mountain

Washington (which probably hasn't been climbed since the loggers left and the second-growth came up thick as hairs on a dog) the surveyor hopes they'll let him know.

**Round trip to Window Point 11 miles, allow 8 hours
High point 2250 feet, elevation gain 1300 feet
February-December**

69

Bald Mountain Overlook (Map — page 70)

Of all the geological oddities in the Cultus Mountains, Bald perhaps is the queerest. This walk gives a close look at the crazy thing — and also a gasper of a panorama across the Pilchuck Creek-Lake Cavanaugh valley, south through the Cascades, and over lowlands to cities and saltwaterways. The route is a great snowline-prober, ascending an early-melting south slope, with big views starting at moderate elevation.

From Highway 9 just north of milepost 44, at the south end of Big Lake, make an acute-angle turn south onto blacktop Cavanaugh Road. Houses and blacktop end at mile 5. At a scant 7¼ miles is an intersection, 800 feet. Go left, and at a Y in a few yards, left again on SW-B-1000, part of a DNR/Georgia-Pacific road system. In 3¼ miles is a switchback from west to east, and in ¼ mile more is a Y; go right on 1000. In 1¼ more miles is another Y; again go right on 1000.

In 2¾ more miles, 7½ miles from Cavanaugh Road, is a Y at 2100 feet. After the long climb in a green tunnel, hereabouts the big views begin; a snowline-probe that starts farther down and reaches this high will yield contentment.

The right fork, 1000, contours east, crossing Bear Creek and at 1½ miles ending (1978) at a washed-out bridge. Just below through clearcut and forest is Bald Mountain, only 2501 feet high but a prominent feature, its peculiar sugarloaf structure thrusting out of the hillside for no apparent reason. Curious souls may wish to thrash through the slash to examine close-up the boggling 1000-foot walls on the valley side of the dome.

For the overlook hike, however, drive left from the Y on SW-B-1500, ascending in ½ mile to a Y at 2400 feet. The left, 1500, leads to Table Mountain and Split Rock Meadows (which see). Go right, on 1510, shortly crossing Bear Creek and, in ¼ mile more, another piece of Bear Creek, with a lovely waterfall under a splendid rock buttress. Park here, elevation 2500 feet.

Yes, though steep and rough the road usually is drivable beyond, but the

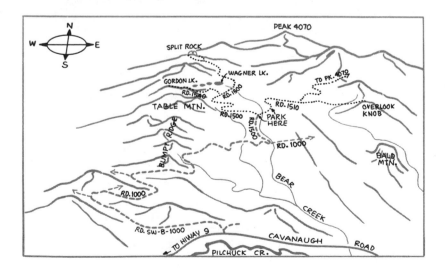

Mt. Pilchuck, Lake Cavanaugh, Frailey Mountain, and not-so-bald Bald Mountain from Bald Mountain overlook

views are such you risk crashing into stumps; it's time to ditch the wheels and soak up scenery at a respectful footpace. Ascending, then contouring, in 1 mile the way comes to a triple-fork Y at 2900 feet. The left climbs to on-going logging that by 1981 or so should complete the scalping of Peak 4070, which then will become a prize goal for viewfinders. For now the supreme gawking is had by taking the right and contouring 1 mile to Knob 2950, clearcut and burned in the mid-1970s, capped by an outcrop of greenish metamorphic rock atop which is a perfect sitting stump.

Sit and look. Directly below is ridiculous Bald. Farther down is summerhome-ringed Lake Cavanaugh, the source of Pilchuck Creek. Above it is the long ridge of Frailey, which connects to Washington, which connects to Stimson, the three forming an "island" cut off from the main range by the Deer Creek valley flowing from the Cultus Mountains to the Stillaguamish. Southward are Jumbo, Whitehorse, Three Fingers, Pugh, Glacier. And sprawling Wheeler, and Olo and Blue, Pilchuck and Rainier. Westward are "Bumpy

Ridge" and Table Mountain, the Stillaguamish delta, many fingers of saltwater, Camano and Whidbey Islands, the Olympics.

Ponder this strange valley and its mysteriously-muddled drainages. Speculate about the push of the Puget Glacier up the valley, the flow of the Big River around the ice front, at different times both to the west and the east of Frailey, and things like that. And what the hell caused Bald Mountain.

Round trip 4 miles, allow 3 hours
High point 2950 feet, elevation gain 450 feet
April-November

Table Mountain and Split Rock Meadows
(Map — page 70)

A person suspicious of Nature's intentions may well feel his scalp prickling during walks around Cultus Mountain. What's the story here? Why the Big Hole, Devils Garden, Bald Mountain? No scene is more bizarre than ineptly-named Table Mountain, with its "Bumpy Ridge" and strange clefts and lakes speaking of faults and earthquakes and glaciers and golly knows, and nearby Split Rock, which maybe can only be explained by UFOlogists. But aside from eerie mysteries there is beauty, too — broad views, subalpine meadows.

Drive from the Cavanaugh Road on the route to Bald Mountain Overlook (which see) and park at the Y at 2400 feet. Yes, park. The road continues and you may be excused for driving about ¾ mile more, but definitely must be afoot before the switchbacks.

But better start at the Y, taking the left fork, SW-B-1500. The views (see Bald Mountain Overlook) are already stupendous in the vast clearcut and grow by the step in the switchbacks that start after ¾ mile. Beyond these, at 1½ miles, is a Y at 2900 feet. Both forks must be taken.

Table Mountain

Go left on 1540. Across the gulch of a Bear Creek tributary is "Bumpy Ridge," the series of knobs on a crest descending from Table Mountain. The highest knob, 3200 feet, is on the map next to the words, "Table Mountain." But it's no table, it's a cleaver, so precipitous it hasn't been logged; if it were, the view would be fantastic. The road ends on a narrow ridge nearly as high, 3125 feet, no table either. Logged clean in 1976, it lies between a saddle separating it from Peak 3200 and another saddle containing the little Gordon Lakes, ringed by subalpine meadow-marshes. Here, ¾ mile from the Y, are views northward over the Nookachamps valley to Hugeview Corner on Cultus, down to Big Lake, Devils, Little, Ika and Goat Islands in Skagit Bay, Erie, San Juans, and the Skagit River meandering to Mount Vernon. Where's the table?

Split Rock Meadows

If you think that's a funny place, you ain't seen nothing yet.

Back at the Y, take the right, road 1500, and surprisingly pass from stumps into genuine subalpine meadows, topping out on a 3100-foot plateau-

Split Rock

saddle-pass. Proceed through parkland, by ponds. (Is this the table?) And then — good grief! — what's that ahead?

Split Rock! A great naked hunk that doesn't grow out of the mountain but alienly sits there, split by giant cracks, feeding a talus of huge boulders beneath its 150-foot vertical wall. It appears to be a foreign body that dropped from the sky and broke in the crash. An asteroid? The arcane cargo of a misfortunate freighter from Alpha Centauri?

Whatever, it's pretty. Curving around the jutting gray base is a soppy meadow ¼ mile long, coursed by a creek flowing from one tea-dark, spookily-deep pool to another.

The road drops off in the Nookachamps valley, connecting to the route to Donkey Vista (which see). The views from the road are about the same as from Table Mountain; for the best, scramble up the forested backside of Split Rock to the summit, 3250 feet, 1¼ miles from the Y.

Complete round trip 7 miles, allow 5 hours
High point 3250 feet, elevation gain 1100 feet
April-November

Devil's club leaf

Mt. Baker and Skagit River from site of Skagit City

SKAGIT RIVER

Draining a third of the north-south length of the Washington Cascades plus a chunk of Canada, the Skagit is far and away the largest stream of the Puget Sound region. It's a big river and a big country — to walkers from homelands of cozier dimensions, overwhelming. There's too much. The spirit fails. The present survey strives humbly to cope, first, by treating only the delta and mountain front, omitting upstream wonders — the miles protected under the federal Wild and Scenic Rivers Act, the Bald Eagle Natural Wildlife Area. Second, since the distance from Puget Sound City bends the Two-Hour Rule, the province is not exhaustively mined but only high-graded; no merely adequate trips are described, it's all strictly A material, good enough to justify the highway travail.

Glories are many: the plain so vast a walker feels at sea in the green; the come-ashore San Juan Islands, islands of rock amid delta alluvium; the fault-block mountains and valleys; the handiwork of the Puget Glacier, nowhere so awesome as here near Canadian sources of the ice, where lobes widened and deepened the fault valleys, rode over the highest summits of the mountain front; and finally the startling bulge of the Cascades west to saltwater.

The province is virtually total farm: down low, fields of corn and cows and cabbages, hay and tulips; up high, trees on state (DNR) and private lands, dominantly Georgia-Pacific. But there is also one of the state's largest wildland preserves outside the alpine mountains, 2000-acre Larrabee State Park. Ranging from sealevel to 4000 feet, the province offers walking the whole year: valley flats are particularly popular in winter when clouds of wildfowl are on vacation here from the frozen North; enormous-view heights, appealing for snowline-probes, are dependably open in fall and late spring.

Most distinctive of the subprovinces is, of course, the delta-floodplain, unquestionably Number One in the region. To be duly impressed by the river, one ought to stroll the dikes in floodtime. Stroll or wade. On second thought, scratch that idea. Let the river subside a respectable bit down the dikes that, beginning a century ago, bit by bit claimed this agricultural treasure house from primeval tidal marshes and floodplain swamps. A person doesn't walk here long without becoming a connoisseur of 19th century three-storey farmhouses and majestic old barns. The proposed Pacific Northwest National Scenic Trail would pass through on the way to Montana; that plan aside, certainly there should be a Skagit Trail extending from the Puget Sound Trail to — to where? Well, how about the Fraser River?

South of the valley, forming not the true front of the Cascades but a false front, is the fault block of the Devils Range, isolated by the block valley (former glacier trough) now occupied by a string of lakes. Rising sharply from the delta, the 25 square miles of second-growth forests, peaks, and secluded-nook lakes are an amazing wildland at the edge of pastoral civilization.

The true front is Cultus Mountain, south portal of the Skagit valley, a bully of a peak hulking 4000 steep feet above the barns. Its 100-odd square miles of tree-farm wildland are well-known to loggers but terra incognita to all but a handful of hikers, few of whom even know the name. Too bad. The views drop you to your knees. And there's the funny stuff — the Big Hole and the Devil's Garden.

Finally, north of the delta is the big push of the Cascades to their terminal plunge to the beaches. This section of the range is unique for that, but also for being split by the north-south valleys (faults, glacier troughs) of Oyster Creek, Friday Creek-Samish Lake, Lake Whatcom-Samish River, and South Fork Nooksack River-Jones Creek, these valleys separating the "island" mountains of Chuckanut, Blanchard, Anderson, Lookout, and — the north portal of the Skagit valley, making a pair with Cultus — Woolley Lyman. Again, loggers know the area best. However, the 10,000 combined acres of State Parks and DNR wildlands on Chuckanut and Blanchard one day will be very famous among hikers. From some of these heights the views of the delta and the San Juan Islands are sensational. From others the close-ups of the steam-leaking Great White Watcher are scary.

USGS maps: Conway, Mount Vernon, Clear Lake, Wickersham, Alger, Bow, Bellingham South

Skagit River near Burlington

Skagit River Banks (Map — page 78)

It's a big river and takes a lot of learning. The lesson for today is the transition from the outer delta (see Puget Sound Trail) to the Cascade front. There is the monster stream to study, fascinated and — in high-water season — a bit nervous or a whole lot frightened. Views of mountains are mingled with views of crops and barns. And steelhead fishermen.

At present it is not possible to walk straight through on either side of the river; much of the route is on private property where trespassing is tolerated but some fences are of the "mean-it" variety — the barrier of barbed wire and the array of KEEP OUT signs show the folks aren't fooling. However, five walks, on one bank or the other, cover most of the river's sinuous length between Conway and Burlington.

Round trip total, all hikes, 23½ miles
High point 43 feet, minor elevation gain
All year

Fir Island-Skagit City

Between the distributary forks of the Skagit is Fir Island, reeking of agriculture and history.

Drive I-5 to Exit 221 and go off through Conway and over the South Fork Skagit River. Immediately turn right on Skagit City Road and park near the little white church. Elevation, 15 feet.

The dike-top strolling is easy, with only a few easy-over fences (for keeping stock in, not people out). Should the situation change and mean-it fences arise, the country lane is close for detouring. The view west is to wonderful old barns and the cultivated plain, east over the river to Little, Devils, Scott, Cultus, Baker.

In 2 miles is Moore Road. It's mandatory to walk west ¼ mile to Skagit City

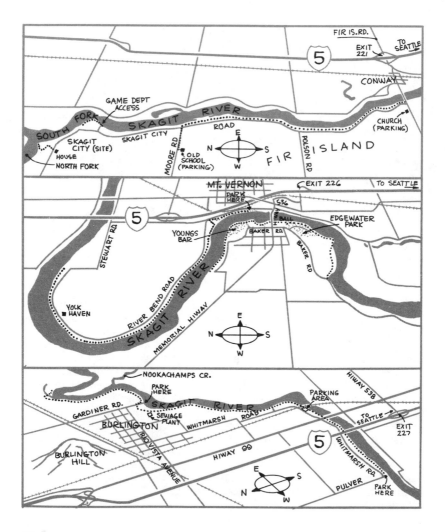

School, closed in 1940, maintained by local history buffs. You can't do without a photo. To go with the one you took of the church.
Round trip 4 miles, allow 3 hours

Unfortunately, the next 1½ miles of dike are practically walkable only by high-jumpers. A Game Department access then provides a way to the river, but just to look, not to walk much. A pity. Upstream ½ mile, access rendered arduous by dike fences and tanglewood brush, a marvelous sandbar thrusts into the angle between the North Fork and the South Fork. This, the wilderness tip of Fir Island, is a grand spot to sit and look. Ought to be a park.

Here was Skagit City, which from a campsite in 1856 and trading post in 1869 grew to the metropolis of the delta, the head of navigation. But in 1879 the giant log jam that made it so was removed, Mount Vernon grew, and Skagit City died. Not a trace remains. A park would at least provide a place to muse. Legally.

Edgewater Park-Youngs Bar-Mount Vernon
Sandbars and public parks make the walking free and easy.

Drive I-5 to Exit 226 and follow Highway 536 west through Mount Vernon and over the Skagit River. Just nicely across, turn left on Baker Road and proceed around Edgewater Park 1 scant mile. Where Baker, here atop the dike, hits the river, park in the wide flat by the bank.

Walk upstream on the splendid broad sandbar to the end. Detour by brushy banks on tire tracks in a flood-open woods being considered for an enlargement of Edgewater Park, which is quickly reached. A Game Department access here. Interesting perspectives over the river to beautiful downtown Mount Vernon, dominated by the noble old Hotel President.

At park's end a detour on streets is necessary. Follow Ball north over Division (Highway 536); beyond a trailer court regain the river on Youngs Bar, a beauty, enormous, and with a Game Department access. The river now bends west away from the city. The grassy dike goes ½ mile more by fields and barns to a house and mean-it fence.
Round trip 4 miles, allow 3 hours

Mount Vernon-Big Bend
Overlapping the previous walk is this one on the other side of the river.

Park in Mount Vernon — a suggested spot is the Lions Club-Kiwanis Parks beside the river on Freeway Drive on the north edge of town.

Walk the shoulder of Freeway north ¼ mile and just short of River Bend Road go left on a woods road and climb onto the lawn-kempt dike. Stroll from city to farms, from freeway to Yolk Haven, hobnobbing with fishermen and ducks. The panorama north and east over the delta is grand to Blanchard, Anderson, Woolley Lyman, Cultus, Little, and Devils. Here is the waterworks for Anacortes, which purifies a piece of the river and pipes it west to refine oil.

Rounding the Big Bend and heading east, at ¾ mile short of I-5 the route is blocked by houses built on the dike by people who love the excitement of flood season.
Round trip 6 miles, allow 4 hours

Skagit River near Burlington

Big Bend-Burlington Sewage Plant

Recross the river. Now there is a definite feel of moving from delta to mountain-walled floodplain. Devils presses close from the south, Cultus nears to the east; northward the delta "sea" is dotted by the "islands" of Burlington Hill and Sterling Hill.

Drive I-5 to Exit 227 and go off east on Highway 538. In ¼ mile turn north on old Highway 99, cross the Skagit, and turn west on Whitmarsh Road. In 1 mile, where the road turns north to become Pulver, park on the shoulder.

The dike-top view extends over to Mount Vernon, up the valley, out to the San Juans. The sky is vast, there's an infinity of air around. The way goes beneath I-5 and old 99 and the mainline railroad bridge. Construction of I-5 without a drawbridge moved the Skagit head of navigation downstream to here (though at very low water the sternwheelers might get under).

At 1½ miles, by the railroad bridge, is a public parking area. Here the river bends north and the dike diverges; the walking route is on a bankside grassy lane leading to another large public parking area accessible from Whitmarsh Road.

The walking is pleasant, the stock fences all easy-over or easy-around. Across the river is a long stretch of wildwoods, a lovely sandbar (how do you get there?). A boat moorage harbors a row of those charmingly graceless boxes-on-rafts characteristic of the Skagit fleet.

The best route shifts to the cow-cropped dike top. The mountain front looms

closer, taller. To the left is the sewage plant of nearby Burlington. A pair of mean-it fences discourage.
Round trip 6½ miles, allow 4 hours

Burlington-Dike's End

Immediately over the two mean-it fences begins the final walk.

Drive north on Whitmarsh Road into Burlington, turn east on Rio Vista Avenue ¾ mile, and then south on Gardner Road several hundred feet to the dike. Park on a shoulder or, if not daunted by mudholes, continue over the dike, past some mysterious old structures, to the riverside sandbar.

Walk upstream on the sandbar. Where it ends, push into woods, skirt a stock fence via riverbank riprap, and proceed in pleasant pastures below the dike. Look across the river to the mouth of Nookachamps Creek; in winter watch for the flocks of swans that frequent close-by Barney Lake.

The river turns east to the end of the dikes that began at saltwater, to the head of boot navigation. In low water a little slough can be hopped over to a fine sandbar at the top of the meander, a lovely wild spot, no houses visible, tanglewoods around. Beyond, progress is possible only for critters that slink through brush or those that swim or fly. Peaks of the Cascade front hang heavy, heavy over thy head. Listen to the swans bark.
Round trip 3 miles, allow 2 hours

Little Mountain (Map — page 81)

If the mountain is little the view is anything but. Lifting abruptly from flat delta, high enough for a broad panorama but not so high as to lose intimacy, the summit is unsurpassed for studying the geometry of green squares (black after the rich soil is plowed). Bring maps and spend hours tracing bends of the Skagit River, peaks of the drowned mountain range of the San Juan Islands, bumps of the Cascade front. Bring binoculars and watch the grass grow in the fields through which roars the swath of I-5.

Drive I-5 to Exit 224, go off east, then north on Cedarvale, and turn east on Hickox Road. In 1 mile, spot on the left a plank and a post marking the

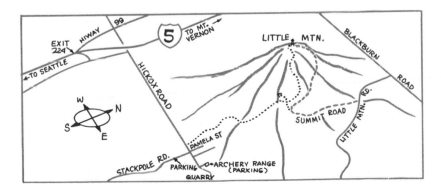

Skagit Flats and Olympic Mountains from Observation Point on Little Mountain

trailhead, elevation 60 feet. No parking is possible here so continue a bit. In less than ¼ mile, just past Stackpole Road going right and then Pamela Street going left, is a Y; the left goes a couple hundred feet to an archery range where parking seems tolerated; if the situation changes, find room on a shoulder south on Stackpole Road ⅕ mile.

The trailhead is a ditch plank red-and-white lettered "Do Not Remove. Little Mountain Trail Head." Information on the post: "Hiker Trail Only. Permission for use revokable at any time; first ½ mile is private property." The maintenance is the contribution of local philanthropists.

Marked at the start by plastic ribbons, the path crosses a field and enters woods and climbs the steep slope. In 1 mile is an intersection; proceed straight ahead and up. (The right goes several steps to the 610-foot switchback on Little Mountain Road; the left was not surveyed.) In a final ½ mile the trail climbs by view windows (gasp and rave) and contours westward in dense summit forest to the Highway Patrol microwave tower. A few steps beyond over glacier-polished slabs of sandstone and conglomerate is the road-end parking area, 934 feet. But there are 50 more feet to climb, up steps of the observation tower that is the center of this Mount Vernon city park.

The view? Words fail. It's a 250-degree sweep, with only the arc east to Cultus and Baker blocked by trees. Homes and farms of the emerald plain, silver meanders of Skagit distributaries, Skagit Bay and Padilla Bay and

Samish Bay, Camano and Whidbey and Fidalgo and Guemes and Cypress and Orcas Islands, the Olympics.

Bring a flashlight to allow a night descent and stay for the gaudy sunset and the dazzling electrical show.

Round trip 3 miles, allow 2 hours
High point 980 feet, elevation gain 950 feet
All year

If ever the trail should be closed, the Little Mountain Road provides assured access to the city park.

Drive as for Devils Mountain (which see). At ½ mile past the right (south) bend where Blackburn Road becomes Little Mountain Road, see an unsigned but prominent gravel road diverging right. Park here, elevation 370 feet, or drive ¾ mile to the first big switchback right, 610 feet. Here is a small parking area and an official city-park "hiker only" sign marking the trail that leads in ½ mile to the top.

Scott Mountain (Map — page 83)

Not the true front of the Cascades, isolated as it is by a fault-block valley, the fault block of the Devils Range is the false front. And the front of the front, the most prominent peak of the range, is Scott. The ascent begins at the edge of the vast Skagit delta, climbs old woods roads along a loud white creek, passes ancient mine diggings in gaudy rocks, and culminates in a series of smashing views. A richly varied, highly diverting trip.

Drive I-5 to Exit 224, go off east, then north on Cedarvale, then east 1 long mile on Hickox Road, then south ⅕ mile on Stackpole Road to an unsigned gravel drive on the east, identifiable by a double entrance with a pair of boulders between. Park here, elevation 30 feet.

Walk the private road ¼ mile to an enormous gravel mine and a T. Go right over a branch of Carpenter Creek, leave the pit, and ascend a logging road southward, dodging lesser spurs. At ½ mile from the pit, where the main road

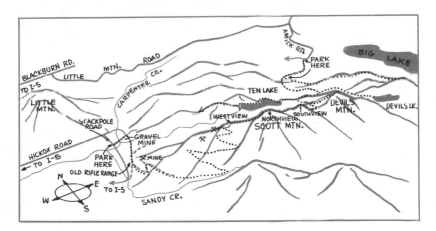

Mt. Baker and Lake Ten from Scott Mountain

switchbacks left (on a route, not surveyed, to Ten Lake), it crosses a lesser road. Go right on this and contour south ½ mile, through more logging and finally above the field of an old rifle range. At the field end is a T at 200 feet. This is the old mine road; turn left. (The right drops to private homes and Stackpole Road.)

Little-wheeled, creek-gullied, pleasant ambling in mixed second-growth, the road heads south from the junction, switchbacks north, then south. (At this second switchback a rude path leads off the end, around a mossy corner, to a very old mine.) The road bends east into the valley of Sandy Creek, inviting sidetrips to waterfalls and pools. At 580 feet the road switchbacks out of the creek valley onto upper slopes of Scott. At 1020 feet, 1¾ miles from the rifle range, is a Y. The left quickly deadends, the right climbs another ¼ mile, switchbacking right, then left, by a gray wall of glacial till, to the mine, the mouth partly open in a cliff of iron-yellow rock the miners thought was nickel ore, back in the 1920s or whenever. Everywhere around here and below are hillside terraces, garbage heaps, rotting timbers, and junked cars from that episode.

Now, the views. Backtrack from the mine to the till wall. Crawl up the left side a hundred slithers on a clay-slick path. Here on a patch of grass at 1200 feet, 3¼ miles from the start, is Westview Nose. Bam. Admire the delta quilt of emerald-green, coal-black, straw-brown squares, dotted by farmhouses and barns, crossed by the bug-busy gray swath of I-5. And gleaming-silver distributaries of the Skagit River entering Skagit Bay. And the Stillaguamish delta, too, and saltwater and islands and Olympics. Turn back now and you've had a trip.

If you please, there's more. A boot-beaten track shoots straight up from the Nose, at 1370 feet attaining a grotesque rock outcrop on the ridge crest and relenting in grade. The path follows the rocky spine, burrowing through salal and spindly conifers. Dodge confusing sidepaths, stick near the spine, exclaim at a granite erratic deposited here by the ice, and in ⅓ mile from the Nose reach Northview Summit, 1580 feet. Zowie. An alarming precipice drops north to secluded Ten Lake. Beyond are Little, Barney and Clear Lakes, Skagit River, Burlington and Sedro Woolley, Cultus and Woolley Lyman and Anderson and Blanchard and Chuckanut, and Samish Bay.

You can't stop now. The entertaining trail proceeds by windows and rock grotesqueries ¼ mile to Southview Summit, 1620 feet, marked by an ancient concrete octagon — foundation of a lookout? A tea house? The panorama — gadzooks. The Skagit mouths and Fir Island, Whidbey Island and pulpmill plume of Port Townsend, Stanwood at the mouth of the Stillaguamish, pulpmill plumes of Everett. The silver sinuosity of rivers snaking over the green plain. Trains rumbling and hooting through farms.

Note: The trail goes on; to use it for an alternate summit route, see Ten Lake.

Round trip to Westview Nose 6½ miles, allow 4 hours
High point 1200 feet, elevation gain 1200 feet
All year

Round trip to Southview Summit 7½ miles, allow 6 hours
High point 1620 feet, elevation gain 1600 feet

Big Lake and Mt. Baker and slope of Cultus Mountain from Devils Mountain

Devils Mountain (Map — page 83)

Since removal of the fire lookout the summit of Devils has rated an E for scenery; for the A view, climb adjacent Scott. Indeed, that can be done from Devils. But there is also, from the east side of the Devils fault block, a unique view east over the Big Lake fault-block valley to the true front of the Cascades, Cultus. Score a B at least. And for an A+ day, combine it with Scott and/or Ten Lake.

Drive I-5 to Exit 225, go off east a short bit on Anderson Road, and turn north on Blodgett. In a long ½ mile turn east on Blackburn Road, which in 1 mile bends south and becomes Little Mountain Road, which winds through the Devils Range 3 miles to a T. Turn right on gravel, deadend Amick Road. Dodge confusing sideroads a bit more than 1 mile; around a bend several hundred feet past milepost 1, spot a fair sideroad on the left, maybe marked by an old, leaning, ax-hewn post, the white paint nearly weathered away, and also by a 3-foot-diameter charred stump. Park in a non-obstructive manner on some nearby shoulder, elevation 750 feet.

Ascend the narrow, drivable road in lush mixed forest, passing driveways to homes. In a scant ½ mile, at 900 feet, is a Y — a better place to park than Amick Road and thus an alternate starting point.

The right fork is the route to the summit of Devils, the alternate way up Scott, and Ten Lake (which see).

Take the left and ascend steeply in good woods, contour around a corner to the east side of the mountain, the background roar of I-5 fading, dip to a ravine, and climb a last bit to a ridge plateau at 1150 feet and a clearcut of the late 1950s. Where the road starts down, at 1½ miles from the Y, beat left through salal a hundred feet to a little knoll of ice-scratched sandstone.

Below is the wide trench of the downdropped fault block; the glacier rumbled through here, and the meltwater river roared. Now there is Big Lake, 3 miles long and ½ mile wide, surrounded by farms and homes (hear the dogs bark, the cows moo). And beyond looms the true front of the Cascades, massive tall Cultus, 4000 feet above the trench. See fields of Fire Mountain Scout Reservation at its base in Walker Valley, and the valley of Nookachamps Creek, and the chaos of Devil's Garden, and the Big Hole, and Donkey Landing, and Hugeview Corner. Tear your eyes off Cultus and look north to the Skagit valley, Chuckanut, Lummi Island, Sedro Woolley, Woolley Lyman, and Baker. Look south to clouds or maybe Three Fingers and Glacier.

Round trip 4 miles, allow 3 hours
High point 1150 feet, elevation gain 400 feet
All year

Ten Lake (Map — page 83)

What a surprise! Accustomed at this elevation to shallow lowland lakes that are being transformed into peat bogs, a hiker is astounded to find deep waters in a rock bowl, seeming a veritable cirque lake. Ringed by steep forests of Devils and Scott Mountains (both of whose summits can be neatly combined with a visit to the lake), the bowl belongs in spirit to a highland wilderness in the heart of the Cascades.

From the 900-foot Y (see Devils Mountain) take the right fork up a little valley, by a lily-pad pond behind an ancient beaver dam. In ½ mile, 1100 feet, is a pass. (Not surveyed, a wheelers' track goes through the pass and ½ mile down to Devils Lake, 826 feet.) The narrow road steeply climbs from the valley in excellent mixed forest and at 1420 feet, 1¼ miles from the Y, flattens to a parking area on the crest of a shoulder. From here three objectives can be attained.

The road switchbacks a final ½ mile to the 1727-foot summit of Devils, offering no views now the lookout tower is gone, only prestige.

However, several minutes up the road from the shoulder, at 1520 feet, a sideroad drops right a short bit to a quarry. From here an old road quickly becomes a trail that climbs to Southview Summit, 1620 feet, of Scott Mountain (which see), reached at ½ mile from the Devils road. As a sidetrip from the Ten Lake trip, this adds a roundtrip distance of 1½ miles, elevation gain 250 feet — an extra hour or so.

But now, for the lake. A few steps up the road from the shoulder, beyond the gate, a big, obvious, unsigned, wheelfree trail takes off right and in a very scant ¼ mile plummets to the lake, 1200 feet. Continue on the shore trail, a delight, now in cattails, now on outcropping sandstone. In a scant ½ mile the

Lake Ten (in Section 10)

way rounds the far end of the lake to a knoll camp above the outlet. Enough. (The trail goes on. From a camp short of the knoll a plain trail climbs to a ridge crest, proceeds through marvelous big-fir forest, and at ½ mile from the lake plunges off the ridge end, down to an immense quarry — see Scott Mountain. Much-used by locals, accesses to the lake from the quarry area are less attractive to visitors from afar.)

Sit on a rock slab and gaze at rippling waters, green walls of trees rising to Devils and Scott. Listen to birds and breezes. Ignore the chunk-chunk-rattle-bang of the quarry (barely ½ mile distant) and the hum-roar of I-5 (some 3 miles off). Noises from a frantic other world, not this serene one.

Round trip 5 miles, allow 4 hours (for Scott, add 1½ miles, 1 hour)
High point 1420 feet, elevation gain 900 feet
All year

The Devil's Garden (Map — page 89)

Residents of hot lands envision Hell as a furnace, and cold-land folk as an icebox. It follows that for Puget Sounders the lair of the Devil is gray, twilight-gloomy, green-oozy, dank and clammy, slimy and slippery. Yet if it is to be the Enemy's garden, it must fit infernal notions of beauty, which is to say it must be frightening as Hell. Well, something bloody awful happened here. The ranger speculates a gas explosion — a burp from a furnace beneath. The surveyor hypothesizes a cataclysmic landslide, a huge piece of Cultus busting loose. The entire mountainside clear down to Walker Valley is littered with monster boulders, mostly hidden by trees. But here in the Garden they are nakedly in the open, some 50 or 100 acres of rocks as big as houses — a chaos, a catastrophe frozen in the moment of its conclusion. The chilling fact is, this was no slow talus growth of eons, this happened all at once, in minutes — and not in the remote past but, as geologists measure time, just a tick ago of Earth's clock. (The best hypothesis so far is that of Louis Reed, who speculates the landslide fell onto the surface of the Pleistocene glacier, which transported the jumble here. Interestingly enough, the Big Hole in the side of Cultus Mountain is close to the north.)

Drive I-5 to Exit 221 and go off east on Highway 534 to Highway 9. Turn north to Big Lake and at milepost 46 turn east on Walker Valley Road. Drive the blacktop a twisting 2 miles through pastures and woods to a gravel sideroad right, signed "ORV Park."

For the route of the future, turn right on the sideroad 1¼ miles to the ORV parking area, elevation about 750 feet. If lucky you can find a flagged route onto an old logging-railroad grade that leads north 1 mile to intersect the route described below.

The route of the present passes through private property of the Fire Mountain Scout Reservation. Its use is entirely dependent on the hospitality of the Scouts, which is dependent on the manners of their guests. If hikers get in the habit of parking cars so as to clog the road, making it difficult for the Scouts to use their property, they will have no alternative but to cease permitting the

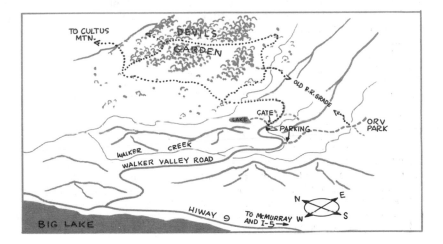

Devil's Garden

public to cross their land. But assuming that has not happened, from the ORV turnoff continue on the county road ½ mile to the end, elevation 400 feet. Opposite the ranger's residence is a shoulder with space for two or three cars. If it's full, drive back to the ORV Park road and park on a shoulder of it — not the county road, which must be kept freely open for Scout use.

Obtain permission from the ranger, granted (so far) in most friendly way, except in fire season when no entry can be allowed. If thoughtless visitors have compelled a change in Scout policy, retreat to the ORV Park (Walker Valley All Terrain Vehicle Trailhead and Picnic Area) provided by DNR and search for the railroad grade.

Where a driveway goes right to the ranger's house, and a gated road left to the camp, take the gated road straight ahead. In about 250 steps is a Y; go left, along the edge of a pasture adjoining the reservation. At the far end, at an elevation of 500 feet, as the road is starting up into forest, note on the right a cat road partly blocked by a heap of gravel. Turn right on this, uphill. At about 750 feet an old railroad grade is crossed; this is the entry from the ORV Park. Proceed on the cat road through a swale and at about 925 feet, ¾ mile from the pasture, spot an obvious trail taking off left.

It's not obvious long because the first boulder field is soon entered. However, the Scouts have marked a route with red and yellow plastic ribbons. NOTE: it's crucial to stick with the ribbons; once off the flagged route, you're in trouble; if you lose the flags, backtrack and pick them up.

Over a hump from the first boulders — horrors! The Garden! How to describe it? With a catch in the breath, a prickling of the skin. Extending some ¼ mile ahead along the slope, and nearly that much up and down, is a "talus" — but no cliff in sight above, just forest all around. Boulders the size of watermelons, and suitcases, and bales of hay, and Volkswagens, and Winnebagos, and summer cottages, and apartment houses, all scattered in disorderly ridges of rocks separated by valleys of rocks, 50-foot towers adored by cragsmen thrusting above black clefts only a caver could love.

Progress is less walking than scrambling, using the hands and the seat of the britches, bewaring of moss-and-lichen slip-and-slide disasters. How far to go? How much time to spend? A person easily could devote a day to exploring trogs and pinnacles. Or could be content to spread a picnic lunch on the green moss table of a boulder and admire the devilishness.

A dodging, clambering, zigging up and zagging down ribboned way crosses to the far side. But just short of there a ribboned escape route leads down into the woods and by more monster boulders, busy growing ferns, to reach the main lower road about ¼ mile from where it was left.

Loop trip 3 miles, allow 4 hours
High point 950 feet, elevation gain 700 feet
All year

Donkey Vista (Map — page 91)

Eye-widening, breath-stopping views from Seattle to the Olympics to the San Juan Islands. To be sure, only a prelude to the brain-spinning panorama from Hugeview Corner on Cultus Mountain (which see). But this route also features a donkey engine peacefully rusting at the landing where the logger walked away from it a quarter-century ago, plus a visit to the Big Hole.

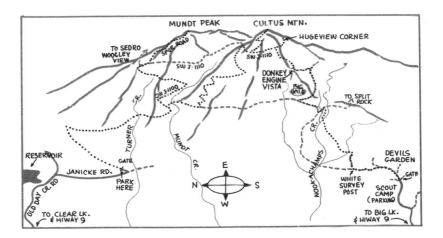

Donkey Vista

Drive to Fire Mountain Scout Reservation (see Devil's Garden). If permission to cross Scout property can no longer be granted by the ranger, retreat to the ORV Park and try your luck from there.

Otherwise, from the reservation entrance at 400 feet set out as for Devil's Garden but where that sideroad turns off, continue on the main road. Ahead is the goal, Cultus, Chinook jargon for "useless"; however, the Skagit Indian name translates as "Fire Mountain," and thus the name of the Scout reservation. Note the forests of white snags from the fires that earned the name.

Passing a sideroad to Scout cabins, in a scant 2 miles the way levels at 900 feet. Ahead a loud creek is heard and in bushes to the right is a white survey post. To save walking a long way around, here take a Scout-built shortcut trail that links old cat tracks and climbs steeply, crossing a branch of Nookachamps Creek, and in 1¼ miles rejoins the road at 1800 feet.

To the right, the road leads 3½ miles to Split Rock Meadows (which see), or in about the same distance to a 3970-foot peak of Cultus. For this trip, go left, lose 100 feet to a plank bridge over tumbling Nookachamps Creek, then contour to a Y at ½ mile from the shortcut trail. The road left is the long-way-around-home; go right, climbing again. At a junction in ½ mile the main road proceeds straight ahead to the Skagit County Watershed (see Cultus Mountain). Take a sidetrip along it the short bit to the Big Hole, where an enormous chunk of mountain slid out, creating this scoop prominent from the lowlands.

Returned, turn right on grassy-grown SW-J-1000. Impassable to wheels, the old road ascends eastward in mostly-alder forest screening a very big picture. In 1 mile, at 2400 feet, a grade obscurely continues ahead; instead, switchback left a final ½ mile to glory. At 5½ miles from the start, at 2750 feet, the road emerges from alders on a wide-open landing. Zounds.

The vista is plenty to keep you wheeling and wowing through lunch. But buffs of logging history will be equally enchanted by the donkey engine left here in 1954 or so by Toughy Boyd when he finished salvage-logging and snag-falling after still another of Fire Mountain's fires.

Round trip 11 miles, allow 8 hours
High point 2758 feet, elevation gain 2500 feet
April-November

On a day when the brush is dry and you're feeling nimble, try the Scout "trail" upward. Just before the landing, note ribbons leading up a cat track. When the track ends at a draw, a rude path continues in a vertical gymnasium, a snarl of fallen logs and a jungle of young greenery, fun for limber youths but very rude indeed to middle-aged trail-trampers. But the acrobatic log-walking and clambering soon yield to easier going and in ½ mile, at 3400 feet, the higher road is reached that leads in ¼ mile to Hugeview Corner.

Cultus Mountain (Map — page 91)

Ramble the high hugeness of Cultus Mountain to Hugeview Corner and exclaim at the panorama from Rainier and Seattle to Everett and the Olympics to Anacortoo and the San Juan Islands. Then ascend to the summit and gasp at the vista over the Skagit valley to Twin Sisters, Baker, Shuksan, and the Pickets. And if not yet helplessly blind-drunk on scenery, stagger to still other vistas.

This approach to the heights of Cultus is on a watershed road that is closed to vehicles (but not feet) most of the year; the route is then peaceful but very long. In the general deer-hunting season starting in mid-October the road is open; weekends then are noisy, but being permitted to drive high gives more time for explorations; an ideal occasion is a crystal-clear midweek day.

Drive I-5 to Exit 227, go off east on Highway 538 to Highway 9, and turn north to the town of Clear Lake. On the north outskirts turn east on Old Day Creek Road and drive by a reservoir signed "Public Water Supply, PUD No. 1 of Skagit County"; the trip leads to the sources of this water. In 3 miles turn right on Janicke Road. In 1 mile, just past a School Bus Turn Around, switchback left on an unsigned road which immediately forks; the left, the trip route, is gated and signed "Public Watershed. To Assure Water Purity Access Is Limited." If the gate is closed, park here, elevation 750 feet.

Walk (this is permitted) by the gate and ascend mixed forest 4 miles to a Y, 1925 feet. The left is signed "Transfer Road, SW-J-1100." The right is unsigned. Driving on is possible, though it will make some cars distraught; for the best trip, park here if not at the gate.

Cultus Summit and Hugeview Corner

Go right from the Transfer Junction Y ½ mile to another Y. The right leads in 1½ miles to the Big Hole and the route to Donkey Vista (which see); go left and switchback steeply up the edge of Mundt Creek valley in second-growth from the 1950s, the first windows opening to start the day's ravings. In 2 miles from Donkey Junction is a T at 3250 feet. The left, unsigned here, is Hookup Road, swinging around the head of Mundt Creek 2 miles to Transfer Road, offering the option of a loop return. Go right on SW-J-1110.

In ½ mile, at 3400 feet, the road levels. Spot a somewhat washed-out grownover sideroad left. This ascends in ¾ mile to the summit of Cultus, 3950 feet. Thoroughly jungled by 25-year-old scrub, the top lacks an all-around view. The window west, by a radio tower and shack, is stunning but smaller than the prospect from Hugeview. But there is more reason for the sidetrip than just to bag the peak — the wide window north and east to Twin Sisters, Baker, and Shuksan, the Skagit valley as foreground. What a show.

Returned from the sidetrip, past a serpentine-quarry helispot and the side-trail down to Donkey Vista, at 1 long contouring mile from Hookup Junction is Hugeview Corner, 3400 feet. Having fainted and fallen down and revived and gotten up, while the echoes of your bleats reverberate, sit and gaze: South — to Stimson and Frailey beyond Pilchuck Creek, Wheeler beyond the North Fork Stillaguamish, Pilchuck beyond the South Fork, Haystack and Si beyond the Skykomish, Rattlesnake and Issaquah Alps beyond the Snoqualmie, and Seattle and Rainier. Southwest and west — down to the Scout camp and green pastures of Walker Valley, Big Lake and Lake McMurray, Devils and Little, Everett and Possession Sound, Camano and Whidbey Islands, Port Townsend and the Olympics. Northwest — the shining Skagit winding through green floodplain and delta, Craft and Ika Islands in Skagit Bay, Erie on Fidalgo Island, the other San Juan Islands, Vancouver Island, Strait of Juan de Fuca. East — over headwaters of Nookachamps Creek into the maze of the Cultus Mountains. Sometime, bring overnight gear and camp, adding dimensions of the night, the lights of civilization and outer space.

Round trip to Hugeview Corner from gate 15 miles, allow 9 hours
High point 3400 feet, elevation gain 2650 feet
May-November

Round trip to Hugeview from Transfer Junction 7 miles, allow 5 hours
High point 3400 feet, elevation gain 1500 feet

Round-trip sidetrip to Cultus summit 1½ miles, elevation gain 450 feet,
add 1 extra hour

Mundt Peak

Go left from the Transfer Junction Y on Transfer Road 2 miles to a Y, 2760 feet.

The left (straight ahead) fork, Transfer Road, is worth walking 1 scant mile to

Mt. Baker from summit of Cultus Mountain, looking across Mundt Peak

a rocky sidehill at 2500 feet; here is the champion view down to houses and streets of Sedro Woolley and surrounding farms.

For the feature, ascend right on SW-J-1110. In ¼ mile, where Hookup Road proceeds right, around the head of Mundt Creek (see above), barely-drivable Spur Road goes left. Follow it 1¾ miles and near the end, at a landing marked by propane tanks, take a cat road uphill right the short bit to the summit of Mundt Peak, 3800 feet. In 1976 a couple of acres of the top were bulldozed flat and some sort of communications tower was erected.

If it's a sensational view over the awesome air ocean of the Skagit to Twin Sisters and Baker and Shuksan you want, this is the place. But there's much more: other summits of the Cultus Mountains, Woolley Lyman and peaks in Canada, peaks in the North Cascades south to Glacier and Whitehorse, and lowlands and saltwaterways and Olympics.

Round trip from Transfer Junction 8 miles, allow 5 hours
High point 3800 feet, elevation gain 1900 feet
May-November

Jeep trail to Butler Hill

Butler Hill (Map — page 97)

A former fire-lookout peak, not high enough ever to be very snowy and thus a choice objective in the white times of winter, yet high enough for detachment from the roar of I-5 and mooing of cows, presents a panorama south over the Skagit-Samish delta, dotted by the "islands" of Sterling and Burlington Hills, smeared by the sprawls of Burlington and Mount Vernon, to Cultus and Little and Devils, to Pleasant Ridge and Skagit Bay, Whidbey and Ika and Fidalgo (peak of Erie, oil refineries of March Point) Islands, Padilla Bay and Bay View Ridge. But the star is the green delta neatly cut by right-angle roads and fences into a quilt of farms.

Drive I-5 to Exit 236 and go off east on Bow Hill Road 1 scant mile to old Highway 99. Cross it onto Prairie Road and follow this east over the Samish floodplain 2 miles and turn right on F And S Grade Road. Continue 1 scant mile, cross the Samish River, sidehill Butler Hill, and bend south in a little sidevalley. Just past the bend a gravel road goes right, to a powerline. Across from it on the left is an obscure woods road — the summit route. Park on a shoulder of the powerline or on a second sideroad a hundred feet beyond the first. Elevation, 150 feet.

Rarely bothered by four-wheel sports nor with intolerable frequency by two-wheelers, the old lookout road climbs through nice mixed forest and big stumps. A green tower of ivy and ferns and moss is passed — a rock tumbled from cliffs above. Then the road ascends by some of these cliffs, mossy-velvet. Switchbacking and twisting and turning, in 1½ miles the way comes to a turnaround circle in a tree-ringed summit bowl.

Sentimentalists will want to walk the path to the right up the mossy slabs to the top, 886 feet; the only traces of the tower are anchor bolts in the rock. Not until the Second Skinning will there be a view here.

But a view there is. Walk back from the turnaround to a rock buttress and follow a boot-beaten track, then a scrambling route, up and over mossy brows several hundred feet to a wide picture window. It's a satisfying 45-degree arc south and southwest, whence the winter sun beams. Bask. Lulled by barking dogs and rumbling trucks, the noise softened by the distance, nap.

Round trip 3 miles, allow 2 hours
High point 886 feet, elevation gain 750 feet
All year

Blanchard Hill (Map — page 98)

More a Range than a Hill, Blanchard rises abruptly from the north edge of the Skagit-Samish delta and sprawls over a dozen square miles between the broad, deep glacier troughs of Oyster Creek and Friday Creek-Samish Lake. Railroad-logged in the 1920s-30s, it's now a tremendous second-growth wilderness. Second Wave clearcutting has commenced on the 8000 acres held by the DNR, but some provision will be made to preserve foot- and

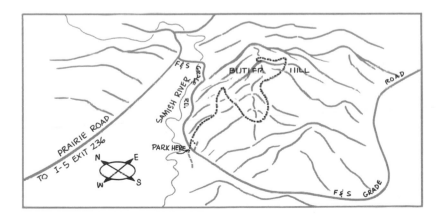

horse-trails. Adjoining, across Oyster valley, are the 2000 acres of Larrabee State Park. What a wildland! Miles and miles of partly-overgrown railroad grades invite days and days of lonesome explorations. Trails presently are few, but this one offers an introduction.

(*Note*: As of 1983 volunteers of the Pacific Northwest Trails Association are building a new trail—a segment of the PNT—over Blanchard. Watch for it.)

Drive I-5 to Exit 240 and go off east on (unsigned) Alger Road ¼ mile, turn south in Friday Creek valley on Colony Road, and in 1¾ miles more turn west on Wood Road. In ¾ mile, at an intersection with no signs, turn north, right, on (unsigned) Springs Road. In some 1¾ miles more, turn left, west, from county road onto a DNR logging road, probably unsigned. (If you reach a T with Shaw Road you've gone ⅓ mile too far.)

The logging road starts west, bends north, switchbacks south, contours around a hill and heads north, passing views of Friday valley and the great white watcher, Baker. At 2 miles from Springs Road, at 875 feet, is a large turnout-gravel pile. Here is the start of a new hiker-and-horse trail to be constructed someday, leading in some 3½ miles to Lily Lake. If you see a trail signed here, take it. Otherwise drive on 1 more mile. As the road is rising to a high point, having just crossed a small creek gully, spot a faint path on the left. Park on the turnout here, elevation 1150 feet. (Up on the cutbank a rotten stump is lettered in red paint, "12.")

A few steps from the road is a Y. The two forks ultimately rejoin and each has its interest; taking one up and the other down is a good stunt. The left, an old log skidway, goes straight up the fall line beside the creek. The right, built by local horsefolk, switchbacks to a rail grade and turns left on it through an old work camp littered with rusty kitchen utensils and chunks of broken donkeys and other machinery. At 1770 feet, a long ½ mile via skidway, a long 1 mile via switchbacks, is the reunion.

In ¼ mile more is a Y. The right leads ¼ mile to the bowl of 1862-foot Lizard Lake, a stump-and-snag-and-log-littered pond only a duck could love. The

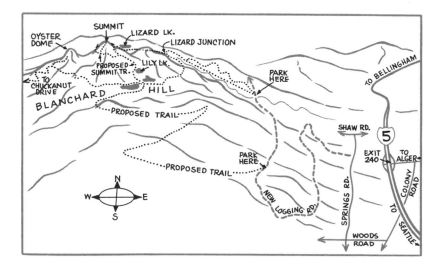

Lily Lake on Blanchard Hill

best feature is a three-storey boulder (where rock-climbers play) and the trog camp it provides.

From Lizard Junction the left fork contours steep hillside on the old rail grade, a lovely stroll in the deep green, tantalized by huge views blocked by the dense screen. (Let daylight in the swamp, DNR.) The trail bends through a rock slot to a forest bowl, passes the stumpy frog wallow of False Lily Lake, and in 1 mile comes to a Y.

Blanchard Summit

Take the right fork ¼ mile to (true) Lily Lake, 2010 feet, a clean droplet ringed by boggy meadows at the foot of the final peak. Once there were, reputedly, summit trails both from here and Lizard Lake, but if any in fact existed they're long since jungle-overgrown. The DNR will, with the aid of volunteers, provide a new summit trail from a camp to be built at the lake. Until then it's a beast. From a woods camp near the north end of Lily the surveyor followed some hatchetings and ribbonings up thickets and slippery slabs to the lovely bald-rock summit, 2300 feet — entirely ringed by 20-foot hemlocks. DNR surveyors have whacked down enough trees to open a window south-easterly to the Samish valley and the upper Skagit, and by blundering around in the bushes a person can see out to the Skagit delta, Cultus, Skagit Bay, and some San Juan Islands. But the one eye-opener is on an open rock below the top, with a stunner of a look at Twin Sisters and Baker. If, when DNR builds the new trail, it does not spare the chainsaw, Blanchard will be a boggling viewpoint of delta and volcano and all.

Round trip 6 miles, allow 5 hours
High point 2300 feet, elevation gain 1200 feet
February-December

Oyster Dome

For the single most striking feature of the entirety of Blanchard Hill (Range), take the left fork from Lily Junction. After ½ mile along ponds of Lily Creek, the trail leaves the old rail grade and plunges down. In ¼ mile, at 1600 feet, find a path going right, over nicely-waterfalling Lily Creek and up the far hillside. Step off the trail a couple feet to a cliff brink and partly-screened views over the Oyster Creek valley to Chuckanut and the San Juans. Proceed a bit more and at 1700 feet emerge in a heap of gigantic boulders at the foot of the slabs, trogs, ribs, cliffs, cracks, chimneys, and bat caves rising vertically to the 2085-foot top of Oyster Dome.

Though not surveyed due to an attack of acute lonesomeness, a route to the summit of the Dome shouldn't be too difficult, starting at 2000 feet from the top of the plunge and beating bushes a scant ½ mile or so. The view ought to be grand.

The remainder of the Lily Creek trail, not surveyed, drops to Oyster Creek and Chuckanut Drive.

Round-trip sidetrip from Lily Junction 2 miles, elevation gain 500 feet, add 1½ hours

Chuckanut Mountain (Map — page 102)

In all the hundreds of miles from California through Oregon and Washington the Cascade Mountains sit far back from saltwater. But here at the north edge of the Skagit delta the range juts to the very shore and from heights above 2000 feet dives to the beaches. Spectacular. Maybe a geologist would say these aren't the Cascades at all, but an extension of the drowned range that forms the San Juan Islands. Certainly here is the most dazzling view of that archipelago.

Each vista point has a variation. Some look so straight down it seems a thrown rock would miss highway and railroad and hit the water. South over the Skagit delta are Devils and Cultus and Rainier, and even the Issaquah Alps and Seattle. Southwest over myriad islands and waterways is the backdrop of the Olympics. But it's the San Juans that enthrall. There is Fidalgo with the hump of Erie, the plumes of refineries. Then low-profile Guemes, then high, double-humped, wild-wooded Cypress. Below, enclosing Samish Bay, is the long hook of Samish Island. West on big Orcas is the high peak (see the summit lookout tower) of Constitution. Mostly hidden, San Juan. North is the tall cleaver of Lummi Peak on Lummi Island. And Vendovia and Eliza and Hat

Telephoto of refineries at Anacortes and Olympic Mountains from Chuckanut Mountain

and Sinclair and Lopez and — well, counting islands is the sport. How many can be seen? About 20, 25? Would you accept 35?

Let it be noted that though Chuckanut has summits as high as 1940 feet, they are wooded and rather viewless and not worth an effort. At 1800 feet on the side of Peak 1940 is Cyrus Gates Overlook, tourist-drivable; at 1¼ miles north of the main entrance to Larrabee State Park, turn right from Chuckanut Drive at the sign, "Cleator Road," and ascend a scant 4 miles to the overlook. Okay for the car-bound, but pitifully inferior to the views gained on foot, because the walking routes get out of the woods into opens of the Chuckanut Burn of the mid-1960s, where fire, salvage-logging clearcuts, and sandstone cliffs have combined to eliminate extraneous greenery.

Drive I-5 to Exit 231 and go off on Highway 11 (Chuckanut Drive). Shortly past milepost 11, on the flat above Pigeon Point, is a large turnout, elevation 150 feet. Park here.

(The loop hike can just as well be done from a north starting point. For that, continue on Chuckanut Drive to ½ mile north of milepost 12 and park at the vista point atop Dogfish Point, elevation 190 feet. Across the highway spot the narrow woods road switchbacking southward.)

Walk north a bit on the highway to a sideroad right, marked by white posts maybe connected by a chain, to an old borrow pit-garbage dump. Ascend the very steep, narrow, gullied woods road, drivable only by sports, who on

Sundays may ruin the peace of the first stretch. The road switchbacks up the ridge west of Oyster Creek, with windows to Blanchard Hill. In 1 mile, at 750 feet, POW! On a point, from an outcrop of sandstone-conglomerate, a window opens wide and so does your mouth. But this is merely the first of the succession of panoramas that by trip's end will leave the hiker drained of shouts. (For a short walk, this makes a satisfying destination, a round trip of 2 miles, 600 feet gain, 1½ hours.)

Continue on, swinging off the point in a small valley; the Y here is of a shortcut, left, and the slightly longer way, right; take either. Rounding another point, the way enters snags of the Chuckanut Burn, passes another great promontory vista, and enters a sizable valley. Here, at 950 feet, 1½ miles from the start, is a triple fork. Climbing steeply to the right is a fun road that quickly deadends. Contouring straight ahead on a contour is the sport-beloved main road, a nice forest walk with (after some brush-beating when the road ends) great views, but no better than those of the recommended route, which is 1½ miles shorter. For the recommended walk, take the grassy road to the left, downhill.

The way climbs from the sizable valley, contours through the burn over a small creek, and halts all wheels by turning straight up the rocks, at 1200 feet, 1 long mile from Triple Fork Junction, reaching a sport-drivable spur of Mountain Road. (Hikers who take the long route will come down from brush on logging cat tracks and this spur to rejoin the route here, having done some 2½ miles from Triple Fork.)

Proceed on the spur, which switchbacks north and descends moderately. In ¾ mile, at 900 feet, switchback south on a lesser road blocked by a mound of dirt. Walk the wide-open ridge crest, dumb-struck by views, fascinated by the geology — the north-south channels along the slope, the little valleylets, the ribs of sandstone. In ½ mile the road ends on a promontory, 860 feet. An old cat track continues, an airy skyway descending the ridge crest, then turning off in a gully, then sidehilling south, passing wonderful sandstone cliffs, weirdly weathered. Switchbacking, dropping into forest, becoming drivable road, at 1 mile from the promontory the way hits Chuckanut Drive. (For a shorter walk, climb from here to the promontory, the views smashing; round trip 2 miles, 700 feet gain, allow 1½ hours.)

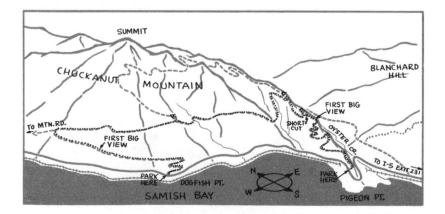

Complete the loop by walking south on Chuckanut, enjoying more views and coal seams and palm-leaf casts, returning to the start in 1½ miles.

Loop trip 6½ miles, allow 5 hours
High point 1200 feet, elevation gain 1100 feet
All year

Lost Lake (Map — page 104)

Geology is the central attraction of the over-the-hill section of Larrabee State Park. The sedimentary structures strike northwest-southeast, dictating alignment of valleys and ridges, and the shales-sandstones-conglomerates differ so greatly in resistance to erosion as to form prominent trenches and ribs and cliffs with the same orientation. Here in the second-growth wilderness a myriad ponds and lakes and marshes dribble together to form Oyster Creek, which exploits a line of weakness to cut between Chuckanut Mountain and Blanchard Hill to saltwater. Occupying one trench in the rocks is Lost Lake. And lost a walker may well feel in these faraway depths where once the Puget Glacier gouged.

Drive Highway 11, Chuckanut Drive, to ¼ mile north of milepost 14. At a broad gravel turnout, Mountain Road (unsigned) takes off right. Elevation, 170 feet. In fire season and much of the winter the road is barred by a big white gate and the hike must start here. That's good; it's a beauty of a footroad when

Bleeding heart

unmolested by wheels, a magnificent snowline-prober. Additionally, if the walk begins at the highway it makes sense to do a loop, taking in Fragrance Lake (which see) on the descent.

Assuming the gate is open and one drives up through the fine fir forest, by the delicious waterfall creeks and sensuous, velvet-like, moss-fern walls, in 1¼ miles, at 675 feet, a sideroad right (signed by a small post with a "1" on the downhill side) leads in ¾ mile to intersect the Chuckanut Mountain hike (which see). At 2¼ miles, marked by the "2" post (on the uphill side, a "3"), is the sideroad right to Lost Lake. Park here, elevation 1050 feet.

In big-fir, maybe-virgin forest, then alders, passing a great window to the San Juan Islands, Skagit delta, and Olympics, at 1 long mile from Mountain Road the way reaches a 1577-foot saddle in the ridge of Chuckanut Mountain. Here is a T. The right, incompletely surveyed, goes out of the park to logging shows on Peak 1860. The left is the way to Lost Lake. Descend an aldery ravine, with looks over Oyster Creek to 1870-foot "Cedar Peak" and 2300-foot Blanchard, and I-5 and Samish Lake, and Cascades beyond.

The road bottoms and levels beneath an imposing cliff. Lost Lake is glimpsed below in big firs. At 1 long mile from the saddle is a T. The left, unsurveyed, is shown on the map as going 3 miles north to the civilization of Bellingham; from that civilization roars a legion of jeepers and razzers to enliven the wilds. Take the right a few yards to a turnaround. A mucky, wheelfree trail proceeds ¼ mile to the head of the black-bottomed, weak-tea lake. Ducks take off, scaring a walker half to death. Where a shore trail goes right, turn left up rocks and follow the sandstone-hearted rib downlake to an excellent mossy slab tilted steeply into the lake, elevation 1182 feet. This is the lunch spot. But by all means continue a bit farther to where lake water pours over a rock sill and sheets foaming-white down black cliffs. Skid down a path for close looks. Below is a beaver pond in another long valley, contained by another long rock rib. And the bottom of the Oyster valley is still a couple hundred feet below, with more lakes, marshes, and a maze of old logging roads. You could get lost, okay.

Round trip from Mountain Road 5 miles, allow 4 hours
High point 1577 feet, elevation gain 1000 feet
February-December

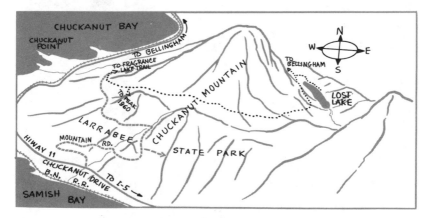

For the looping exit via Fragrance Lake, walk up Mountain Road several minutes to the Fragrance Lake parking area and trail sign. From Chuckanut Drive, this Lost Lake-Fragrance Lake loop trip is 10 miles, elevation gain 2000 feet, a decent day's exercise.

Fragrance Lake (Map — page 105)

When all roads are loud with machines, all beaches hectic with childish laughter, when all the splendid 1965 acres of Larrabee State Park seem groaning under weight of deserved popularity, there is yet a haven, a foot-only trail through marvelous forest to a gem of a lake in a quiet green bowl. And on the way is a superb view over Samish Bay to the San Juan archipelago. What's the fragrance? Peace, it's wonderful.

Drive Highway 11, Chuckanut Drive, to Larrabee State Park. A bit north of the highway-side garages and ranger's house is a parking area and trail sign, "Viewpoint .9 miles, Fragrance Lake 1.9 miles." Park here, elevation 130 feet.

Switchback steeply a short bit up to cross the grade of the old Mount Vernon-Bellingham Interurban Railway — now the Interurban Bike Trail, eventually to extend to Bellingham, and worth a walk in its own right. The good trees begin — and get better. The trail switchbacks up through noble specimens ¾ mile to a saddle. The trail ahead is "Fragrance Lake, 1.1 miles."

First turn left to "Viewpoint .2 mile." In gorgeous forest, firs up to 5 feet thick, proceed to a railing-guarded cliff brink. At an elevation of 650 feet survey the horizon of islands and waters from refineries of March Point on Fidalgo to Guemes and Cypress and Orcas and Samish and Lummi and the rest. And look straight down to the highway and the shores of Wildcat Cove.

Then return to the junction, follow a creeklet down, then again switchback steeply up to another saddle. Here a sidetrail climbs right a few steps to Mountain Road — the short route to the lake. But Mountain Road often is closed in winter and the long trail then is the short way.

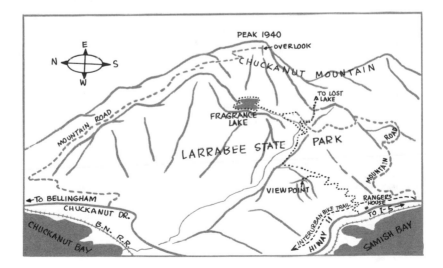

From the junction the trail drops gently ¼ mile along a small vale in tall-tree forest of cedar and hemlock, a lush understory, to the lake, 1030 feet.

Good-to-meager path circles the lake, over creeks, through groves of 8-foot cedars and 6-foot spruces, under gray rock walls half-hidden in greenery. All is silence. Then — "splash!" — a fish leaps.

Round trip 4 miles, allow 3 hours
High point 1100 feet, elevation gain 1000 feet
All year

Woolley Lyman Mountain (Map — page 108)

Presumably the locals have a different name for this map-nameless be-hemoth lumping high (4257 feet) above the Skagit valley, overpowering Sedro Woolley (56 feet) at one foot, Lyman (87 feet) at an other. By whatever name or none, this unquestionably is the premier platform for viewing the vastness of the Skagit delta. And what else? Good grief! Pray that Baker doesn't erupt or you'll get it all over you. More? Yes, a grand total of five (5, count them, 5) mountain ranges. And as a cherry on top, the best-preserved donkey engine found (outside a museum) in the **Footsore** surveys.

Note: This enormous mountain, occupying some 60 square miles, is an "island" cut off from companion Cascades by Skagit south, Samish west, and the Nooksack River-Jones Creek trench northwest-southeast. In addition to the route surveyed to the summit, there are a radio-tower service road up from Lyman and logging roads from Jones Creek-Nooksack River. The surveyed route is the hardest but the best.

Drive Highway 9 north 10 miles from Sedro Woolley to Wickersham, 314 feet, and turn east on Wickersham Road. In ½ mile, just across the puny Samish River, the main street curves left; go off it right on Ennis Creek Road, which seems too meager to get anywhere. Have faith. (However, in ½ mile is a gate, usually open; if closed, the summit is a long ways away.) Narrow and often steep but solid and safe (except when washed out), the road climbs through old second-growth and new clearcuts, starting off southward, switch-backing north, south, north, and, at 2050 feet, a scant 4½ miles from the highway, south. At 5 miles, 2350 feet, hurrah, an open window! Brace yourself — green pastures of the Samish are precipitously below, the bulk of Anderson is huge to the west, and out the slot south is the Skagit and out the slot north is Lake Whatcom. For a snowline-prober starting in Wickersham, ascending the pleasant footroad, this is a dandy turnaround.

It's getting about time to stop driving and start walking. The suggested spot is Snagtop Junction, 2450 feet, 5½ miles. (Note: In case the gate at ½ mile from the highway happens to be closed,here is a satisfying destination. And also for a snowline-probe.)

Even if you vote to drive farther for the main hike, pause here to ascend Snagtop Crag, 2550 feet, several minutes away via an old quarry road. From bald slabs of a greenish metamorphic rock among silvered snags, on the brink of an alarming, overhanging, 180-foot cliff, look to the green checkerboard of the Samish and Nooksack valleys, Lake Whatcom, Anderson, and Skagit valley.

Mt. Baker from Woolley Lyman Mountain

For the main feature, onward. The road swings around the head of Ennis Creek, crossing it; at a Y in ⅓ mile from Snagtop Junction, go right. Climb from the Ennis valley around a shoulder onto the main ridge of the mountain; little windows grow larger, eliciting gee whizzes and wowees, but you ain't seen nothing yet. At 3200 feet, 1½ miles from the Ennis Y, where a lesser road goes straight, switchback left, north. In another ½ mile, at 3500 feet, where a lesser road goes straight, switchback right. If you've not already changed from wheels to boots, do it soon — shortly the road is slid out and unmaintained.

Now in continuous stunning views, the way contours the mountainside just below the ridge crest. The airy, open slopes clearcut in the 1960s or so have only modest shrubbery amid the silvering slash, the splashing creeks. Around a corner the 4257-foot summit appears and then, at 3800 feet, 3½ miles from Snagtop Junction, the road withers away and dies.

A party electing to stop here would not be disappointed; the views are eyeball-bulging, head-spinning. But golly, the summit is close, why quit? You may think of reasons in the next bit, angling uphill from the road-end through slash and marsh marigolds and 12-foot silver firs, but in no more than a couple dozen groans and dirty words, voila, at 3950 feet, hit the Willow Road, a thicket of whips but better than slash. Follow it right ¼ mile and receive your reward— a donkey engine resting on skids, the wooden roof snow-crushed and the ironware rusty and willow-encumbered, but virtually intact; in the boiler fur-

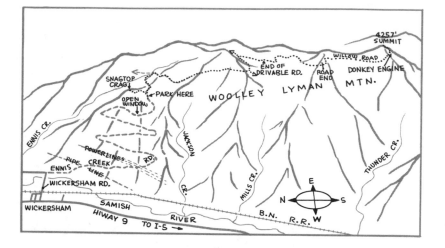

nace the ashes of its last fire (when? 1960ish?) look as if they might still be warm. Worth the trip in itself.

But don't quit now. A couple hundred feet beyond the donkey leave Willow Road and proceed straight up, partly following open alleys, partly thrusting through young trees. The schisty, stumpy summit appears. And in perhaps ¾ mile and 1¼ hours from where the road ended and the silly stuff started, see a huge granite erratic (the Puget Glacier was here!) and then (curses!) a road.

But never mind. Several steps up the road is the top, and here you cannot be bitter. To list a tenth of the sights would require a chapter. But demanding mention are: Skagit valley and delta, and Stillaguamish delta too, from Chuckanut Mountain to Camano Island, Sedro Woolley to La Conner; San Juan Islands and Whidbey Island and Everett pulpmills; Cultus and Three Fingers and Glacier; Sauk Mountain and Eldorado; Lake Whatcom and Bellingham Bay and Garibaldi; fresh clearcuts dropping east to Jones Creek-South Fork Nooksack valley, slopes of the 4100-foot summit just north all freshly skinned, beautifully desolate; iron-red crags of Twin Sisters; five (5, count them, 5) mountain ranges — a great sweep of North Cascades, the Olympics, the San Juan Islands range, Vancouver Island Mountains, and white giants of the British Columbia Coast Range. That's about a tenth of a tenth.

Oh yes, don't forget the Great White Watcher. If it happens to be steaming the day you're here, keep your boots on, ready to run.

Round trip from Snagtop Junction 8½ miles, allow 7 hours
High point 4257 feet, elevation gain 1800 feet
May-November

PUGET SOUND (sic) TRAIL:
EVERETT TO BELLINGHAM

Beyond log-dominated Everett waterfront and Snohomish River estuary the Puget Sound Trail (which by this point has left Puget Sound far behind) regains beach at Priest Point. Thereafter only the briefest residential interruptions break through the tall bluff of glacial drift guarding the wildness; moreover, unlike the shore south of Everett, there is no railroad to mar the meeting of waves and sand. The beach walks along Port Susan Bay are among the very finest so near Puget Sound City.

Then commences the epic Crossing of the Deltas, 70 miles as the dike winds and foot plods, unique among pedestrian routes of the West (and probably the East and South and North). Most walkers are drawn initially by the fleets of waterfowl sailing, mobs of shorebirds hustling, raptors patrolling, songbirds chirping. So famous is the birding that fans often fail to mention the panoramas over marshes and bays to islands and Olympics, over fields of corn and cabbage and tulips and cows to Cascades. Never are the mountains so dramatic as when seen from "at sea" in the overwhelming horizontality, where a walker feels so conspicuously vertical as almost to want to get down in the muck and wiggle.

History is central to the delta experience. Agriculture started even before the 1860s, when dikes began claiming (farmers and engineers insist on calling it "reclaiming," as if they were here first and Nature were the intruder) the riparian and tidal marshes. Hamlets founded in that era remain, charming antiques more or less hale, and everywhere are wonderful old barns and three-storey farmhouses replete with chimneys and gingerbread. The 19th century lives! And dies: there also are derelict houses sagging in the silt, rotten boats moldering in sloughs, doooying pilings thrust out in bays, and names on old maps marking the sites of vanished villages.

Not to be scorned is walking delta roads; the barnwatching is the best, as well as the savoring of the ripe aroma of manure, as characteristic of the delta as pulpmill perfume of Everett. However, the survey sought to follow the outermost feasible line, the boundary dike between crops on one side and tidal marsh or tideflat on the other. As with a river, the dike necessarily is continuous, but as with kayakers, dike-walkers must find places to "put in." Stressed herein are put-ins that have easy parking and unchallenged access to dikes.

"Challenge" is the key word. Dikes belong to abutting landowners; strangers are variously tolerated — or not. In these pages dikes are classified by their status during the 1977-1981 surveys. A Class 1 dike is public (such as, in the Skagit Wildlife Recreation Area) and may be walked by anyone any time. A Class 2 dike is private, may have a few mild signs and step-over stock fences, but is some distance from habitations and ordinarily is passable without objection — though one ought always to be quiet and discreet, and must retreat apologetically if told to do so. Ownership of a Class 3 dike is irrelevant because it is overgrown by thorny thickets of wild rose or that damnable combination of the alien (introduced by the Enemy of Mankind) Himalaya and evergreen blackberries, the clothes-tearing, arm-scratching, eye-gouging, throat-slashing, impassable tangle of "hellberry." A Class 4 dike is strictly off-limits, either because it goes too near homes or because the signs and "mean-it" fences say the residents aren't fooling, they don't want you around. (Class 3 and 4 dikes sometimes can be got by at low tide via saltgrass meadows or tideflats. The old hands among delta walkers wear hip-length rubber boots to permit comfy knee-deep wading of small channels.)

The opening segment of the Crossing is the Stillaguamish delta. Without a break this merges into the Skagit delta, which as traversed on its shore has three parts. First is the "south delta," consisting largely of Fir Island, enclosed between the South Fork and North Fork distributaries of the Skagit that in modern times have emptied the mountain water into Skagit Bay. The south delta ends at the "come ashore" San Juan Archipelago, where rock-hearted "islands" of forest green now ringed by fields indeed were ringed by water before silting and diking combined to dry their feet. Beyond the "islands" of Fish Town and Pleasant Ridge is the "middle delta," where the Swinomish Channel narrowly cuts off Fidalgo into Islandhood. Not for centuries has the Skagit coursed the middle delta to Padilla Bay, though an abandoned flood-control scheme would have transferred part of the flow there by digging the Avon Bypass. The "island" of Bay View Ridge separates middle delta from "north delta," to whose ownership, in absence of the mighty Skagit, the puny Samish River pretends.

The conclusion of the Trail is as unique as the delta. After staying far back from saltwater in all its length from California, here the Cascade Range juts out to the shore and from the loftiness of Chuckanut Mountain plummets to the beach. Except there's darn little beach. Just rock cliffs. Never fear. To the rescue of the hiker comes his old friend from the south, the familiar pair of shining steel rails leading onward from Samish Bay to Chuckanut Bay to Bellingham Bay and the triumphant denouement of the Puget Sound Trail.

USGS maps: Everett, Marysville, Tulalip, Stanwood, Juniper Beach, Utsalady, Conway, La Conner, Deception Pass, Bow, Anacortes, Bellingham South

Mile 0-6½: Everett Waterfront-Snohomish River-Marysville (Map — page 112)

When last heard from (**Footsore 1**), the Puget Sound Trail had left Puget Sound and slunk by the Everett Amtrak Station and plentiful parking, several blocks on Hewitt from the center of downtown Everett.

This opening segment of the Trail northward is excellently grubby-grimy, a delight to fans of the Industrial Revolution. Everett, the premier Milltown, has the region's greatest concentration of wood-processing mills, miles of them, and to keep them busy, lakes of logs, seas of logs, oceans of logs floating in waterways, mountains of logs piled on reclaimed tideflats. Bored with hike after hike of trees-trees-trees? Come see what happens when they're made into logs-logs-logs — and lumber and pulp. Tugs pull logs around, helicopters fly them, ships load them for Japan. And the mills clankety-clank-hiss-boom-bah them into boards and chips and paper.

The Trail sets out north beside the railroad tracks, then switches to Norton Avenue. Star attraction of the host of mills is the huge sulphite (white paper)

Pulpmill at mouth of Snohomish River in Everett

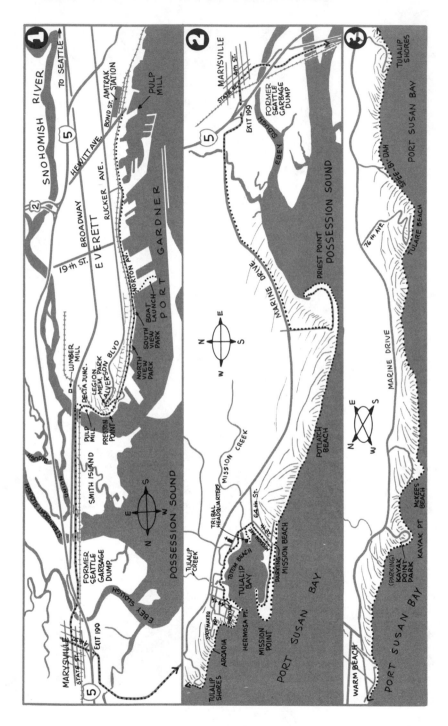

pulpmill (source of one of the three steam plumes that used to identify Everett from distant viewpoints in the mountains but now so cleaned up that Milltown is very hard to spot). At 1¾ miles is the jutting fill of Port of Everett's Norton Avenue Boat Launch; plentiful parking and a jolly good viewpoint of logs rafted in Port Gardner Bay, protected by a breakwater island from stormy winds that blow.

The next mile is a break in the industrial procession — the shore walkway and gardens, parking areas and grand views, of Port Gardner Bay South View and North View Parks.

Where mills resume, Norton climbs the bluff to join Alverson Boulevard. A mandatory sidetrip is the ½-mile walk up the viaduct to Legion Memorial Park and its bluff-top viewpoint. Tremendous. Down Possession Sound to the pastel oil tanks of Mukilteo, over to little Gedney (Hat) Island and long Whidbey Island and the Olympics, to Camano Head and Port Susan Bay, north over the Snohomish estuary to Wheeler, Frailey, Devils, Cultus, Baker.

Back down by the water, the Trail returns to railroad for a mile, rounds Preston Point to banks of the Snohomish River, passes the stupendous hissing rumbling steaming kraft (brown-bag) pulpmill (a plume-maker thriftily running entirely on sawmill waste) to Delta Junction, beside the twin bridges of old Highway 99.

Scramble up the embankment to old 99. There's nothing for it — the surveyor sought a neater route over sloughs and islands but was frustrated — the 2¾ miles to Marysville are all road-walking. But definitely worth it. In succession are crossed: Snohomish River (views downstream to the kraft mill and upstream to the lumber mill, source of the third steam plume); Smith Island (a huge log dump and sawdust mountain); Union Slough and a nameless island (nice boatyard); Steamboat Slough (another pair of drawbridges, for a total of five bridges over it; more views to the Cascades); a large island heaped with Seattle garbage; Ebey Slough (be careful before crossing it to go left on 99); Marysville and a final batch of ducks, boatworks, and mills.

Mile 6½-14: Marysville-Priest Point-Mission Beach (Map — page 112)

Industry and Snohomish River are left behind and the Trail begins miles of bluff-guarded wild beach interspersed with short bits of beachside habitation.

However, forget the first 4½ miles — the route is entirely on Marine Drive with no beach access — and if you could get there, there's no beach, just trash-covered muck of the Snohomish estuary.

At Priest Point (site of a Catholic mission in 1858; the bell is now in St. Anne's Church, Tulalip) true beach resumes. However, getting on the beach there through the solid row of homes is chancy. A wild-eyed (but polite) pedestrian bearing a strange device ("Bellingham or Bust") might be let through; most folks had better do this as a nice 3-mile walk from the north.

But to describe the route from the south: The beginning of walkable beach is at a salvage-tug dock in the angle between river slough and bay beach. The view is grand over Possession Sound to the jetty guarding Port Gardner Bay, to pulpmill plumes, to oil tanks and ferry of Mukilteo, to ships at anchor and ships underway, to rotting old hulks — all in all, the best middle-distance perspective there is on Milltown.

In ¾ mile the low spit of Priest Point, wall-to-wall houses, yields to bluff and houses retreat to the top, always there for the next 1 mile but never a bother.

Sunken boats in Tulalip Bay

Look over the water to Gedney (Hat) and Whidbey Islands, ships and log rafts. If a little tug putt-putts to the beach and a man wades ashore, don't panic — it's the log patrol come to snake off logs escaped from rafts. Look to mountains from Three Fingers to Index. Hear the drone of Everett, savor the rich aroma of pulp.

Staircases down from homes of Potlatch Beach end and for 1 mile the beach is lonesome under tangled forest and naked cliffs of a bluff 100 feet, then 200 feet high. Then begin waterside cottages of Mission Beach.

Drive Marine Drive north from I-5 (Exit 199), turn left on 64 Street (signed "Mission Beach, Tulalip Bay, Tribal Center") a scant ½ mile to a Y. Go left on 28 Avenue ½ mile. Just across the street from the fire station, park in a large, mucky turnout atop the low bluff and follow a roadway down to old pilings of the vanished Mission Beach Boathouse. Walk south.

Mile 14-18: Mission Beach-Tulalip Bay (Map — page 112)

The feature is picturesque little Tulalip Bay, and a cozy spot it is, with a ton of history, much of it painful. Here are headquarters of the Tulalip Reservation to which Governor Stevens and the U.S. Army herded the Snohomish, Stillaguamish, Snoqualmie, and Sammamish peoples.

From Mission Beach the Trail goes 1 mile north on fine under-the-bluff beach to "Mission Point," whose long arm enwraps Tulalip Bay on the southwest. On the bay side a long sandspit invites a sidetrip out in the middle of the bay for close looks at the hamlets of Tulalip, Totem Beach, and Mission Beach. At low tide walkers can then get off the beach onto public road, Mission Beach Drive, and loop back past a fleet of pleasure craft floating, and a fleet sunken, so many moldering wrecks the waters appear to have been the scene of a miniature Pearl Harbor.

Just before the fire station, turn north on Mission Avenue. Joining 28 Avenue at 64 Street, the way passes a broad flat on a stubby peninsula, site of a village far in the past, then of the Indian Agency Office, and now the business and social center of the peoples.

Crossing Mission Creek and passing through Totem Beach, the road passes below pretty and historic St. Anne's Church. From there a new road rounds the bay but the old road, blocked off, can be walked to Tulalip Creek, dammed for a salmon-rearing pond from which the Tulalips have released some 5,000,000 juvenile salmon since 1970. In a scant ½ mile more the road is joined by 44 Avenue and reaches a gap in houses, a mass of logs and pilings, and a large, undeveloped, public parking area, base for hikes south and north.

To reach this parking area, from Marine Drive turn westerly on 44 Avenue, signed "Hermosa Point," and drop ¼ mile to the water.

Mile 18-25½: Tulalip Bay-Kayak Point Park (Map — page 112)

When nominating sections of the Trail for the Best Walks Award, don't omit this beauty. At a half-dozen spots roads have crept down the treacherous bluffs, but these are brief interruptions; there are three 1-mile wild stretches and three shorter ones, and more than half the length is utterly lonesome. The only public accesses are at the ends of the strip.

The way rounds Hermosa Point, with views south to pulpmill plumes, to mountains from Si to Rainier to Olympics. North of the point ¾ mile is the last piling-protected boathouse (of Arcadia) and the start of the first wild bit, 1¼ miles long. From beneath the noble bluff, largely sand with blue-clay cliffs, up to 200 feet tall, the views south to Whidbey Island begin to yield to Camano Head and Island, across the mouth of Port Susan Bay.

A bulge is rounded, views of Tulalip Bay are lost, and homes of Tulalip Shores occupy ¼ mile of a narrow sand flat. A scant ½ mile of empty beach leads to the wide valley and cute old community of Spee-Bi-Dah, one-time summer cottages clinging to forest hillsides above the green vale. In 1 mile more of wildness another bulge is rounded to another inhabited beach bench beneath an imposing 400-foot bluff. This ⅓ mile of Tulare Beach is followed by a ¼-mile wild bit, a lesser bulge, behind which is Sunny Shores, the homes mostly up on the hill. Then comes 1 mile of wild beach — though with several trails down the 300-foot bluff from unseen houses. Now comes McKees Beach, ½ mile of homes on a sandy-flat point. A final ⅓ mile of wild-bluff beach leads to Kayak Point Park.

Beach at Kayak Point (Snohomish County) Park

Mile 25½-32: Kayak Point Park-Warm Beach-Hat Slough
(Map — page 112, 118)

It's ending, it is, the "typical Puget Sound beach." Here is the Trail's final offering of such, a last wild beauty before starting the Something Else of the deltas.

Go off I-5 on Exit 199 and in ¾ mile take the left, signed "Tulalip," and follow this main road (Marine Drive, though not so signed at first) just short of 13 miles to Kayak Point (Snohomish County) Park. Turn left ½ mile down to the beach parking lot.

Do not neglect the superb park, 670 acres with camps and 3300 feet of public beach. ARCO planned to build a refinery here but aroused citizens of Port Susan Bay chased it north to a more compliant county. Not that ARCO took a beating; it stands to make a bundle on real estate games, the value of subdivisions enhanced by this fine park in their midst. Ultimately a trail system will be built through the uplands; presently there are paths worth walking for the forest, including some giant Douglas firs; the long-range dream is for a Kayak Point-To-Cascade Crest Trail. Combining wildwoods and saltwater, the park features a large bird population, notably bald eagles that visit almost daily and often including a veritable herd of herons, and extra-large and bold coyotes.

116

But, to the beach. Once past several homes, the first 2 miles are mostly wild, most houses kept respectfully distant from water by the bluff, up to 180 feet high, of till and blue clay and much-played-on sand cliffs. Views are over Port Susan Bay to Camano Island and Olympics.

A point is rounded and the view opens north to the head of Port Susan, to the Stillaguamish delta, to Chuckanut Mountain. And cheek-by-jowl homes line the beach for the next 1½ miles. This is Warm Beach, where the surveyor swam 50 yards, long ago, to become a First Class Scout. The once-enormously-popular public beach now is entirely private, not so much as a streetend access.

A bunch of old pilings are passed, views begin north to Cultus and Twin Sisters and Baker, and habitations are left behind. So too is "dry land," the bluff retreating inland, the beach yielding to mudflat bordered by delta saltmarsh and tanglewood swamp. At medium tides the tidal channels can be hopped over to reach the dike, a Class 2.

Fields and cows on one side, saltgrass on the other ("meadows" and then mudflats that in low tide can be wandered far out in the bay), the dike twists and turns 1 mile to Hat Slough, at this moment in history the chief distributary of the Stillaguamish River, which makes the head of Port Susan largely a freshwater bay (and that's why, to the amazement of the surveyor on a frigid winter day, it was partly frozen over).

In 1½ more miles beside or near the slough-river, passing low-tide sandbars, horses, crabapple trees, cornfields, a grand barn and (walk softly, politely) a farmhouse, the dike comes to Marine Drive a few steps south of the bridge over Hat Slough.

Mile 32-41: Hat Slough-South Pass-Stillaguamish River-Stanwood (Map — page 118)

After that prelude, here it really starts, the Long March over the deltas; not for many a mile, now, will the stranger with the strange device see more than scraps of true beach. But birds? Wow!

Note: This segment can be done as a 9½-mile loop, hiking the first 8 miles of the Trail and then, rather than proceeding into Stanwood, returning 1½ miles on Marine Drive to the start.

Go off I-5 on Exit 212 and drive Highway 532 to the east edge of Stanwood. Just past the bridge over the railroad turn south on Marine Drive, signed "Warm Beach," 2½ miles to Boe Road. Park near the north side of the bridge over Hat Slough.

Walk Boe Road west ½ mile; where it goes straight, climb atop the Class 2 dike along Hat Slough. In 1½ miles more the dike reaches the slough mouth and turns north. To the right are fields and mountain views, to the left are marshes and open water (or vast mudflats) of Port Susan, beyond which is Camano Island.

In 1 mile more the dike turns inland to the end of Boe Road (no parking) and bends north a winding 1¾ miles to the mouth of South Pass. Emptying into Port Susan Bay, this distributary of the Stillaguamish River connects to another, West Pass, that empties into Skagit Bay, the two providing boats a passage through; the passes also make Camano an Island, here a clam-toss away.

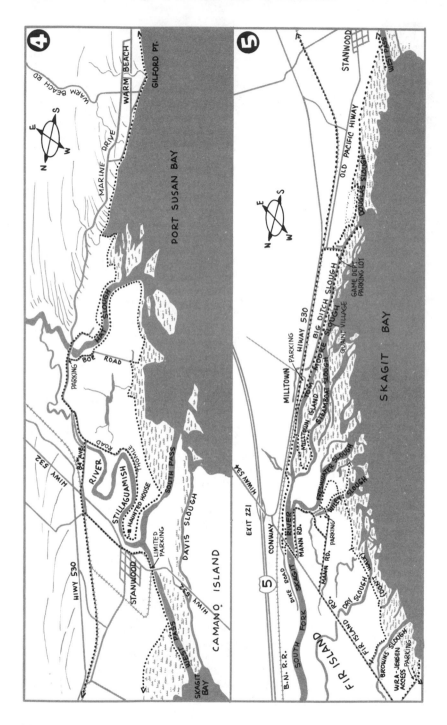

Stillaguamish River from Thomle Road bridge

In 1 mile the dike comes to the division of the Stillaguamish into passes and turns east along the river. The tall smokestack of Hamilton Lumber's long-gone mill marks the location of Stanwood — a location that swings all over the compass as the river meanders east, south, even southwest, then southeast, north, and so on. A sidetrip on cow paths leads to a haunted farmhouse, three storeys, three chimneys, tilted in delta mud, hellberry-overgrown, upstairs windows framing faces of Charles Addams characters.

The next scant 1½ miles continue on the dike, passing across-the-river Stanwood and its industrial cluster, then a line of fishing boats; when the dike becomes impassable, shift onto the farm lane passing headquarters of industrial-farm Twin City Food Inc.

Here begins public Thomle Road, an alternative to the dike when it's too overgrown. In a scant ¾ mile Thomle leaves the river at a northward meander and the hiker is best-advised to do the same, cutting across the neck of the meander, in ¼ mile returning to the river.

In ⅓ mile more on Thomle is a bridge, left on 84 Avenue NW, over the river. (To close the 9½-mile loop, turn right here.) The Trail crosses the river to Marine Drive, passes under Highway 532, and after a final scant 1 mile from Thomle reaches the main drag of Stanwood.

119

Mile 41-45¾: Stanwood-West Pass-WRA Big Ditch Slough Access (Map — page 118)

The Stillaguamish delta is polished off — and the Big Show, the Skagit delta, begun. Now the view is over Skagit Bay to the north end of Camano Island and to Whidbey Island, to peaklet islands of Ika and Goat, and to Mount Erie on Fidalgo Island. Vistas open to more San Juan Islands and over the delta to Little, Devils, Cultus, Woolley Lyman, Chuckanut, Baker.

Note: This segment lends itself to an 8-mile loop, doing the 4¾ miles to Big Ditch, then returning via the Big Ditch Access road and railroad tracks (pleasantly traversing fields and marshes) 3¼ miles to Stanwood.

Go off I-5 on Exit 212 to Highway 532, on the east edge of Stanwood exit right on Highway 530, drop to Stanwood, and park near the railroad tracks (or, if not planning to do the loop, anywhere else in town).

Walk 1 long mile west through town to the river-side factory complex of Twin City Food. Find the deadend rail spur and follow tracks to the split of the Stillaguamish, then north along West Pass under the Highway 532 bridge. Turn left off the tracks on a farm road, in a couple hundred feet climb onto overgrown dike and somehow battle several hundred feet past a farm on Class 3 dike to Class 2, and walk good path to the mouth of West Pass, 1 scant mile from Twin City Food. (This is an iffy bit but there is no practical detour, so be polite and quiet when passing the farm.)

In ¾ nice mile matters are complicated by a couple tough but not rigorously mean-it fences; here the route crosses ditches draining to minor Douglas Slough, the last of the Stillaguamish. Hellberries force short detours off the dike top. Douglas Slough opens to a wide channel in marshes left and the transition begins to Skagit drainage.

In ¾ mile from the complicating fences, the dike turns sharp left and the way becomes good cowpath. A sharp turn right leads by the mouth of Douglas Slough. At ¾ mile from the two sharp bends is a sharp bend right; off left, now, is the mouth of Big Ditch Slough, first of the Skagit. Shortly, where the dike bends left, hellberries make the dike Class 3. So, leave the dike, here with a dam-bridge over the moat ditch, to the field and a ditch-side path leading a scant ½ mile to a public road. This is the entry to the Skagit Wildlife Recreation Area's Big Ditch Access. Turn left over the dike to the parking area. (Or, if doing the loop, turn right on the entry road ¾ mile east to the railroad tracks.)

Mile 45¾-48¼: WRA Big Ditch Slough Access-Tom Moore Slough-Milltown (Map — page 118)

Thanks to the State Game Department, the first Class 1 (hurrah!) dikes of the Trail. But (sob!) leading to classically diabolic Class 3. Before that, though, wow — one of the greatest delta walks.

From the east edge of Stanwood drive north on Highway 530. In 2¼ miles, where 530 drops from the hill to meet railroad tracks and Old Pacific Highway, turn left on the latter, then immediately right on the narrow road signed "Skagit Wildlife Recreation Area, Big Ditch Access," leading ¾ mile to the parking area.

Walk to the road-end at the tide-gate dam and cross the plank bridge over Big Ditch Slough. On the far side a lovely sidetrip goes left on a spur dike ½

Closed-to-vehicles bridge over Tom Moore Slough to Milltown Island

mile to the slough mouth; at low tide one can proceed a mile or more out in the vast sandflat-mudflat, out among the peep.

But to forge northward, turn right and walk the grassy dike between Big Ditch right and cattails left — out there a 2-mile-long line of ancient pilings stands in mudflats north of Tom Moore Slough, part of a "training dike" built by the Army Engineers in 1911. In 1 mile of wonderful walking with broad views over Skagit Bay to islands, over Skagit delta to mountains, is a delightful surprise, a "village." On stilts beside Tom Moore Slough is a row of "duck shacks," ingenious improvisations of driftwood and salvaged lumber, each with its perilous plank walkway from the dike, each with its privy (ah, the tales that are told of midnight catastrophes in the cattails).

Now the grassy dike path yields to a semi-tunnel in hellberries, leading to another village; being careful not to meddle, walk out to the bank of Tom

Moore Slough; upstream at the foot of Milltown Island it is joined by Steamboat Slough, onetime route of sternwheelers.

Beyond this second village the dike trail is irregularly maintained. In late 1977 the surveyor battled another ½ mile, determined to win through to Milltown, but some ½ mile short of the goal, bleeding and groaning, cursing whoever it was introduced Himalaya and evergreen blackberries to our formerly green and pleasant land, confessed defeat. Machetes subsequently reopened this stretch, but when the hellberries again conquer, hikers headed for Bellingham should detour to Milltown via the railroad.

Mile 48¼-50¾: Milltown-WRA Milltown Island Access-Conway (Map — page 118)

The feature is a sidetrip in the great wildland-reclaimed-from-agriculture of Milltown Island.

Leave I-5 on Exit 221 and drive Highway 530 south a scant 2 miles to no mill, but the lone domicile announcing itself as Milltown. A stub road west, signed "Skagit Wildlife Recreation Area, Milltown Access," climbs the dike and goes north ⅓ mile to a parking area.

The main thing to do here is cross Tom Moore Slough on the ancient, rickety-looking, slippery, unsafe-feeling, closed-to-vehicles, plank-and-steel-truss bridge, a beauty of a relic. A dike formerly protected Milltown Island from the enclosing Tom Moore and Steamboat Sloughs, but floods sliced through and the critters love it, all marshy fields and swampy tanglewoods. A person can walk the Class 1 dike upstream ½ mile to a gap. If willing to get wet knees, he can cross the soggy spot to a resumption of dike and proceed an unsurveyed distance, 1-2 miles, around to Steamboat Slough.

But, for Bellingham, turn north from the parking area, follow the pleasant Class 1 and 2 dike a scant 1 mile to the splitting of the two sloughs at the island head. Here use the railroad to cross a ditch, return to the dike, now a pasture, and in 1½ more miles, where the South Fork Skagit splits into Steamboat and Freshwater Sloughs, hit Fir Island Road. To the right is Conway, whose chief industry is antiques, and among whose gracefully-old, well-kept houses is gracefully-old, well-kept "Conway Tavern 1932." (How many of you kids out there have heard of "Repeal"?)

Mile 50¾-53¼: Conway-Fir Island-Skagit WRA Headquarters Access (Map — page 118)

The dikes of Fir Island tend mostly to be Class 4, though a lone walker on weekdays can find some of them Class 2. However, here also are splendid Class 1 dikes and the most popular walks in the Skagit Wildlife Recreation Area.

Leave I-5 on Exit 221 and where Highway 530 goes left, go right into Conway. Park on the west side of town by the fire station or, before the bridge over the river, go right on Dike Road and immediately left to the river and a pretty picnic area.

Cross the bridge to Fir Island; just below, the South Fork Skagit splits into Freshwater and Steamboat Sloughs, each of which splits again, the river splintering to a maze of distributaries.

Turn south on Mann Road (the appealing dike along Freshwater Slough is

Mt. Baker and snow geese in Skagit Wildlife Recreation Area

too inhabited). The road bends right, leaving the dike where it is in a fee-hunting area covered with duck shacks, crosses Wiley Slough, and turns north. Here Game Farm Road goes left ¼ mile to Skagit WRA Headquarters Access, which requires an essay to itself.

Skagit WRA Headquarters Access (Map — page 118)

Encompassing sloughs and islands, tideflats, swampy woods, marshes of saltgrass, cattails, and sedge-bulrush, and farm fields and dikes, the 12,761-acre Skagit Wildlife Recreation Area is the most important waterfowl area in Western Washington; wintering or nesting, 26 species of ducks are found here and three of geese, and brant and whistling swan and sandhill cranes. There are also 200 species of songbirds, plus harbor seal, river otter, mink, deer, and beaver. The 20,000-35,000 snow geese that winter are the superstars, but if a walker misses their show, he won't fail of other bird experiences, ranging from flitters in the bushes to great blue herons to clouds of sandpipers wheeling and diving in tight formation.

123

Way out here, "at sea" in the vast flatness of the delta, there are long views: south to Camano Island and Rainier, west over Skagit Bay to Whidbey Island and Olympics, east to Devils and Cultus and Whitehorse and Big Four, and north to Ika Island, Erie on Fidalgo, Baker and Shuksan and snowy peaks in Canada.

Offering all this, and on a purely Class 1 hassle-free easy-strolling route, the Skagit WRA Headquarters Access is far and away the most popular walk on the delta. Eventually there will be a wildlife interpretive center, viewing "blinds," and additional trails.

From Conway drive Fir Island Road, taking either the east or west entry to Mann Road and the WRA sign, "Headquarters," pointing down Game Farm Road. In ¼ mile pass the headquarters compound, cross Wiley Slough, and turn left on the dike road to the large parking area.

The walk is a loop, with sidetrips, around a nameless island between Wiley and Freshwater Sloughs. From the parking area walk the dike downstream along Freshwater Slough, tanglewood swamp left and drainage ditch right, at a couple points crossed by footlogs permitting roving in the fields. The dike bends right and in 1 mile crosses the marsh island to Wiley Slough. Here is an intersection. To the right is the dike leading back 1 mile to the parking lot, completing the basic 2-mile loop.

But for the full treatment, first go left. Pass a causeway right, over Wiley Slough (for a sidetrip off the sidetrip, take the causeway and proceed ½ mile, until halted by a mean-it fence). Hundreds of weathered tree roots in the marsh speak of past floods. As do rotten rowboats sunk in the reeds. The dike ends in ½ mile at the mouth of Freshwater Slough, a supreme viewpoint over the waters. — Or mud: at low tide one can wander far on the sandflats.

Complete dike tour 4 miles, allow 3 hours

Mile 53¼-56½: WRA Headquarters Access-WRA Jensen Access (Map — page 118)

The Ideal Trail would proceed on the dikes from Headquarters Access, but ½ mile from the Wiley Slough causeway the way becomes firmly Class 4; folks at the gun club are hostile to non-member birdshooters but absolutely choleric about birdwatchers. The Practical Trail, therefore, follows country lanes. Go north on Mann Road, then west on Fir Island Road, crossing Dry Slough and Browns Slough. Where Browns Slough Road turns north, go straight ahead on Maupin Road, in ½ mile reaching the turnoff, left, to WRA Jensen Access.

Proximity to masses of the public makes for a low level of toleration, and Jensen Access is hedged by animosity. The surveyor walked the dikes all the way from Headquarters to North Fork, but was shouted and glowered at and had the dogs set on him. So, except at low tide, when one can roam saltgrass and tideflat (and bypass the dikes), Jensen Access is just a place to come and look for snow geese.

Incidentally, though the original intent of the WRA was to provide birdshooting, the hunting has gone steadily downhill since the 1930s and become fifth-rate. This is not, as a few misinformed hunters suppose, due to mobs of birdwatchers tromping the dikes, frightening the birds with the click-click-click of cameras, but to the education of the birds. For the smashing finale of a walk during hunting season, wait until 15 minutes after the close of legal shooting hours and see the thousands of fowl fly in from the bay, where they have safely been sitting out the day, watching the clock.

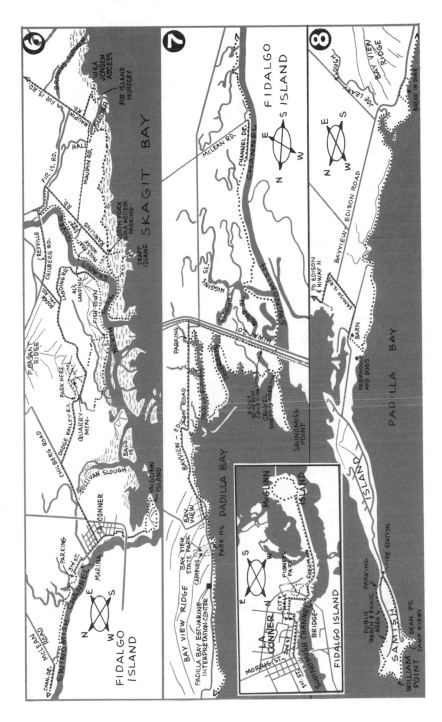

Mile 56½-58½: WRA Jensen Access-WRA North Fork Access (Map — page 125)

The Practical Trail follows Maupin Road north to Rawlins Road, turns east to Fir Island Road, and goes north on it to leave Fir Island on the bridge over the North Fork Skagit, 2½ miles from the turnoff to Jensen Access.

However, though iffy, the Ideal Trail is here regained at first reasonable chance. Walk Maupin Road ½ mile from Jensen Access turnoff and just past Hall Slough unobtrusively get on the dike, which is posted by a gun club but never goes near manned observation posts and thus is technically Class 4 but on lonesome days is really Class 2.

The dike passes the mouth of Hall Slough and turns northwest. Here it is partly on natural beach, protected from wave action by a line of pilings. In a scant 1 mile from Maupin Road are the WRA boundary and secure Class 1 dike. Trail burrows through the dike-top thicket of baldhip roses (the hips appearing in winter to be millions of cherry tomatoes). The bay-side walking is great at high tide, two spur dikes permitting sidetrips up to ¼ mile out in the water. At low tide the sea-meadow and tideflat roaming is endless. In a scant 1 mile from the start of public dike is the parking area of the WRA North Fork Access. Again, a separate essay is needed.

Skagit WRA North Fork Access — North Fork Mouth, Craft Island (Map — page 125)

More of the same — and something completely different — a couple things. Unlike the many-sloughed South Fork, the North Fork hugely flows to the bay all in a single surge. And here the flatness of delta bumps against hard rock and startling eminences of peaklets of the San Juan Islands.

Drive Fir Island Road to just south of the bridge over the North Fork and turn west on Rawlins Road, signed "WRA North Fork Access." In 1¾ miles the road ends at the dike; park on the shoulder.

A full, rich day can be spent here. At high tide walk south on Class 1 dikes (see above) totalling nearly 3 round-trip miles. But medium tides offer the big thrill, off the dikes, out in the sea meadows.

From the road-end walk the dike-top trail ¼ mile to the North Fork — broad, deep, swift, impressive. Turn downstream through a sand-floored alder forest to meadows. Across the river are startling cliffs of "Fish Town Island." In ½ mile on the bank is an indistinct Y of paths. Both are essential. (For an alternate approach to the Y, from the road-end cross the dike and follow the obvious path out through the meadows.)

The right fork continues on the banks in grass hummocks and bulrushes; across the river are clifftop cow pastures, then the bizarre village of Fish Town. At ½ mile from the Y the river at last splits. Bend left a final ½ mile to the mouth of the south distributary. A genuine mouth of the Skagit! Views are superb of incredible Ika Island, a mountain rising 450 feet abrupt as a cinder cone.

The left fork crosses wet-foot meadows ⅓ mile to the fairyland of little Craft Island. Clamber up a bit of rock and spend hours (but watch the tides, in order not to spend a whole lot more hours) poking around green benches of moss and lichen and grass, in masses of ferns, miniature forests of small cedar and juniper, fir and madrona, thickets of snowberry and rose. The knobby algae-

Fish Town cottage next to the North Fork Skagit River

colorful walls of conglomorato arc croded by tides in weird textures. In spring it's all a flower garden.

Though only 75 feet high, amid such flatness of delta and water the mountain seems enormously taller. The view is from Rainier to Canada, Olympics to Baker, and all around to the green delta and the island-dotted waters. On the survey, some 30 herons were spotted perched on logs and roots, pretending to be part of the woodwork. Beware of gulls dropping clams on the rocky island to break them open; the shell fragments show it's a popular sport here.

Round trip, all tours, 7½ miles, allow 5 hours

Mile 58½-62¼: WRA North Fork Access-North Fork Skagit Bridge-Dodge Valley-Landing Road (Map — page 125)

As described above, from the North Fork Access walk north ¼ mile to the river. Turn upstream ½ mile on wide, grassy dike to a boathouse with boat moorage, boats for rent, restaurant, cabins, and picnicking — and of interest to long-distance hikers, the only overnight camping for miles.

Cow-cropped Class 2 dike continues 1½ miles between river and fields to a farm road giving access to Fir Island Road where it rises to bridge the North Fork and leave delta flats of Fir Island for rocks and forests of "Pleasant Ridge Island." Homes prevent the route from turning down along the river; go inland on Chilberg Road and turn left on Dodge Valley Road, dropping to a finger of delta amid island heights. In ¾ mile is the turnoff left on Landing Road.

Mile 62¼-65¾: Landing Road-Al's Landing-Fish Town-Quarry Mountain (Map — page 125)

The Official Trail must stay on Dodge Valley Road the 1¼ miles to the Fish Town Trail (see below). However, the Ideal Trail takes the long way around, which wavers between Class 2 and 4 and can only be recommended for quiet, no-dog, solitary, humble, respectful, occasional walkers. Do not throng here.

Turn left on Landing Road and cross Dodge Valley to rock-hearted "Fish Town Island." Public road ends, yielding to the driveway to Al's Landing, with boat-launching and mooring and limited public parking.

The Trail from here is partly trail, mostly route. A woods road from the Landing climbs above a couple houses and ends at a tumbledown barn in a field atop a cliff plummeting to the river. The next ⅓ mile of decent forest trail, brushy trail, pure fumble-around brush, and cow paths leads to a clifftop pasture. Proceed along the brink, staying respectfully, quietly distant from the pasture-top farmhouse, admiring views over the North Fork to the delta and Skagit Bay. At pasture's end is the first subdivision of Fish Town, a collection of shanties on the mountain slopes — and a live-in old boat moored in a slough below. Genuine trail drops from this neighborhood down to the conglomerate rock nose of Gage's Point, rounded on slippery planks which continue into the swamp. Walk the planks — the main street of Fish Town — by the houses on pilings, on floats, on footings of conglomerate, houses built of driftwood and scrap, mostly weathered gray, innocent of paint. (The **white** shack with a 10x10-foot **lawn** is the eccentricity here.) If such a community of free spirits had a king, his castle would be the three-storey tower perched atop a big boulder.

By the castle is a Y. The Ideal Trail goes left, climbs a forest knoll, and drops to a dike passing a western suburb of Fish Town. This dike gives promise of leading past Ika Island and grassy barrens of Bald Island and directly to La Conner. It doesn't. It becomes a Class 3 hell, forcing a walker to take a farm road to Dodge Valley Road, reached at 1¾ miles from Fish Town. Because this involves invading a farmyard, don't do it.

Instead, go right at Castle Y — on a route scarcely inferior to the Ideal. The trail crosses a low valley in "Fish Town Island," ½ mile through a wildland forest of 4-foot-diameter firs and spruces and cedars, fern-hung, mossy, marvelous. A path then follows a ditch ½ mile through cornfield and cabbage patch to Dodge Valley Road, reached at a sharp bend. North several hundred feet, past a handsome yellow farmhouse, is a wide parking area (connected to a county-owned quarry) used by Fish Town residents.

Quarry Mountain (Map — page 125)

A sharp little peak at the tip of a peninsula of "Pleasant Ridge Island" provides a broad view over delta farms and bay waters.

From La Conner drive east 1 mile on Chilberg Road and turn south on Dodge Valley Road. In 1 mile the road rounds the foot of the mountain, here deeply quarried. Park a bit south of the quarry.

For a mountain that measures just ¼ mile square and is but 260 feet high, there's an amazing amount of walking — 2 miles and more of horsetrail and footpath wandering all over the slopes, some virgin-forested with big firs, a pocket wilderness.

To be properly introduced, walk the quarry road (no public wheels allowed) up from a low gouge to a middle one to a high one, from which a woods road curves around to a meadow bald on a 190-foot promontory. Gaze over the middle and northern deltas to La Conner, Chuckanut, and peaks in Canada, and westerly to Erie and Bald Island. The explorer then can find good trails to skimpy paths that lead to the 260-foot summit, just below which is a lonesome mossy-rock knoll with a broad view over Skagit Bay.

Round trip to summit 2 miles, allow 1½ hours

Mile 65¾-68¼: Quarry Mountain-La Conner (Map — page 125)

The Practical Trail goes 1 long mile north in farms on Dodge Valley Road, then 1 long mile west on Chilberg Road, over Sullivan Slough, by the Pioneer Memorial and the famous Tillinghast Seed Company into La Conner. Before the Bellingham-or-Bust pedestrian can turn north, he absolutely must pause for a sidetrip.

La Conner-McGlinn Island (Map — page 125)

Not many towns are worth walking (personal opinion) but this one definitely is. Located where the San Juan Islands "come ashore" in the Skagit delta, beside Swinomish Channel which connects Skagit and Padilla Bays and makes Fidalgo an Island, the old fishing-farming village become artist colony is thoroughly engaging. As a bravura finish, a trail leads into the pocket wildland on the miniature mountain of McGlinn Island.

South entrance to Swinomish Channel from McGlinn Island

Drive from I-5 or Highway 20 to La Conner and park on First Street where it and Morris Street (the in-town name of Chilberg Road) meet.

From the Magnus Anderson log cabin, built in 1869 on the North Fork Skagit and moved here in 1952, walk south on First by shoppes and old houses and museums, by fishing boats and pleasure craft and tugs towing log rafts, with views over to the Swinomish Reservation, to which Governor Stevens assigned the Skagit and "South" Indians. Where First enters an industrial concern, jog left, then right on Second, by the City Hall (1886) and the La Conner House (1878). At San Juan Islands Cannery turn left on (unsigned) Caldonia, then right on Third, then right on Sherman at the foot of "Pioneer Park Mountain." Leave the street and climb the trail into the forested park (camping permitted) dedicated "In memory of Louisa A. Conner, for whom La Conner was named in 1870." Pass the High Orange Bridge to Fidalgo Island (but first walk out on it for the view up and down the Channel) and drop back to Sherman at the New England Fish Company, a scant 1 mile from Morris Street. Proceed out of town on the tideflat neck connecting "Pioneer Mountain Island" to "McGlinn Island Mountain." At about 1 mile from New England Fish the public road ends at an old quarry with plentiful parking for those wanting a shorter walk.

Unsigned but obvious trails lead from the quarry but for the best start go east a few feet to a turnaround and find a big trail into the forest of fir and madrona.

The ¼x½-mile "McGlinn Mountain" towers 125 quite vertical feet above saltwater and marshes. The interlacing paths require no guidance. Poke around and find a little sandy-beached cove at the mouth of Swinomish Channel, and another cove harboring a houseboat. Other paths open to grassy brinks of alarming 100-foot cliffs dropping sheer to the water. Look over the jetties guarding the channel entrance, the enormous rafts of logs, to the towering 450-foot peak of Ika Island, and to Goat and Bald and Craft Islands, and over Skagit Bay and delta to Three Fingers and Pilchuck. From another spot, look over the delta to the white cone of Baker. Note large granite erratics dropped by the glacier that gouged the cliff-walled outlet of Swinomish Channel.

Round trip 5-6 miles, allow 4 hours

Mile 68¼-73¾: La Conner-Swinomish Channel-Padilla Bay-Swinomish Point (Map — page 125)

The way subdivision is going, the Ideal Trail may not be walkable long; go soon, before a Practical Trail on roads must be taken.

Drive to La Conner and park on First Street where Morris Street (Chilberg Road) intersects.

Walk north on First by docks on banks of the Swinomish Channel. At the start of the huge Port of Skagit County Marina jog right on Third and proceed by thousands, millions, googols of swift, superpowered pleasure craft, the same that erode the underpinnings from La Conner and, on summer weekends, make the San Juan Islands an uproar. At the north end, Third turns left and ends by the Channel. Here, a scant 1 mile from Morris, is a large parking area and alternate start.

Cross a great sandy flat awaiting subdivision to hit the Class 2 dike north of a dike-top house. Boats boats boats in the Channel. Birds birds birds there and

Telephoto of Whitehorse Mountain (left) and Three Fingers (right) from Indian Slough dike

in the fields. Views to Canada and Chuckanut and terrific Baker, over the delta to Cultus, south to Pilchuck. In 1¼ miles the dike (increased in width to permit house construction atop) is met by McLean Road, coming from the La Conner-Bayview Highway 1¼ miles east.

At McLean, which bends north as Channel Drive, houses of Skagit Beach Lots occupy and block the dike, forcing a switch to the road for 1 scant mile to the road-end (late 1977). Unobtrusive parking may be possible here for a walk start. But subdivision stakes march north.

If and where houses end, return to the dike, which in ½ mile turns inland around a slough-bay to a junction of Higgins, Telegraph, and Blind Sloughs. Vapor clouds rise above forests from unseen refineries. The San Juan Islands, from Cypress to Lummi, grow. South are Index and Rainier. At 1¼ miles from the junction of sloughs the dike crosses under the two high new highway bridges over the Channel. It is necessary here to walk circumspectly from the dike by a house to westbound Highway 20, cross it to a private lane past a cluster of shacks, then return to dike and quickly hit the railroad tracks where they cross the Channel mouth where it widens into Padilla Bay. Here is a large gravel factory.

Swinomish Point (Map — page 125)

Clouds of peep dipping beaks in mud, fleets of ducks sailing, "Christmas trees" of March Point oil refineries, a stunning panorama of San Juan Islands from Fidalgo (Mt. Erie) to Hat to Guemes to Cypress to Orcas (Mt. Constitution) to Samish to Lummi, peaks in Canada, Chuckanut, Skagit valley and Baker and Shuksan. All from a saltmarsh peninsula, enlarged by sand dredged from the Swinomish Channel, thrusting far out in Padilla Bay.

Drive Highway 20 west from I-5 (Exit 230) to the truck-weighing station ⅓ mile east of the bridge over Swinomish Channel. Park here, out of the way of trucks.

East a few feet from the weighing station a gated road crosses the railroad tracks and parallels them west ½ mile to the gravel factory. Skirt the edge and walk north over tidal meadows; choose a medium tide. In ¾ mile seagrasses end at low mounds of dredged sand. At low tide wander out on miles of flats.

Round trip 2½ miles, allow 2 hours

Padilla Bay National Estuarine Sanctuary (Map—page 125)

For nigh onto a century a string of entrepreneurs plotted to convert Padilla Bay variously to an oyster farm, oil refinery, industrial port, or—by filling and dredging—a city of plastic boxes, each with its plastic stinkpot moored beside the patio. This last scheme came perilously close to succeeding. However, establishment in 1980 of the Padilla Bay National Estuarine Sanctuary—one of only eight such preserves in the nation—saved the habitat of black brant, eagles, herons, snow geese, river otters, harbor seals, clams, crab, and dozens of species of fish.

Ultimately the sanctuary will encompass 11,600 acres, mostly salt marsh and tidelands. For walkers, the dike system described in following pages is the best way to explore the riches. Before or after or during a hike, a visit is mandatory to the interpretive center, located on the 64-acre homestead of Edna Breazeale, who led the battle to save the bay, donated the homestead, and at the age of 87 was the star of the 1982 dedication ceremonies.

A ¾-mile nature trail starts at the center and explores bay beaches and upland woods. A 7-mile shore trail is planned.

Drive Highway 20 west from I-5 (Exit 230) and turn north on Bayview-Edison Road to Bayview State Park. Continue ½ mile to the center.

Mile 73¾-84½: Swinomish Point-Bay View State Park (Map — page 125)

In some opinion the dike-walking around southern Padilla Bay is the best of the Skagit delta. Though the route technically is Class 2, most is a de facto 1. A series of sloughs are crossed, the peninsulas between them reaching out in the bay, and the birds and farmhouses are continuously fine, and the views to refineries and San Juan Islands and supertankers, delta and "come ashore" islands, Cascades and Canada, steadily delight.

Because this segment of the Trail intersects public highways at the ends and three spots in the middle, parking and dike access uniformly easy, the imaginative walker can devise all manner of short looping hikes, using public roads for shortcut returns after long twisty-turny stretches of dike.

From the gravel factory (see Swinomish Point) get onto the start of the Padilla Bay dike; actually, tall grass on the top makes for harder walking than the sand-mud beach, when tide permits. The dike bends out to a little point of salt meadow, a marvelous vista of birds and horizons, then south over the mouth of Blind Slough, now mostly converted to cornfields. Detour by hellberry thickets via dike-base meadows to improving dike path. Pass more peninsulas, marsh islands, concrete-box duck blinds where hunters lie in ambush; again, the dike becomes so overgrown the only passage is along the foot, at a medium tide. The way bends southerly up Telegraph Slough, full of ducks and peep, and at 2¼ miles from the gravel mine comes to railroad tracks and Highway 20, either of which can be walked back to the weighing station for a 3¼-mile loop.

From here the Short Trail goes east from Telegraph Slough 1 mile on railroad tracks and north ¼ mile on Bayview-Edison Road to Indian Slough. The Long Trail is a splendid 3½ miles on dikes, partly open, partly tangled (the slopes walkable), around the magnificent peninsula between Telegraph and Indian Sloughs. The two trails combine for a neat loop.

Just short of the bridge over Indian Slough is parking for several cars, a good base for walks in either direction.

Easy, unposted dike goes down Indian Slough to a point at the mouth of a nameless slough, across which is an old dock, interesting junk, and a handsome farmhouse, and then up Nameless Slough to the highway, this tour covering 1½ miles, hitting the highway ½ mile from the previous parking place. (Here is parking for a couple cars on the shoulder.) The 2-mile loop is among the best short dike walks on the whole Trail.

The next 2 miles, to the dike end, are also terrific. Having come up one side of Nameless Slough, the Trail now goes down its twists and turns on the other side a long ½ mile to Indian Slough, turns north by a grand white farmhouse, uninhabited, then a couple inhabited houses — never seen if one is walking beside the water at low tide. The way is then clear the ¾ mile to the mouth of Indian Slough, where marsh islands and points are foreground for Padilla Bay, 120,000-ton supertankers anchored off March Point, and San Juans. The final ¾ mile is along bay shore, by a long line of pilings (for what?); seameadow isles decorate the bay, hawks patrol the fields, views are tremendous. Now the dike ends, the Trail bumping against the rise of "Bay View Ridge Island."

Beach! (Not much, very narrow, and only at medium tides.) A bluff of glacial till! (Only a few feet high, though.) Long time since the Trail has seen these!

To complete a dandy 4½-mile loop, climb from the dike to the Bayview-Edison Road and walk it south 2¼ miles, in fine bay views, from the island heights, then over delta flats, to Indian Slough.

To proceed north, at high tide walk the highway north 1 mile to Bay View State Park; at low, take the beach, detouring up to the highway briefly to get around docks at the hamlet of Bay View.

Mile 84¼-90¾: Bay View State Park-Samish Island (Map — page 125)
Bay View State Park is a good base for walks north and south. Of interest to long-distance walkers is the campground on the uphill side of the highway.

Modest eminences provide the climax views of March Point refineries and supertankers and steam plumes, and glorious perspectives on the San Juan Islands, of which long long Samish now grows prominent.

Drive Highway 20 west from I-5 (Exit 230) and turn north on Bayview-Edison Road to the park. Be sure to visit the Padilla Bay Interpretive Center, ½ mile north.

The Practical Trail for Bellingham pilgrims takes to public roads at the park — to the north 3 miles is a mean-it fence. However, the Ideal Trail here described makes a good up-and-back walk from the park those first 3 miles. The transition is made from "Bay View Ridge Island" to the northernmost of the three segments of the Skagit delta, the final views are had over Padilla Bay to refineries and Olympics, the panorama of San Juans grows, and the vista opens over the northern delta to steadily-growing Chuckanut and Blanchard, Baker and peaks of the British Columbia Coast Range.

The first long ½ mile is on skinny beach beneath a short till bluff. Then delta meadows sneak around a corner of the "island." On their southernmost reach is a cluster of beach houses, followed by open pasture-saltgrass.

At 1¼ miles from the state park a dike thrusts out from the bluff and turns north. This easy walking may be a snare and a delusion because the reclamation effort has been abandoned; in ¼ mile is a hole in the dike too big for a Dutch boy's finger; the crossing is dryfoot at low tide, wet-knees at middle tide, wet-eyebrows at high tide. In the latter case, retreat the ¼ mile, fight and whimper inland on a rose-garden (thorny, that is) path, and after ½ mile on the highway find an obscure path dropping through woods to another dike leading outward to the shore dike, regained just north of the breach.

Now with cornfields on the right, the Class 2 dike winds and bends 1 mile to the mouth of, then the head of, Joe Leary Slough, bounding the north foot of "Bay View Ridge Island." A meadow delta invites a sidetrip to the slough mouth and a fine view south to Ika and Erie and March Point, north to San Juans, notably Lummi Island, and long views up the Skagit valley, framed by Woolley Lyman and Cultus. Turn back here for a nice 6-mile round trip from the state park.

Hellberry tangles force detours off the dike to tidal meadows. Fences, including a mean-it, plus close-by farmhouses, probably will daunt all but a lone, quiet surveyor keeping a low profile on a winter weekday.

After this close encounter, though, come 3 miles of unmolested solitude at sea in the delta. Most of the way guarded from wave erosion by old pilings rotting at the bases, dotted by duck hunters' ambushes, the easy-walking Class 2 dike meanders along little points and bays in constant views westward over the broad flat bay, eastward over the immense flat delta, the walker an anomaly in Flatland.

But this superb dike hike, one of the very best of the entire Trail, not only has a mean-it fence at the south entry but a sloppy exit on the north. At the neck of Samish Island a farmhouse perches atop the dike and a pack of large, loud dogs forbids passage. So, ¼ mile short of this dangerous obstruction, where an old barn can be seen due east, it is necessary to leave the dike and muck-wallow a field-edge path ½ mile to the highway, attained beside the old barn. Shoulder-parking nearby permits the segment to be walked from this point on Bayview-Edison Road, route from the state park of the Practical Trail.

Samish Island (Map — page 125)

Actually two islands joined by a sand neck, and now really a peninsula, Samish Island is a trip to sea. Miles and miles it reaches out from the delta, dividing Padilla Bay from Samish Bay, seemingly striving to escape the mainland and join companions of the archipelago. Views are spectacular from the San Juan-typical grass-moss balds, flowers and Douglas firs and madronas atop, rock cliffs and deep water beneath.

Drive I-5 to Exit 231 and go off west on Highway 11, Chuckanut Drive. In 6½ miles, at Bow Postoffice, turn left 1 mile to Edison. South of that quaint village a scant ½ mile, turn west on Bayview-Edison Road. In a long 1½ miles, where that road turns left to Bayview State Park, go straight, then turn and twist, to Samish Island. Beaches of the first island and the sand neck are elbow-to-elbow private, a total loss. Just where the neck connects to the second island is a junction, identified by the fire station on the left. Turn right and drive ⅓ mile along the north shore to the Samish Island Public Beach and Picnic Site. Utilizing 1500 feet of public tidelands and a bit of upland donated by local folk in 1960, the state DNR saves a portion of Samish for the public.

Descend the staircase to the beach (at high tide there is none), guarded from houses by a bluff of glacial drift. In ¾ mile begin cliffs of metamorphic rock. Take an obvious path up to the flattish island top, elevation 100-150 feet. Paths crisscross and fade but by trying this and that, trending inland from the bluff edge, a walker shortly emerges on an old, undriven woods road into a field and orchard, by a collapsed farmhouse, to an old quarry. From here several paths lead northward to the nameless "North Point." From a clifftop sea meadow the views are grand to Guemes, Cypress, Orcas, Vendovi,

Snowy owl perched on barn near Edison

Sinclair, Eliza, and Lummi Islands — the latter revealing its amazing 1500-foot summit-to-beach western precipice. Only a scattering of distant houses are visible, the San Juan Islands seem a wilderness, and this point part of it. Precisely here the Snohomish County PUD planned to build a nuclear power plant, the output to be shared by Seattle City Light. Locals yelled, the cost of a nuke became too great, and the land's fate now is in doubt. The PUD is trying to peddle the land to subdividers; Skagit County is trying to stop that; to the surveyor's knowledge, nobody has publicly mentioned that this potentially is one of our greatest saltwater parks.

After a certain amount of trial-and-error probing, the correct path can be found southward from the quarry area to William Point, site of a beacon light atop another sea-meadow bluff. Now the views are southerly. A short way from the point a path switchbacks down cliffs to beach (reached in perhaps 1½ miles from the leaving of beach on the north side of the island) that extends onward to Camp Kirby, property of the Samish Council of Camp Fire Girls. Public use of this beach is strictly on the basis of trespassing, usually tolerated on miserable winter days but actively discouraged in high-use summer periods.

At 1 wonderful mile from William Point is the tip of the long spit of Dean Point, where a person stands swept by winds, far out in the waters, the cross-chopping waves a foreground for views over Padilla Bay to Guemes and Jack and Hat and Fidalgo Islands, refineries on March Point, supertankers at anchor and supertankers underway north to Cherry Point refineries; south over the Skagit delta are Cultus and Devils.

Proceed ⅓ mile along the south side of the spit to the bluff and find a steep path up the jungled cliff to the public road, attained near and outside the entrance to Camp Kirby. Walk the road a scant 1 mile back by the fire station to the picnic area.

Loop trip (with sidetrips) 5 miles, allow 4 hours

Mile 90¾-98¼: Samish Island-Blanchard (Map — page 137)

The last of the delta is some of the best. Easy dikes, de facto Class 1, with good parking and unbarred access at both ends, round the shores of Samish Bay. Samish Island bounds the view south, perspectives change on the San Juans; drawing very near, now, are Chuckanut Mountain, with its steep dun slopes of sandstone-banded brush dating from the mid-1960s forest fire, and the grand canyon of Oyster Creek.

The opening of this segment isn't all that good. Shore houses and gun clubs force abandonment of the Ideal Trail; most of the shore is lonesome but people block access to the dikes. The Practical Trail thus follows Samish Island Road to Bayview-Edison Road to Bow-Edison Road (Highway 237), on the way crossing the little Samish River to the crooked-street hamlet of Edison, the road walk covering 3½ miles.

For the great (and open) walking, drive to Edison (see Samish Island) and park near the Edison School, on the north outskirts of town.

Across the highway from the school an unsigned street goes off from a highway bend. Follow it past houses and church and, where a driveway goes left to a last pair of houses beside Edison Slough, bend right on a farm lane that parallels an inland, secondary dike; at a scant ¾ mile from the highway is

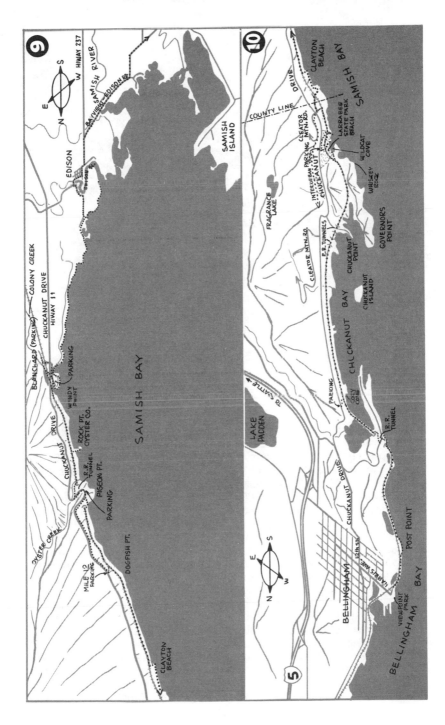

Railroad crossing Colony Creek

the shore dike. Here, at a turnaround, a path leads up on the dike, which may be legally as well as de facto Class 1.

For an excellent sidetrip, walk the dike trail left to the mouth of Edison Slough, then upstream to the end, ¾ mile from the turnaround. This is a nice and tidy and bird-busy 3-mile round trip from Edison.

But Bellingham calls. From the turnaround walk the farm lane a short bit, then where the dike top becomes open, climb aboard. Driven just enough to keep down hellberries and grass, the easy-strolling dike rounds little peninsulas and little bays, passes rotting-away pilings reminding of frontier forts, and duck blinds where gunners crouch, making noises they think sound like ducks. The ducks mostly think otherwise and stay out of range. See mallards and bufflehead and goldeneyes, brant and snow geese, herons and gulls and hawks, plovers and peep.

A short bit of overgrown dike is easily skirted on saltgrass, then good trail resumes to the dike end at the mouth of Colony Creek, 3¼ miles from Edison.

This 6½-mile round trip from Edison, totalling 8 with Edison Slough thrown in, is a smashing finale to the delta journey. It also makes a splendid day's walk, done from either end. Here at the north, on a peninsula at the mouth of Colony Creek, is spacious public parking amid debris of a long-gone oyster company. Drive Highway 11 to where it is just starting up to the bridge over Colony Creek. Legg Road (unsigned) goes right, into Blanchard. A narrow dirt extension goes off left and parallels the highway north ¼ mile to the dike and the parking.

So, Colony Creek. End of the dike hike that began lo these 70-odd miles ago. The delta is over but the memory lingers on.

Mile 98¼-104: Blanchard-Larrabee State Park (Map — page 137)

Now for something completely different. Sacre bleu! Who'd have thought the old Earth had so much elevation in it? After days and miles of delta, viewing the abrupt verticality of Blanchard and Chuckanut, this precipitous plunge of the Cascades to saltwater, gives a neckache. Yet, surely, it's entertaining after sand and mud to slice cliffs of sandstone, conglomerate, shale, coal, and fossil beds. Differential erosion by waves sculpts odd knobs, scoops, rock filigrees. Views change of beaches, points, bays, San Juan Islands, and barges, tugs, sailboats, oyster dredges, and supertankers.

The Trail is plainly marked by two parallel steel rails, all too infrequently traveled by the choo-choos, yet often enough that a person must maintain constant vigilance not to be snuck up on from behind. As always, passage is by trespassing, not invited or encouraged or condoned by the company but normally tolerated if not too many hikers obstruct traffic by getting themselves run over. The shore is always close below, just steps away, but there is very little beach. Close above is Chuckanut Drive, providing frequent accesses for short walks.

Go off I-5 on Exit 231 and follow Highway 11, Chuckanut Drive, over the delta to the foot of Blanchard Hill. At Legg Road either turn left to the parking at the mouth of Colony Creek (see above) or turn right to park in the heart of moldering (1885) Blanchard.

The railroad tracks cross the mouth of Colony Creek and thereafter are beside the water, passing Windy Point, views over Samish Bay to Samish and other San Juan Islands, Olympics and all. Ahead are the striking barrens of the mid-1960s Chuckanut Burn.

At 1¼ miles is the Rock Point Oyster Company, selling fresh oysters. The family-run operation is open to examination from the dredge to the oyster-sorting room to the retail store. No parking except for customers.

Just north are the siding of Samish, the mouth of Oyster Creek, and Pigeon Point, bored through by a ¼-mile tunnel too dangerous to walk. So, at the mouth turn off on a path to the Rock Point access road, climbing to Chuckanut Drive. A few yards north, past milepost 11, is a parking area atop Pigeon Point, 2¼ miles from Blanchard and a good spot to hike south or north from.

A private (but walking allowed) chain-barred lane drops back to the tracks north of the tunnel. The way goes 1 mile by cherry trees and a huge heap of ivy-overgrown oyster shells to a pretty waterfall; here a trail climbs easily to the highway, attained just north of milepost 12. At the parking area here, find the trail on the water side of three large firs, two with leaning trunks that form a V.

In ½ mile the Trail rounds Dogfish Point, whose impressive sandstone cliffs are fenced by a wire mesh that catches small rocks and has a sensor wire to warn trains of big rocks fallen, and the bodies of idiots who try to come down here from the highway. A grass-topped sandstone point is a nice spot to sit and look south over the Skagit to Cultus and beyond, north to the tall bulk of Lummi Island.

Lovely madronas hang over the water. Blackened fir trunks tell that the Chuckanut Burn came down to the very shore. At 1 mile north of Dogfish Point

139

Larrabee State Park

the tracks are separated from the beach by a sand terrace; go onto it, or onto Clayton Beach, marked by stubs of old pilings — relics of the Mount Vernon-Bellingham Interurban Railway.

In ¼ mile sand ends at sandstone and the best part of the whole Blanchard-Bellingham segment of the Trail. Moth-eaten sandstone with lenses of conglomerate forms buttresses enclosing tiny coves. A bit of Larrabee State Park takes in a piece of the beach but the rocks are a private inholding that absolutely must be added to the park. From the beach a trail goes inland to the tracks.

For the shortest access to this glory spot, drive Chuckanut Drive to milepost 14, enter Whatcom County, and pass the unsigned south entry to Mountain Road; just beyond is a sign, "Emergency Phone ¼ mile," and then on the left are three white concrete posts and a sizable parking turnout. From here a trail reverse-turns south, following the grade of the old interurban railway down through lovely woods, over a nice creek, to reach the tracks in ½ mile, a short bit from Clayton Beach.

From the beach the tracks go inland; paths lead out through the sandstone knolls to lovely coves. In ¾ mile is the main developed section of Larrabee State Park.

Mile 104-107½: Larrabee State Park-Chuckanut Bay (Map — page 137)

The park is the big business of this segment, which aside from that has nice parts but is mostly cut off from the shore by private property.

Just south of milepost 15 on Chuckanut Drive take either entry down into Larrabee State Park, park at any lot, and take any path down to the tracks and the shore. Only about ⅓ mile presently is public. But good, but good. The beach of cute Wildcat Cove is a delight, as are sandstone cliffs of points south and north and of nearby Whiskey Rock.

But Bellingham calls. Proceed north, crossing public roads stoutly warning, "No Beach Access." Thus pass Governors Point and Pleasant Bay and Chuckanut Point, total losses. The way is now along Chuckanut Bay, little Chuckanut Island a foreground grace note to looming Lummi. The tracks traverse two short tunnels dated 1912, cross two wild ravines, pass waterside houses and also blufftop houses, until the cliff rises too high and steep. Great tilted slabs, 200 feet high, suggest fantastic rollerskate runs, one ride to a customer. The way enters the north arm of Chuckanut Bay, enclosed on the west by a long point with sprawling mansions of the beautiful people at the rocky tip. Then, just past a private road down to a beach home, is a little rock point, a white all-shell beach on one side, a cozy cove scooped in the other. A wondrous spot. And wild, because here the steep, forested slope rises 200 feet to Chuckanut Drive. Note railroad gravel sloping into bushes, marking a trail outlet.

To use this access to the Trail, drive Chuckanut Drive to just south of milepost 18. By the sign, "Entering Bellingham," is a turnout on the inland shoulder with room for several cars. The obvious trail sidehills south in marvelous big firs up to 4 feet in diameter, then drops — clay-slick but safe — to the tracks at Cozy Cove.

Mile 107½-110¼: Chuckanut Bay-Bellingham (Map — page 137)

Though Cozy Cove is a convenient access to the south end of the home

141

stretch, the most popular start is the north end (see below).

The Trail crosses the head of Chuckanut Bay on a causeway of granite blocks. The west shore is enchanting, ribs of sedimentary rock poking in the bay, sides eroded in pockmark cave scoops. Here is the mouth of a tunnel, dated 1913, that is long and curving and forbidden.

The detour over the top is not a lot of fun, but not tough either, and safe if done with care. To the left of the tunnel mouth a meager path ascends, swinging south to skirt cliffs, requiring use of hands at one spot (no danger, though). Then the way becomes vague, indistinct branches this way and that. Aim for the telephone-wires swath, follow near it to the hilltop; for the easiest route, take a fork across the swath and find an old woods road that leads to a private blacktop road. Coming the other way, spot this woods road by the large rotten log blocking it. Coming from either direction, this short stretch requires some fooling around — and care to avoid cliffs.

Walk south down the private road to the telephone swath and turn right on the obvious trail leading easily down to the tracks, coming out on the south side of the tunnel mouth. On the way pass a fork left to panoramas over Bellingham Bay. This point with its maze of paths in open, broad-view forest is a favorite destination for walkers south from Bellingham.

The way north passes a series of lagoons impounded behind the track causeway. Wild woods on the bluff yield to homes. At 1 long mile north of the tunnel is Post Point. Ah, joy. Slabs shelf into water, separating private sitting nooks. Two trees on the grassy point pose prettily for the camera. The view over the broad reaches of Bellingham Bay is dominated by the massive bulk of Lummi Island and the long thrust of Lummi Peninsula, but there are still Orcas, Constitution close enough to see the summit tower, and Cypress, Guemes, Samish, and Fidalgo with its hump of Erie and steam plumes of refineries. And there are more plumes north, beyond now-appearing Bellingham, salaam salaam.

At ½ mile from Post Point is a sewage-treatment plant and then a superb viewpoint park provided by the Port of Bellingham. If not the heart of beautiful downtown Bellingham it's close enough.

To start walks here, follow Chuckanut Drive into Bellingham; past Fairhaven Park and Bridge it becomes 12 Street. At the second stoplight turn west and descend Harris Avenue to the water. Since the park closes at dusk, if planning a late return leave the car outside the gates in the industrial area.

Okay, it was there and you did it, the 110¼ miles (not counting sidetrips) from Everett. Accept adulation of the welcoming crowd, the keys to the city, the tickertape and confetti, the kisses of the pretty maidens (or whomever), the Hero Medal, be modest and jolly and rumpled for the teevee, murmur oracular aphorisms for the press, sign the book contract, and, as the band strikes up "When Johnny Comes Marching Home Again," or perhaps "It's a Long Long Way to Cougar Mountain," start back.

Bellingham landmark

Bald eagle on snag overlooking beach

THE NORTHERN ISLES:
CAMANO, WHIDBEY, FIDALGO

If no man can be an island, and always tolling in the ear must be that infernal bell, at least a person can hie to an island and put some water between him and the din.

The 20-mile length and 1-to-4-mile width of Camano are rounded by a beach of some 50 miles, mostly "Puget Sound type" of pure Grade A, though up to 1½ round-trip driving hours farther than the mainland across Port Susan Bay, bending the Two-Hour Rule. Glacier-drift bluffs rise as high as 450 feet — and that's why, on an island so long a favorite for summer (and now retirement) homes, and with only scraps of public tidelands, there's so much wild walking. On the principle that residents of Puget Sound City seeking woodland strolls have much closer options, the interior was not surveyed. To reach

Camano Island, drive I-5 to Exit 212 and from there follow Highway 532 across the Stillaguamish delta to the bridge over West Pass, whose narrow width is all that makes the island so.

Second-largest island in the United States, 36-mile-long, 1½-to-6-mile wide Whidbey once was a chain of islands, the northernmost of which was not uniformly glacier drift but had (has) the rock heart of a true San Juan. On the approximately 135 miles of shore only maybe 30-40 miles of tidelands are publicly owned, but bluffs to and above 300 feet protect the solitude of perhaps twice that many more miles, and except in some new, uptight subdivisions the populace is pretty relaxed about foreigners afoot. Perhaps that's because Island County presently has barely 37,000 residents, mostly on the northern third of Whidbey, huddled around the Navy airfield, and presumably nerves will rub raw when and if all the 40,000 undeveloped platted lots are built on, raising the population (even with no more plat plots) to 170,000. The efforts of such groups as Save Whidbey Island for Tomorrow, Friends of Ebey's Landing, and Evergreen Islands are directed toward saving such ecological and scenic climaxes as Crockett Lake and Ebey's Prairie and several surviving forests, preserving the basically rural character of the county, and preventing the overloaded islands from sinking under the waves.

The east side of Whidbey, the lee shore with the deeply-indented bays, was first to be built up. Beaches are quiet-mood "Puget Sound type." History is rich and charm thick in the old towns.

The southwest is a wildly-exciting weather shore, superbly scenic, featuring the magnificent tall bluffs that are famous landmarks throughout the region. A distinct advantage over more northern beaches is a round-trip driving time at least 1 hour less.

(Speaking of approach, the normal best is to drive I-5 to Exit 189, go off west to Mukilteo, ferry to Columbia Beach, and drive the main island road, Highway 525, which becomes Highway 20. On jammed-up summer Sundays the long way around via Deception Pass Bridge may be the shortest way home.)

The "West Coast Trail" is something else. A visitor from Puget Sound City feels an exhilarating escape from claustrophobic, mountain-walled confines of the inland sea, a wondrous enlargement of the world, in gazing to the water horizon of the Strait of Juan de Fuca. On a clear day you can see Asia — from whence roar the gales that stir oceanic surfs, sculpt the bonsai forests, wave the grass of the Mendocino-like sea meadows. Despite the recent invasion by subdividers braving the winds to trash the flats, the bluffs remain unconquerable and here is the longest stretch of undeveloped beach this side of Olympic National Park. There are other attractions, too: the umbrella of the Olympic rainshadow that also covers Fidalgo; Main Street traffic of ships and boats; the Weird Pits of Point Partridge, old-lakebed Ebey's Prairie, spits and baymouth bars and lagoons; mementoes of ancient wars, and the Ebey's Landing National Historic Preserve climaxing all.

Fidalgo is merely high-graded here. Partly this is because the island is treated in detail by Marge Mueller's book, **The San Juan Islands, Afoot and Afloat.** Mainly, though, it's because over many years the forests and peaks were permitted to become one of the worst motorcycle hells in the Northwest. Happy to say, the City of Anacortes and Washington State Parks are now cooperatively developing a management plan for some 2400 acres of city land and hundreds more of state land that will, when implemented in the 1980s, make Fidalgo a supreme glory of American pedestrian sport.

USGS maps: Mukilteo, Maxwelton, Hansville, Freeland, Langley, Juniper Beach, Camano, Coupeville, Port Townsend North, Utsalady, Deception Pass, Anacortes

Camano Island — North End (Map — page 146)

Where the Stillaguamish delta wraps around the end of Camano Island are two fine non-private, okay-anytime shore walks.

Davis Slough
A dike hike along Davis Slough, a small tidal channel connecting Port Susan Bay and Skagit Bay.

Drive a scant ½ mile west on Highway 532 from West Pass Bridge to a parking area on the south, signed "Skagit Wildlife Recreation Area — Davis Slough Access."

Walk the dike path south 1 mile, between salt meadows and slough on the right, farm on the left, birds everywhere. At the waters (or mudflats) of Port Susan Bay the dike turns east, passing a grassy peninsula that leads out through ducks and dunlins to South Pass, one mouth of the Stillaguamish. Look down the west shore of the bay to Barnum Point and the Olympics, down the east shore along the Puget Sound Trail.

This is the most interesting part of the loop. However, to complete it, follow South Pass to farmhouses and the split of the river, continue on West Pass to the highway bridge and walk the shoulder back to the car.

At a low enough tide one can cross under the highway bridge and walk saltgrass meadows 1 mile north to the mouth of West Pass in Skagit Bay. Also, dikes and roads north of the highway, not surveyed, follow Davis Slough toward Skagit Bay.

Loop trip 2½ miles, allow 1½ hours

English Boom
Here's the compulsory north-end trip. Views are breathtaking over Skagit Bay and delta to the mountains. History is thick, and so are the birds.

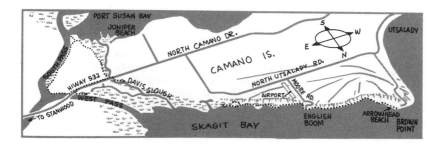

Mt. Baker from English Boom on Skagit Bay

Drive Highway 532 just beyond milepost 2 and turn north on Utsalady Road-Arrowhead Road, as the sign calls it. In 2 miles, just past an airstrip, turn north on Moore Road ¾ mile to a large parking area by the beach. The public swarms here with no apparent objection (1978).

This is the site of the booming grounds of the English Logging Company, where logs were assembled and enclosed by booms in rafts for towing to the mill. That's what the forest of old pilings was for.

The wild shore, secluded by a tanglewood bluff, is open both ways. West 1 mile on gravel-cobbles is Arrowhead Beach on Brown Point — houses and a turnaround. East the delta immediately begins; creek-incised saltgrass meadows were surveyed 1 mile, and perhaps can be walked 1 more to the mouth of West Pass.

Views on a crisp-clear winter day are stunning. The ice mound of Baker and Twin Sisters dominates but also grand are peaks enclosing the Skagit delta — Woolley Lyman, Chuckanut, Blanchard, Devils, Cultus. South are Three Fingers, north are Canadian giants. The centerpiece is the broad expanse of Skagit Bay from Whidbey Island to Ika and Craft Islands, the entire Fir Island segment of the Skagit delta, and the whole Stillaguamish delta.

Round trips 6 miles, allow 4 hours

147

Camano Island — East Side (Map — page 148)

The lee, Port Susan shore of Camano is infested with houses, only becoming wild near Camano Head. However, two tolerated public accesses permit sampling nice bits on this side of the island.

Barnum Point

A naked bluff at the mouth of a spit-closed bay attracts eyes and feet from afar.

Drive Highway 532 to its end at a large signboard directory to island businesses. At the Y here (Terrys Corner) turn left on East Camano Drive, then almost immediately left again on Sunrise Boulevard. In a long 2½ miles turn left on Iverson Road. At a T in ¼ mile turn left and drop to a dike-enclosed beach flat. Just after hitting the flat is a shoulder with room to park.

Take several steps to Lona Beach Road, where houses are behind the dike, and turn south ¼ mile to a beach access. Public feet seem tolerated (1978).

This near the head of Stillaguamish-silted Port Susan Bay, at low tide the mudflats are vast. At the foot of a 100-foot bluff of sand and till the erratic-decorated beach leads 1 mile south to where the bluff lowers to naught at Barnum Point. At the tip is an orchard and farmhouse; step quietly, politely around to cute Triangle Cove, across whose mouth is a bar solid with homes.

Views are fine over the bay to the delta of the Stillaguamish and wide valleys of its two forks, to Baker and Cultus and Three Fingers and Pilchuck, and down the bay by Warm Beach and Kayak Point to Gedney (Hat) Island beyond Camano Head.

Round trip 2 miles, allow 1½ hours

Cavelero Beach County Park

A public park! On Camano Island! You can eat your tuna fish sandwiches and drink your strawberry pop at a veritable public picnic table! The mountain views are exciting, too.

From the end of Highway 532 go left on East Camano Drive 2½ miles to a Y. Camano Hill Drive goes right; stay left on East Camano Drive another 2½ miles and turn east on Cavelero Road ½ mile to the park.

Read the peaks from Baker to Cultus to Pilchuck. On glummy winter days when nobody's about a person may be tolerated by the small groups of

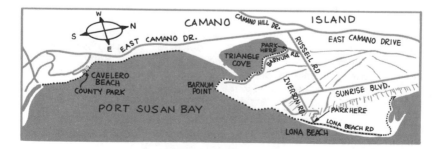

Beach north of Barnum Point

houses adjoining the park on both sides and can then walk north 1¼ miles, and south ½ mile, beneath nice wild bluffs, before rows of houses end the fun.

Round trips 2½ miles, allow 2 hours

Camano Island — West Side (Map — page 150, 151)

Though Whidbey takes the brunt of howlers from the ocean, the west side of Camano Island, the weather shore, gets its share of waves and thus has the pounded look walkers like. Saratoga Passage is busier than Port Susan, fishing boats going to and fro and log rafts south to Everett mills. Two wild stretches of beach offer good lonesome walking, and both have waterside public parking, oh joy.

Onamac Point (Map — page 150)
A thrusting spit is the start for journeys north and south almost without ends. From the Y at the end of Highway 532 go left on East Camano Drive 2½

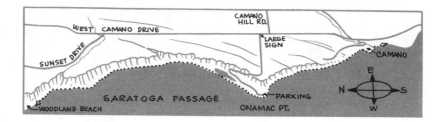

miles to a Y. Go right on Camano Hill Road 3½ miles to West Camano Drive. Turn north a bit to the large subdivision sign, "Onamac," and drive west on the private road ("Visitors Welcome") switchbacking down the bluff ¾ mile to a large driftwood-side parking area on Onamac Point.

From the beach-driftwood-dune-lagoon start the beach proceeds north into bluff-guarded wildness. Erratics are notable. On a minor point at 1¼ miles are the kitchen midden of an ancient Indian camp and a forlorn, ruined, beach cabin. In ¼ mile more are houses, the Sunday turnaround. On winter days, though, the route could be extended on and on, small villages alternating with bluff-protected peace.

South from the lagoon the beach, sporting monster erratics, is bluff-safe 1 mile to the old town of Camano, the Sunday turnaround. But beyond there 3½ miles to Camano Island State Park are only several short inhabited stretches.

Round trips (okay Sundays) 5 miles, allow 3 hours

Camano Island State Park (Map — page 151)
Aha. Whatever becomes of tolerated trespassing, there'll always be these 134 acres of public forest, path-interlaced, and 1 mile of splendid public beach rounding Lowell Point.

From the end of Highway 532 take the left, East Camano Drive, 6 miles to a Y, both forks confusingly signed "East Camano Drive." Go right, signed "state park," 2 miles to an intersection at Elger Bay Grocery. Turn west on West Camano Drive 1¾ miles and turn left on Park Drive. The park is entered and in 1 mile the headquarters passed. Just beyond is a Y, the left leading to parking on the beach at Lowell Point, the right to parking by North Beach. Take your pick.

A 6-mile perimeter trail through the woods is planned. Presently there is a bluff-top, wide-view path, the north end at the switchback on the road to North Beach, the south end in a ravine cutting the Lowell Point road at the foot of the bluff.

From North Beach to Lowell Point is 1 long mile of 100-foot cliffs of sand and varved blue clay and gravel, madronas hanging over space above. Views extend across Saratoga Passage 2 miles to Whidbey Island, the Olympics beyond, far north up the waterway, and south to the island end at Camano Head and beyond to Gedney (Hat) Island.

Keeping in mind that in sunshine and on Sundays the walking off the end of public parks irritates residents and is banned by rangers, still it must be noted, for lonesome seasons and days, that north of the park the beach is marked

Saratoga Passage from Camano Island State Park

only by scattered communities the scant 4 miles to Onamac Point, and southward the shore goes 2 miles into and around Elger Bay and another 3 miles to Mabana Shores (see Camano Head).

Round trip (Sundays) 2 miles, allow 1½ hours

Camano Head (Map — page 152)

Whatever else you do while on the island, don't fail to drive to the southern tip, Camano Head. From the airy brink of the 320-foot bluff that plummets to the beach, look giddily down naked cliffs and sliding tanglewood to the waves, and out over Possession Sound to Hat (Gedney) Island and Port Gardner Bay and Everett's ships and pulpmills, and to Mukilteo's ferry and pastel oil tanks and, on the hill above, enormous buildings of Boeing's Paine Field complex, and to Cascades and Olympics. As of early 1978 this incredible viewpoint was "for sale by owner." Owner! Nobody but the Almighty "owns" such spots. It ought to be dedicated as a temple. At the very least made a public park. Go see before the access (at the U-bend where West Camano Drive becomes East Camano Drive, a woods road goes to the brink) is closed off; write a letter to Island County or State Parks demanding justice.

Further, the beach walk around the base of Camano Head is a classic of the inland sea, 3 miles purely wild beneath that formidable cliff, the rest only spottily inhabited. But the beach is all private and the putting-in and taking-out must be done circumspectly not to bother residents; the loop trip suggested is best done by small parties on lonesome weekdays. Never on Sunday.

Drive to Elger Bay Grocery (see Camano Island State Park) and continue on West Camano Drive a scant 4½ miles to the Mabana fire station. Don't park here — find a shoulder nearby on subdivision sideroads off Dallman Road.

To do the loop counterclockwise, from the fire station walk west ¼ mile on Highland Parkway. Where it bends right, take the gravel road switchbacking down to the boat-launch, which is public but not so signed, lest the neighborhood become unlivable.

(Note: Not surveyed but mighty attractive is the shore north 4 miles to Elger Bay; a beachwalker down there below the bluff would scarcely see a house the whole way.)

The beach goes south under a bully sand cliff footed by blue clay. Jungle then alternates with bare walls; trails and perilous ladderways, and one aerial tram, come from unseen homes 100 feet up. At 1¼ miles a road descends to a dozen homes on a beach-invading fill that must be passed via an inland detour. Then beach solitude resumes to Pebble Beach at 2½ miles; the jutting

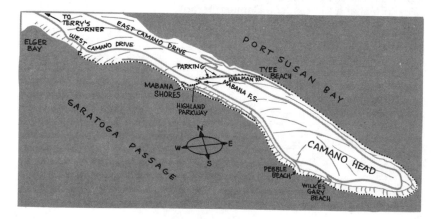

West side of Camano Island, on the way to Camano Head

spit encloses a lovely driftwood-filled lagoon; several houses are here. Immediately south is Wilkes Gary Beach, ¾ mile of cottages, and then commonooc undiluted wildness

Across Saratoga Passage are Langley, on Whidbey Island, and Sandy Point and Columbia Beach, the ferry shuttling to Mukilteo. Now, around the bend, appears Hat Island — and Everett. The bluff rears up to its full 320 feet, becomes beautifully-naked white till and brown sand and blue clay, horridly vertical. At 4½ miles from the put-in the shore turns sharply.

What a spot! Camano Head. Sit for lunch. From remote wildness look to the harbor of Everett and buildings downtown. See the ferry and sailboats and mountains.

Now turn north into Port Susan Bay. The bluff is less steep but still an appalling (to property owners) 300 feet high. The view is over to the Puget Sound Trail and Index, Pilchuck, Three Fingers. On the survey a pair of (nesting?) bald eagles were seen, and herons and ducks and fishing boats. A concrete chunk jutting into the beach suggests an old boat-tieup for a camp. Loot of recent cedar-mining has been hauled away by small boat. Nearly rusted-away iron rails in the beach, set in aged concrete, and an odd gully above, suggest a log skidway — from a hundred years ago? The view opens to the head of the bay, Chuckanut, Baker. At 2½ miles from the Head start houses of Tyee Beach. In a scant ½ mile a community boat-launch serves as take-out onto the road, which climbs the bluff ½ mile to East Camano Drive. Cross to Dallman Road and in ¾ mile return to the fire station.

Loop trip 9 miles, allow 7 hours

153

Whidbey Island — East Side (Map — page 155, 158)

The lee shore of Whidbey, more comfortable for living than the stormy west and thus more built-up, also can appeal to a walker on days when the weather of the weather shore is too exciting. If the beaches are generally less dramatic, they're still good, and the views easterly are distinctive and the history rich. A number of short-to-long strolls sample the scene.

Langley (Map — page 155)
The cozy old village, not fancy but cute, offers calm pleasures — views over Saratoga Passage to Camano Head, Everett pulpmills, and Cascades.

From Highway 525 turn north on Langley Road. In town follow signs down to the beach and parking at Phil Simon Memorial Park.

Walking is permitted on the private beach ½ mile south; beyond is mostly wild for 1 scant mile to houses of Sandy Point.

Round trip 3 miles, allow 1½ hours

Holmes Harbor (Map — page 155)
Though the populated beach lacks marine distinction, walking it is the way to soak up the aura. Named in 1841 by Wilkes, the 6-mile-long, up to 2-mile-wide inlet was a center of farming, then logging, and briefly after 1901 harbored a socialist colony.

Drive Highway 525 to Freeland. Turn right on an unsigned road across from a pizza joint and drive to Freeland (Island County) Park.

West from the park is most of the history — old docks and pilings. Under a bluff up to 100 feet high, the beach east, then north, is mostly wild for 2 miles. The photographer saw two eagles.

Round trip 4 miles, allow 3 hours

North Bluff (Map — page 155)
Public beach across gives entry to a fine stretch of wild shore under the 200-foot, mostly-wooded wall of North Bluff, a dominant feature of the Saratoga Passage shore.

Drive Highway 525 north from Greenbank ¼ mile and turn right on North Bluff Road. In 2¼ miles turn right on Beachcomber Road and switchback ½ mile down to the beach. Turn left on a dirt road ¼ mile to the parking area.

Civilized only by a trail or two, the beach proceeds north under partly-naked bluff, in views to Camano Island, 1½ miles before a subdivision intrudes. If this can be passed, immediately north are nearly 2 miles of public tidelands to which the public has only boat access.

Round trip 3 or 7 miles, allow 1½ or 5 hours

Coupeville (Map — page 155)
A bit artsy-craftsy but genuinely charming is Coupeville, a hotbed of history. The views and beach-walking also are nice.

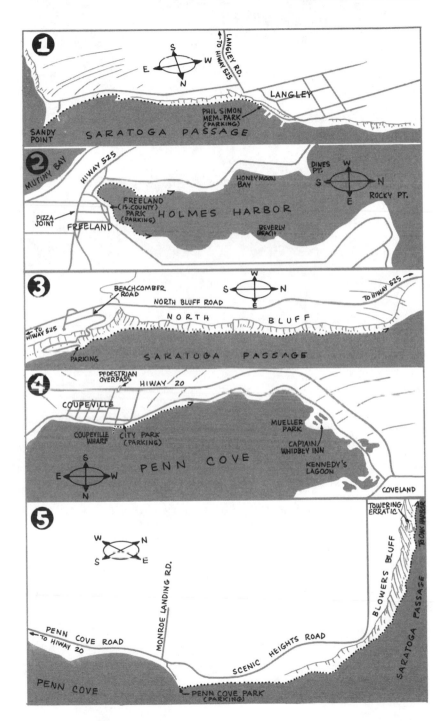

Coupeville Wharf

Drive Highway 525, then 20 to Coupeville and just before the pedestrian overpass turn right into town. At the waterfront turn left to Coupeville City Park.

With only a small gap, the tidelands are public west from the park 3 miles, to the head of Penn Cove, to lagoons and peninsula of Mueller Park, where is located the old (1900) log restaurant, Captain Whidbey's Inn, and to delightful Kennedy's Lagoon. Except for the first mile from the park it's not wild walking, but very pleasant.

As for the history, it began (Indians aside) in 1840 when Father Blanchett came to instruct the Skagits; a bit of the cross they made for him is preserved here. In 1852 Thomas Coupe took up a donation land claim; his 1853 house is here, as is the Methodist church (1853) and the Alexander Blockhouse built for the troubles in 1855. Across the street is the museum of the Island County Historical Association. From Coupeville Wharf (1900) the views are grand out Penn Cove to the white loftiness of Baker, Cultus and Devils above the Skagit delta, and Stanwood beyond the tip of Camano Island.

Round trip 6 miles, allow 4 hours

Penn Cove-Blowers Bluff (Map — page 155)
California-like golden fields slope gently down to the hamlet of San De Fuca

on the north shore of Penn Cove, which comes within a mile of cutting Whidbey Island in two. At the turn of the shore is impressive Blowers Bluff.

Drive Highway 20 north from Coupeville to the dangerous T. Follow the highway right ¾ mile to San De Fuca and turn right on Penn Cove Road. In 2 miles, where Monroe Landing Road goes left, turn right to the public boat-launch of Penn Cove Park, unsigned.

From a wide sandspit-lagoon the beach is close under the road ½ mile. Then the bluff leaps up and enwildens the way. The view back to the head of Penn Cove includes Coupeville and the Olympics. As the shore bends, the view is over Saratoga Passage to Pilchuck and Three Fingers, Cultus and Higgins, Baker and Shuksan. Rounding more, the view is into Oak Harbor and the Naval Air Station and out to Strawberry Point.

Meanwhile the bluff has grown to 150 feet, including a stretch of vertical till. At 2¼ miles is the chief spectacularity, a monster erratic of quartz-veined gray metamorphic rock, 20 feet high, topped by till and grass. Beyond this Towering Erratic the bluff leaps to 200 feet, steep and naked. In ¾ more mile bluff and wildness drop off to the mouth of Oak Harbor.

Round trip 6 miles, allow 4 hours

Oak Harbor Beach Park (Map — page 158)

The Whidbey megalopolis, Oak Harbor, essentially is an overgrown cluster of fast-food franchises serving a transient Navy population. Nevertheless, a Great Fire in July of 1921 burned up most of the waterfront structures and the rest rotted, opening space for a pretty city park, a base for beach walks.

Drive Highway 20 to the south end of Oak Harbor. At the stoplight where the highway turns left, turn right to Oak Harbor Beach Park. (Farther in town are other park accesses and parking areas.)

The view is mouth-watering to the picturesque peninsula of Maylor and Forbes Points, but these are part of the Oak Harbor Seaplane Base, as is the cute tombolo of Point Polnell. Off-limits until declared surplus and made a park.

However, the way south is open and mostly wild the 2½ miles to Towering Erratic (see above).

Round trip 5 miles, allow 4 hours

Strawberry Point (Map — page 158)

Now, this is more like. The longest recommendable walk on Whidbey's east side only quits when feet and tide dictate; actually it goes on and on to Deception Pass. Saratoga Passage now ends and the views are over Skagit Bay past the tip of Camano Island to the awesome width and flatness of the Stillaguamish-Skagit deltas, the Cascades jutting abruptly up beyond. As the miles wear on, there come into view the funny little islet-peaks of the south-ernmost San Juans, in the head of Skagit Bay.

At the south edge of Oak Harbor, where Highway 20 turns left, go straight

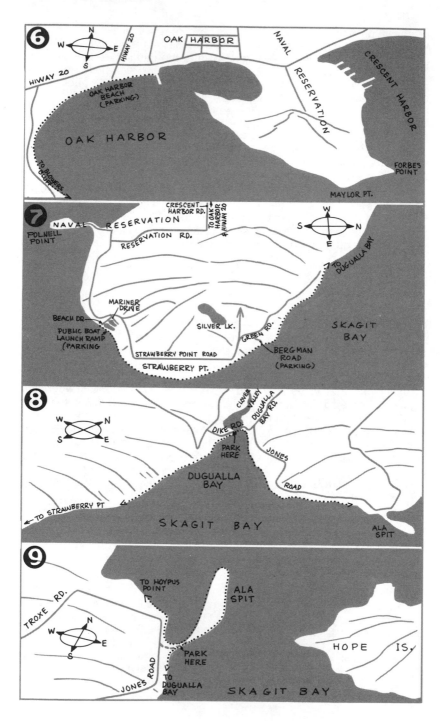

through town to the boundary of the Navy reservation. Turn left along the base boundary, first on 70 NE, then right on Crescent Harbor Road, which becomes Reservation Road. At a long 9 miles from the Oak Harbor stoplight, turn right into the Mariners Cove subdivision and follow Marina Drive, then Beach Drive, ½ mile to a public boat-launch.

After several hundred feet on the baymouth bar blocking off the lagoon (now dredged for yacht basins), the bluff of glacial drift rises up, and except for brief breaks remains at 50 to 150 feet to Dugualla Bay, permitting only small and scattered structures on or near the lonesome beach.

In 1 mile from the boat-launch is Strawberry Point, bringing in sight the long, low horizon of the Skagit delta dikes. An ancient boathouse of big timbers bears the faded advertisement, "Apples For Sale 50¢ Sack."

At 2 wild miles from the point are a wide valley, several houses, and a public beach access at the deadend of Bergman Road. (Drive past Mariners Cove on Strawberry Point Road, as Reservation Road becomes, 2 miles; where it turns left, go right on Green Road, then ½ mile right on Bergman Road to the beach.)

Wildness resumes. Nice creeks are crossed. Alders lean a hundred feet over the beach. Enormous erratics are passed, one as big as a house, a forest of ferns atop. Each bulge in the shore yields new views north — to "Fish Town Island," Ika and Bald and Craft and Goat Islands, Quarry Mountain, the mouth of Swinomish Channel, Hope and Deception Islands.

How far to go? There's nothing stopping feet or dulling interest in the 5 miles to the next put-in, take-out on Dugualla Bay.

Round trip up to 10 miles, allow up to 7 hours

Dugualla Bay (Map — page 158)

The bay mudflats, covered with log rafts and assorted trash, do not invite the boots, but the bay itself is interesting and the dike leads to fine beaches south and north.

Drive Highway 20 north from the Oak Harbor stoplight 6 miles and turn east on Dugualla Bay Road. In a scant 1 mile turn right on Dugualla Dike Road ¼ mile to a dike-top parking turnout.

The bay is the east end of the swale, Clover Valley, that extends across Whidbey Island; when sealevel was 35 feet higher it split off Whidbey's north tip in a separate island. Now the vale contains a large lake, formerly a tidal lagoon, a great flat farm, and a jet airfield that harasses the countryside for hundreds of miles around.

The easy-access dike leads to wild beach 5 miles south to Strawberry Point (which see) and 3 miles north to Ala Spit (which see).

Round trip to Ala Spit 6 miles, allow 4 hours

Ala Spit (Map — page 158)

Magicland! Particularly appealing for a short, slow, musing walk among the birds and toy islands, the spit also is an assured public put-in for long walks

Abandoned barge visible at low tide on Ala Spit. Mt. Erie beyond

south to Dugualla Bay and north the scant 2 miles, wild all the way, to Hoypus Point in Deception Pass State Park (which see).

At the Y where Dugualla Dike Road goes right (see above), go left on Jones Road 3 miles. Upon descending to the shore, take the unsigned dirt road right, down to public parking on Ala Spit.

Ah! On one side of the ½-mile-long driftwood-heaped spit is the bird-busy lagoon. On the other, across the narrow channel, are grass-tawny rock buttresses of Hope Island. South in the bay are Deadman Islands, Seal Rocks, Goat and Ika Islands, the opening to Swinomish Channel. North are Skagit and Kiket Islands — and, of course, Fidalgo. Here the glacier-drift islands end, the rock-hearted San Juans begin.

Round trip 1-4 miles, allow 1-3 hours

Whidbey Island - Southwest Shore (Map — page 163)

From beaches far south on Puget Sound, from peaks high in the Cascades, the tall, naked bluffs on the south end of Whidbey Island are prominent landmarks. A person canny in the ways of the inland sea admires them from afar and suspects they must be dramatic places to walk. And so they are, so they are. Between broad, shallow, storm-open, useless bays, the jutting bluffs feature solitude, a chaos of erosion, and a big parade of Main Street water traffic — tugs towing barges and log rafts, ships going to and from the ocean, fishing boats, pleasure boats, ducks.

Possession Point

The southern tip of the island, separating Puget Sound from Possession Sound.

Drive Highway 525 a scant 2 miles from the ferry and turn left on Campbell Road. In ¾ mile turn left on Cultus Bay Road. In 4 more miles, where this turns right on shores of the bay, go straight on Possession Road and follow it through turns and switchbacks 2 miles to Possession Beach and the road-end in School Bus Turn Around. Needs of the bus limit public parking to one or two cars, and the private beach requires toleration, so this is strictly a walk for winter weekdays.

After ¾ populated mile the bulge of a 100-foot wall of vertical till is the gate to lonesomeness. Views north to Mukilteo ferry, Three Fingers, and Baker yield to views to the Edmonds-Kingston ferry, Seattle's West Point, and Rainier. The bluff leaps to its towering maximum of 380 feet and the shore rounds to views of the Olympics. After 1 mile of wild beach are the flats at the entry to Cultus (Chinook jargon for "useless") Bay and great masses of houses.

At low tide Cultus Bay utterly empties; the sand-mud might be walkable the ⅔ mile across to Scatchet Head for a continuation of the route.

Round trip 4 miles, allow 3 hours

Indian Point-Scatchet Head

Though a bit less high, the bluff from Indian Point to Scatchet (a variant of Skagit) Head is longer — more than 2 continuous miles — and more vertical — a steep leap of 300 feet — and more naked. It thus is unmolested by subdividers, the longest stretch of wildness on the island's southwest shore.

Drive Highway 525 from the ferry 3½ miles and turn south on Maxwelton Road 5 miles to Maxwelton. Park at Dave Mackie Memorial (Island County) Park.

Walk the beach away from the village-on-the-sandflats of homey old Maxwelton in views over Useless Bay to Double Bluff, out to ship traffic of Main Street (here, still Puget Sound), the winking light of Point No Point, Foulweather Bluff at the mouth of Hood Canal, and Olympics from Angeles to Zion to Constance and south. In ¾ mile is Indian Point and its 200-foot cliff, at first tanglewooded, then bare. The precipice steepens, rises to an awesome 260 feet in one lift from the beach, bare drift capped by vertical till. Among clay beds is a layer of leaves, twigs, logs, cedar bark, and fir cones — not years or decades old, but eons. So steep the bluff becomes, the top a straight-up 300 feet, that chunks constantly fall, slides of huge clay boulders tumble out in the water to be battered by waves.

At 1½ miles from Indian Point a nameless point thrusts out, the bluff lays back, and a well-used trail descends from the rim, 340 feet up. Now the view is

Bluff overlooking beach near Maxwelton

south up the Sound to Edmonds, the ferry, Appletree Point, West Point. The bluff loses its woods and is again steep and naked to Scatchet Head. A final ½ mile leads to a boulder bulkhead and a subdivision that is not thriving, due to the heavy heavy hangs over thy head location of the homesites.

(Note: The beach from Maxwelton northward on Useless Bay is mostly wild, the guarding bluff as high as 240 feet. The beach is solid with houses ¾ mile from the county park; beyond, there seems no obstacle for 3 miles to Deer Lagoon.)

Round trip 5½ miles, allow 4 hours

Double Bluff

The sand cliff of Double Bluff is truly a noble eminence, the most prominent naked bluff on the entire inland sea, rising 367 feet from the water in one

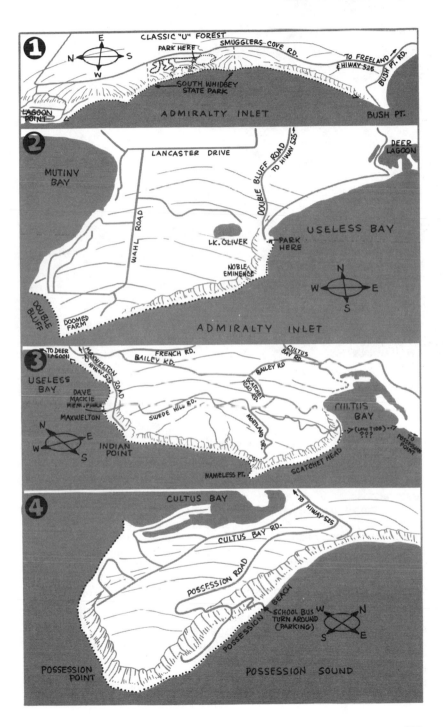

Admiralty Inlet from Whidbey Island

sweep. A public access, and protection of an (undeveloped) state park, draw Sunday throngs to the superb wildland beach.

Drive Highway 525 from the ferry 9¼ miles and turn left on Double Bluff Road, which proceeds 2 miles to Useless Bay and ends in a (whoopee) public beach access.

The splendid sand beach quickly leaves domiciles and bumps against the foot of the noble eminence. A safe if exhausting path weaves between sand cliffs to the top for a majestic panorama of seas and shores. Hereabouts the name of Main Street changes from Puget Sound to Admiralty Inlet; the traffic is the same — heavy. Directly across the street is Foulweather Bluff at the mouth of Hood Canal, south is Edmonds, north Marrowstone Island. Beyond rise the Olympics, from foothills of Zion and Walker to snowy heights of Townsend and Constance. Himmel.

Jump-slide-erode back down to the beach and proceed by an exceptional variety of glacial drift from at least two ages, by discontinuities, by eagle snags and maybe the eagles, by a Grand-Canyon-like gulch sliced in the sand.

The bluff dwindles and at 2 miles rounds a point, atop whose low bank is a light and a spacious green cow pasture, now as for nigh onto a century. An idyllic scene. And as of 1978 slated to be cut up in lots and de-idyllized. Oh the bitterness. In ½ mile more is the point named Double Bluff on maps, but that seems a mistake; surely the noble eminence is the nameworthy feature of the vicinity. Anyhow, here starts Mutiny Bay and another mob of houses, so turn back.

Round trip 5 miles, allow 4 hours

South Whidbey State Park

A unique combination for southern Whidbey — not only beach, but a gorgeous old-growth forest. Walk on the sands, walk in the woods. The great old Douglas firs and associates are the more exquisitely enjoyed for being an island of antiquity in second-growth, and green-twilight woods and sky-open waters combine to produce an experience greater than the sum of the parts.

Drive Highway 525 north from the Freeland turnoff 1 mile and turn west on Bush Point Road, which becomes Smugglers Cove Road and in a scant 5 miles from the highway reaches South Whidbey State Park. Enter, turn left into the picnic area, and park.

The Big Blowdown of 1979 extensively remodeled the park, among other things opening broad new vistas where formerly was only cloistered greenery. The rebuilt trail system roams through the giant trees, both fallen and still standing. Two paths descend to the beach. Walking the beach ¼ mile joins the ends for a loop.

(Note: Across the road from the park is a 255-acre tract of partly old-growth firs and hemlocks and cedars owned by the University of Washington. It was the attempt by the state DNR to clearcut this "Classic U" forest that triggered the lawsuits, legislation, and general uproar culminating in the "Plaintiff Trees" affair.)

Total woods trips 3 miles, allow 2 hours
High point 200 feet, elevation gain 200 feet

The 85-acre park includes nearly 1 mile of public beach. Off the ends are good stretches of wildness where trespassing usually is tolerated, at least on murky Thursdays. South it's 2 miles beneath green riot of bluff to the village which has smeared Bush Point (beyond which, after ¾ mile of houses, is wild beach again for 2 more miles into Mutiny Bay). North it's 1½ miles to the village on devastated Lagoon Point; after 1¼ miles of homes, wild beach resumes for 2 miles to Lake Hancock (which see).

Beach round trip 2 or more miles, allow 1½ or more hours

Whidbey Island — West Coast Trail (Map — page 166)

Why is this the most-famed, most-acclaimed beach of the inland sea? Because of the vigorous weather, and surf, of the weather shore, where

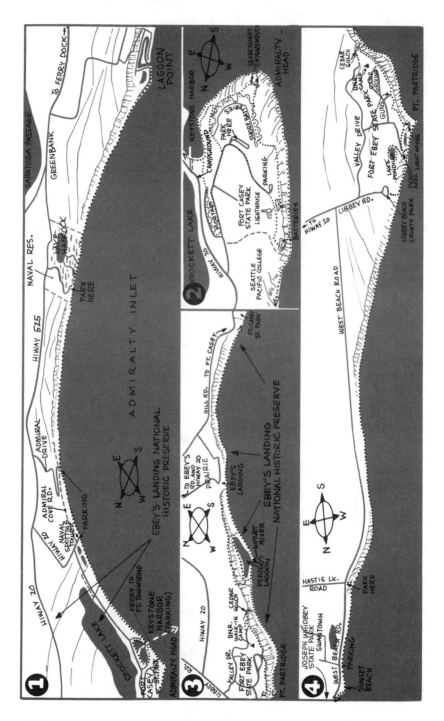

storms blow freely in through the Strait of Juan de Fuca from the ocean. Because of the wildness that prevails due to the discouragement of dense habitation by the weather plus the sea cliffs. Because of the storm-tortured forests, so much like those of the ocean coast, and the tawny sea meadows, so much like those of green-and-gold California. Because of the busy Main Street waterway, always something going this way or that, somewhere, and views from Baker to the San Juans to the Olympics to Rainier. Because of eagles and old forts. That's some of it. And unlike the Wilderness Ocean of Olympic National Park, it's all close enough to Puget Sound City for easy day hikes.

Though the proposed Pacific Northwest Trail follows most of the route, the usual walk on the West Coast Trail is, of course, this segment or that, short or long, from any of some 10 public parking and beach-access points along the 25 miles which (by definition here, if nowhere else) constitute the Trail.

Mile 0-2½: Lagoon Point-Lake Hancock

Despite a reputed 4-acre Lagoon Point (Island County) Park, this stretch is most esthetically walked from the north to avoid the ecological disaster on the point.

Drive Highway 525 north from Greenbank 1½ miles, to just past views down to Lake Hancock. At the end of the fence marking the boundary of the Naval Reservation, turn left on a narrow woods road. A long-unused gate has a faded sign announcing "Danger. Absolutely No Trespassing. Bomb and Rocket Target Area." But no longer to be seen here is the rockets' red glare, bombs bursting in air, and the road proceeds ¾ mile by tidal marsh to a parking area, informal but heavily used, at the beach.

A junior version of Crockett Lake, Lake Hancock is a lagoon largely filled with driftwood and reeds and meadow-marsh and a ton of ducks; it ought to go directly from the Navy into public park or wildlife refuge.

The baymouth bar extends ¾ mile south. Then glacial-drift bluff rears up to 200 feet, guarding the shore from property owners the 1¾ miles to Lagoon Point.

Mile 2½-6½: Lake Hancock-Admiralty Bay-Crockett Lake

With accesses at both ends, this segment is lovely bluff-wild most of the way, only the north bit depressingly house-jostled.

In places vertical and bare, rising as high as 150 feet, the till-sand-clay bluff is particularly striking in the till section just north of Lake Hancock, where erosion has carved a badlands of arretes and chimneys and pillars. Totally lonesome except for a dozen houses on a slump terrace at the halfway point, the pebble-agate-concrelion beach extends 3 miles to the start of the baymouth bar cutting off a former portion of Admiralty Bay, enclosing Crockett Lake. Civilization begins, marked by a community swimming pool and parking lot (reached from the highway via Admiral Drive, usable on winter weekdays as a put-in for hikes south).

The next 1 mile of beach, along the bar, is elbow-to-elbow houses of Admirals Cove subdivision; for hikes starting at the north end, walking the shore road may be preferred to being stared at by all those picture windows.

Mile 6½-8¼: Crockett Lake-Keystone Harbor

The birding in the lagoon of Crockett Lake is famous. The public-tidelands beach (efforts are being made now to acquire the adjoining lands of the bar to

Old gun mounts at Fort Casey

prevent more Admirals Cove houses) is walkable in the driftwood line at the highest tides.

Where Highway 525 ends, turn west on Highway 20 and follow its turns a scant 2 miles to the beach. The highway turns right; a spur goes straight ahead to a Navy spotting tower (for gunnery practice) and a public parking area, base for hikes south to Lake Hancock and north.

Crockett Lake, named for Colonel Walter Crockett, who as a companion of Colonel Isaac Ebey took up a donation land claim in 1850, is feeding and resting ground for hundreds of waterfowl at a time, plus herons and, some winters, snowy owls. This finest of Whidbey's lagoons so far has been saved from becoming another yacht basin, but is still in private hands and insecure.

Bar and beach end at the old, abandoned Keystone Ferry dock, and the new dock in the harbor dredged by the Corps of Engineers in 1948. Here is the boundary of Fort Casey State Park, and more parking.

For a dandy sidetrip, voyage to and from Port Townsend (as would the proposed Pacific Northwest Trail, after coming down the island shore). Because it must thread through ship traffic, barge traffic, tug-and-lograft traffic on Admiralty Inlet, the ferry sometimes takes an hour for the crossing — which in a storm is thrilling if not paralyzing.

Mile 8¼-9¾: Fort Casey State Park

History, beach, and views, plenty to keep you busy and happy if high tide prevents long shore hikes.

Drive Highway 20 to Keystone Harbor and park at the boat-launch area. (Other large parking areas are across the harbor at the entry to the campground and at several places inside the park on heights of Admiralty Head.)

From Keystone Harbor along the beach by the campground, around Admiralty Head, and north to the park boundary is 1½ miles, a first-rate walk.

However, another 2 miles or so of great strolling are on the trail system through the old fort, of which 137 acres have been preserved in park. Built starting in 1897, Fort Casey was one of the "Death Triangle" (or "Devil's Triangle") guarding Puget Sound from nebulous enemies. Gun batteries, spotting bunkers, and searchlight emplacements remain. Also mandatory on the tour is the neat-and-tidy lighthouse — metalwork black, walls white, roof red. The first light here was installed in 1860, the present one, retired and now serving as the park's interpretive center, in 1902.

Admiralty Head is the climactic viewpoint of the West Coast Trail. North are San Juan Islands, farther around Vancouver Island, and then, out the water horizon of the Strait of Juan de Fuca, China. There are Olympics from Angeles and Blyn Hill and Big Skidder Hill to Zion and Walker and Constance. In the distance is the plume of the mill at Port Angeles and directly across the waters is the pulpmill plume of Port Townsend; the lighthouse winking at the tip of Point Wilson marks the location of Fort Worden State Park. Farther south is the third member of the Death (Devil's) Triangle, Fort Flagler (State Park). And here is the most exciting Main Street marine-traffic view in the region — merchant ships and fishing boats and tugs and barges and pleasure craft and Navy vessels and, dodging through it all, the Keystone-Townsend ferry.

Mile 9¾-12¼: Fort Casey State Park-Ebey's Landing

At the park begins the longest stretch of undeveloped beach on the island, extending with only the most minor disturbances of wildness north 9½ miles to Hastie Lake Road. Washington State Parks is acquiring a 6-mile shore strip up to 400 feet wide connecting Fort Casey State Park to Fort Ebey State Park. As of 1981 the only gaps are between Fort Casey and Ebey's Landing and on Perego's Bluff.

With good parking and beach access at both ends, these 2½ miles are purely lonesome except for old fort buildings at the south end, used by Seattle Pacific University and off-limits. The distinctive "Ebey-type" sand bluff (composed largely of loess blown here by dry glacial winds) rises up, lowering on the north to Ebey's Landing. The walk from park to Landing is exceeded in beauty and popularity only by the walk north from the Landing.

Mile 12¼-14¾: Ebey's Landing-Perego's Lagoon-Cedar Gulch (DNR Point Partridge Recreation Area)

With a bluff trail permitting a walk even at high tide, and connecting to the beach at Ebey's Landing and Perego's Lagoon, the 3½-mile loop trip north from the Landing is unsurpassed for scenery and popularity, is universally acknowledged a supreme classic of the inland sea.

To reach Ebey's Landing, drive from Fort Casey State Park entrance, keeping left at junctions, 3 miles. Or, on Highway 20 just north of the Coupeville pedestrian overpass, turn south on Terry Road, which becomes

Perego's Lagoon and Strait of Juan de Fuca from bluff north of Ebey's Landing

from the highway. Parking is fairly plentiful along the shore-road shoulder.

Ebey's Landing National Historic Reserve, established 1978, is purchasing land and development rights in the area of Smith's and Ebey's Prairies, Crockett Lake and Coupeville, including the site where Ebey took up his donation land claim in 1850, and where in 1857 Haidas came down from the north and chopped off his head.

The beach is wonderful the 1¾ miles north to spit-enclosed Perego's Lagoon, picturesquely filled with bleached driftwood. But the return trail that climbs the tawny sand and grass slopes from the lagoon is unique, and must be walked for at least one leg of the loop. On the bluff lip, as high as 240 feet above the brown-white driftwood line, the gray beach, the white breakers, and the gray-green sea, views are glorious over Main Street traffic to three mountain ranges — Vancouver Island, Olympics, Cascades. And way out there is the water horizon, the edge of the world, source of the winds that so buffet the Douglas fir and Sitka spruce they have the appearance of being tortured for centuries by a Japanese bonsai artist. Then, at trail's end, is the stunning overlook of the emerald plain of Ebey's Prairie, elevated 80 feet above the beach, a green billiard table except where plowed a rich lakebed-alluvium black, one of the longest continuously-farmed tracts in the state.

(*Note*: The high water of early 1983 breached the Perego spit and converted the lagoon to a tidal reservoir, its outlet river wadable only at a low tide. Since the gap is near the north end of the spit, through hikers should go inland to the bluff foot.)

From Perego's Lagoon the Trail goes on, but strictly on the beach, though a continuation of the bluff trail is planned. In ¾ mile is the prominent V notch of

Cedar Gulch, down which is a path from the state Department of Natural Resources Point Partridge Beach Area.

To reach this DNR site, a good base for walks south and north, drive Highway 20 from Coupeville 3½ miles to a dangerous T where the highway turns right. Go left on Libbey Road, signed for the state park. In ¾ mile turn south on Valley Drive and follow state park signs left on Floral Circle and past Fort Ebey State Park and through the Weird Pits; at 1½ miles from Libbey Road is the parking area, from which one trail leads up on a Weird Ridge to walk-in camps, and another down Cedar Gulch to the beach.

Mile 14¾-16¾: Cedar Gulch-Fort Ebey State Park-
Libbey Beach County Park

Another dandy loop presents itself, on beach from Cedar Gulch to the north end of Fort Ebey State Park, returning via a high-tide-open bluff trail, by military artifacts, for a total of 3½ miles.

From the Cedar Gulch trail north under the light on Point Partridge, by a small lagoon, to the beach-access trail from Lake Pondilla, is 1½ miles.

However, to back up and take the bluff route from the south: From Cedar Gulch a meager, boot-beaten track, often treacherous, but to be improved someday, follows the brink a long ½ mile to the 50-site campground of 227-acre Fort Ebey State Park. A good trail leads a scant 1½ miles through the park and out the above-mentioned beach-access trail to the lagoon. Built for World War II because it commanded a straight shot out the Strait of Juan de Fuca, Fort Ebey has a pair of mounts for 6-inch guns, which are on the trail, and a picturesque inland water tower which is not. The most conspicuous relic of military days is gorse, planted by the Army as a substitute for barbed wire, making sentimentalists about things Scottish sighful, when they're not shrieking with pain as the spikes penetrate. The trail also passes the lighthouse and, finally, the picnic area above Lake Pondilla; the bilious green water is beloved of ducks but is of chief interest to humans for occupying the most notable of the Weird Pits. Holes up to 100 feet deep pock the landscape eastward across the width of the island to Penn Cove, separated by knife-edge ridges just as mysterious. What are they? Ancient gravel pits (dug by Ancient Astronauts)? No. It is hill-and-kettle topography formed by melting of a stagnant section of the Puget Glacier.

Drive to Fort Ebey State Park via Libbey Road, Valley Drive, and Floral Circle, following signs (see DNR Point Partridge). At ¾ mile from Libbey Road turn right into the park. Park roads lead to parking and trailheads at the Lake Pondilla picnic area, the gun sites, and the campground.

From the Lake Pondilla beach-access trail it's a scant ½ mile more on the beach to Libbey Beach (Island) County Park.

Mile 16¾-19¼: Libbey Beach County Park-West Beach-
Hastie Lake Road

For every dozen hikers who head south from Point Partridge, only one heads north. That's a mistake. If different, the beach north is equally fine and, in its own specialties, more spectacular.

From the dangerous T on Highway 20 drive Libbey Road west 1¼ miles to the end at Libbey Beach County Park.

Public tidelands extend 6 miles north from here, guaranteeing freedom of the sands. On this 2½-mile section the bluff rises to over 200 feet, stunningly precipitous much of the way, keeping houses from the beach the entire distance. Unlike the "Ebey-type" sand bluff south of Point Partridge, here the mix is a more standard clay and sand and gravel and till, some rocklike, from older glacial times, forming noble tall cliffs.

The view rounds to northward vistas into Rosario Strait, past the lighthouse on Smith Island and supertankers carrying oil to the refineries, to the San Juan Islands, rising to the heights of Erie and Constitution.

Then the bluff drops to houses and Hastie Lake Road.

Mile 19¼-22: Hastie Lake Road-West Beach-Sunset Beach

From Highway 20 drive Libbey Road west ½ mile and turn north on West Beach Road 2¼ miles to Hastie Lake Road, which ends in a public beach access to public tidelands extending south and north.

Beach houses quit when the bluff rears up. In 1 mile the beach rounds 100-foot-high "Vertical Till Point" and enters a shallow cove. Now the clay-sand precipice rises steadily higher, finally to 250 feet — as exciting as anything south of Point Partridge. In a most impressive "Grand Canyon" stretch the alternating strata of sand and clay form steps, resembling a wall of the famous canyon of the Southwest.

Then the bluff drops to nothing and man snuggles up to the water. A public parking area and beach access here are reached by driving West Beach Road north 2½ miles from Hastie Lake Road.

Mile 22-26: Sunset Beach-Joseph Whidbey State Park-Clover Valley

The cutoff old bay, now Swantown Valley, presents 1 mile of Sunset Beach houses, not appealing. However, at the north end on West Beach Road is a public parking area, boundary of undeveloped Joseph Whidbey State Park, 112 acres leased from the Navy.

Actually, the park ends in a long ½ mile, but when the Navy isn't shooting rifles the local folk walk on. For 3 miles the beach is lonesome-wild except for two Navy-only recreation sites. At 1¾ miles, beyond still another cutoff bay, drift bluff briefly rears up. The beach at the point here is distinguished by exposures of non-glacial bedrock, picturesquely eroded by waves. In another 1¼ miles of solitude a little bluff rises to a Navy park. Beyond its bulge are Clover Valley and Ault Field, off limits. Across the mile-wide gap West Beach walking resumes, as described in Deception Pass State Park.

Deception Pass State Park (Map — page 174, 178)

If a person were compelled to select a single spot for all wanderings of saltwater shores and forests, there could be no better choice than Deception Pass State Park. One would think Mother Nature felt cramped for space in Creation, forced to stuff such richness of goodies in such small room: virgin forests of Douglas fir up to 9 feet in diameter; other forests of grand fir, Sitka

Deception Pass from Bowman Hill trail

spruce, shore pine, juniper, and madrona contorted and sculpted by storm winds blowing from the Pacific Ocean with naught in the way to blunt their fury; grassy sea meadows, flower-bright in season, and rock gardens of moss and lichen on headlands looking out to the San Juan Islands; a myriad surprising little coves and secluded pocket beaches, and islands and off-shore rocks, and former islands (tombolos) connected to the mainland by sand necks; kelp beds and rafts of waterfowl, seals cavorting, eagles nesting and hawks soaring, and mobs of herons flying to and from a rookery; pretty-pebble beaches, tidal marshes, and a sand-floored, tea-water, sealevel lake, enclosed by a baymouth bar topped by the best sand dunes on the inland sea; buttresses of heavily-metamorphosed volcanic rock polished and rounded and scratched by the Puget Glacier. To this man adds small boats (and sometimes, amazingly, log rafts pulled and pushed by tugs) navigating cliff-walled Deception Pass, where at turns of the tide the water runs river-swift and turbulent; and history of Indians, explorers, the CCC — and a penal colony. All in the rainshadow of the Olympics, where mossy citizens of Puget Sound City flock in winter for a chance to see the sun.

The bulk of the modern park was preserved in virginity (or near) as a military reservation until turned over to the state in 1925. In 1933 the Civilian Conservation Corps, supervised by the National Park Service, began developing roads and trails and building shelters, the craftsmanship in stone and timber contributing a rustic charm. Presently consisting of 2600 acres and likely to grow ultimately to 3000, the park hosts some 1,800,000 people a year for camping (254 sites), swimming, boating — and hiking the dozens of miles of trails and beach.

So many are the delightful nooks, so intricately interwoven the paths, and so many the convenient parking areas, a pedestrian can assemble the ingredients into a virtually infinite number of superb recipes. Short walks can be taken, a mile or less, yet fun enough to keep a child — or adult — entertained all day. Or these can be linked in longer rambles. Described here, to stimulate the imagination, are combinations that among them pretty well sample the park.

Note: the park is notable for cliffs from which the rangers annually rescue scores of bold idiots trapped by their bravery. Please stay on safe paths and beaches.

From I-5 drive Highway 20 onto Fidalgo Island and take the south arm, signed "Deception Pass." The park is entered at Pass Lake and lies on both sides of the highway and both sides of Deception Pass.

Rosario Head-Bowman Bay-Lighthouse Point-Canoe Pass (Map — page 174)

Quintessential, that's what it is — most of the raptures promised by the introduction are delivered here. Three short strolls can be taken separately or combined.

From Highway 20 at the south end of Pass Lake, turn right, signed "Rosario." Pass the sideroad down to Bowman Bay (closed in winter, but in other seasons an alternate parking and starting point), continue 1 mile, and turn left down to the Rosario Beach parking and picnic area.

Stroll #1, a ½-mile loop. Walk out the grassy neck of the picnic area and up the forest-and-meadow heights of Rosario Head, with broad views over Rosario Strait to Lopez Island, little lighthouse-blinking Smith Island, and the

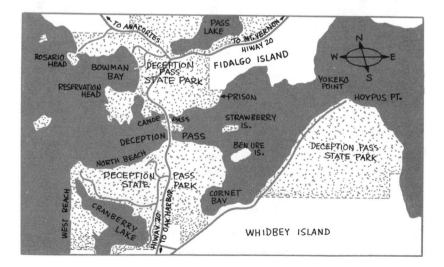

water horizon of the Strait of Juan de Fuca. Look across Northwest Pass to Lighthouse Point, next on the agenda.

Stroll #2, 1 mile to junction, then a 1-mile loop. Returned to the picnic area, take the "Canoe Pass, Lighthouse Point, Bowman Bay" trail by the restrooms, into woods, along cliffs, ½ mile to Bowman (Reservation) Bay and the picnic area. On trail or beach proceed ½ mile more, by a boat-launch and one-time fish-rearing ponds and old dock, along a marsh, to a wooded sidehill above the low neck connecting to Lighthouse Tombolo. Here is a Y; take the right, down onto the neck. On the far end the trail goes left around a corner and starts up the hill; spot a less-good path taking off from it straight up the hill — this is the return of the loop.

Frequently on the brink of alarming precipices plunging to the water, the way proceeds through meadows, tree sculptures, seascapes, knolls, tiny beaches, from one oo-and-ah pause to another. Keep left at forks. At the far outside of the loop the main island is separated by a chasm from the islet-peak of the light (not a house), which ain't worth the danger; forget it; at least six other meadow-bald promontories offer the same view — into Deception Pass, across to North Beach and West Point, and over Bowman Bay to Rosario Head. Beware of clams dropping from the sky; if gulls hover above, prepare to dodge.

Actually, the best plan is to return the way you came, on good trail. But by picking rude paths carefully to avoid peril, one can finish the loop in order to experience all variations on the view.

Stroll #3, a 1-mile loop. Returned to the Y, take the left, round forest slopes, pass a sidetrail left (the loop return), switchback up a peaklet, and contour. Then take a sidetrail down to overviews of Canoe Pass, Deception Pass, Canoo (Pass) Island, the bridge, and boats; another path drops to the beach at the west entrance of Canoe Pass. Complete the loop back through a saddle and return as you came to Rosario Beach.

Three-stroll round trip 4½ miles, allow 3 hours
High point 150 feet, elevation gain 500 feet

Pass Lake-Lake Campbell (Map — page 178)

A recent acquisition, around and north of Pass Lake, is as yet undeveloped, respecting the privacy of the couple, the Heilmans, who tended and loved this land so long and fended off taxmen and developers to preserve it for the people. Eventually a trail system through the forest, selectively logged before World War II but very lovely, will connect duckpond-quiet Pass Lake and Lake Campbell at the foot of Mount Erie.

Adventurous walkers can sample the area on a fire-protection trail and rude fishermen's paths, as roughly indicated on the accompanying sketch map. If the trees aren't huge the woods are really wild; on the survey in a winter twilight were heard alarming crashings in the brush, one merely a deer but the other suspected of being a chimera or basilisk.

Loop trip 3 miles, allow 2 hours
High point 500 feet, elevation gain 400 feet

Bowman Hill-Canoe Pass-Prison Camp (Map — page 178)

The Bowman Hill segment never was developed by the CCC, the only travel routes being long-overgrown military patrol roads and brushed-out powerline service roads, along which walkers have beaten out a rude trail system. The rangers would just as soon not have too many folks getting lost here and falling off the cliffs, so the area is suggested only for the experienced hiker. The accompanying sketch map indicates the general route, starting from the turnout just north of the bridge.

The scenery is more of the same (terrific), though with a different perspective. The history is novel: From 1909 until 1923, an average population of 25 prisoners lived on a bench by the shore and worked the quarry in the north wall of Canoe Pass. Concrete footings and a large concrete cistern are about all the traces of the colony to be seen; the quarry is best viewed from Canoe Island.

Round trip to prison camp 2 miles, allow 2 hours
High point 450 feet, elevation gain 800 feet

Canoe (Pass) Island (Map — page 178)

No short walk in the park is more scenic, more popular, and more dangerous. So take it easy. But by all means take it.

Drive the highway over the bridge to the island-top parking area and go. Descend the alpine-meadow-like rock-garden path, strawberry-blossom-bright in spring, and with grass widows and mahonia blooming as early as February, to the east tip of the island and look east to Strawberry Island and Hoypus Point and Yokeko Point. Stroll close by frightening eddies and whirlpools of loud waters, under the bridge, to the west tip and look west to Deception Island.

You're really in the middle of things here, in the waterway called "Boca de Flon" by a Spaniard in 1791 and given the modern name next year by Vancouver, who'd been deceived into thinking he'd found a peninsula until his man Whidbey explored the passage.

Round trip ¾ mile, allow 1 hour
High point 175 feet, elevation gain 250 feet

West Beach-Sand Dunes-North Beach-Cranberry Lake
(Map — page 178)

Here's another melange of three strolls, partly quintessential but also with two unique features — unique not only in the park but the entire inland sea. Though each stroll can be a delicious afternoon by itself, the combination is suggested because the contrasting flavors enhance each other.

The combination can be done from several parking areas. For one (no better than the others) drive the highway south of the bridge to the park headquarters entry. Following West Beach signs, drive to the large parking area at West Beach.

Stroll #1, a partly-looping round trip of 4½ miles. Head south on West Beach, walkable at all tides, in views to San Juans and Olympics and the water

Canoe Pass and Deception Pass bridge

horizon of the Strait of Juan de Fuca. At ¾ mile is the park boundary, beyond which houses have invaded the dunes, but are set back far enough not to disturb enjoyment of waves and waterfowl, and the parade of ships south to Puget Sound, and the Liberian merchant marine carrying billions of quarts of oil to the refineries. At 1⅓ miles from the park the walk must halt, blocked at the outlet creek of Cranberry Lake by the U.S. Naval Reservation and Ault Field; the danger in going on is not so much in being captured as a suspected spy but in being on the beach when a jet fighter passes inches overhead, the noise turning you into a vegetable.

The beach is great. An inland-looping return, however, leads to The Unique. Here where the rainshadow sun shines and the wild west winds blow there were, until the recent past, 3 continuous miles of sand dunes, far and away the grandest such display on the inland sea. National Defense clobbered more than a mile of glory, and developers are mutilating another. Even so, the ½ mile preserved by the park still is the grandest such display on the inland sea. In

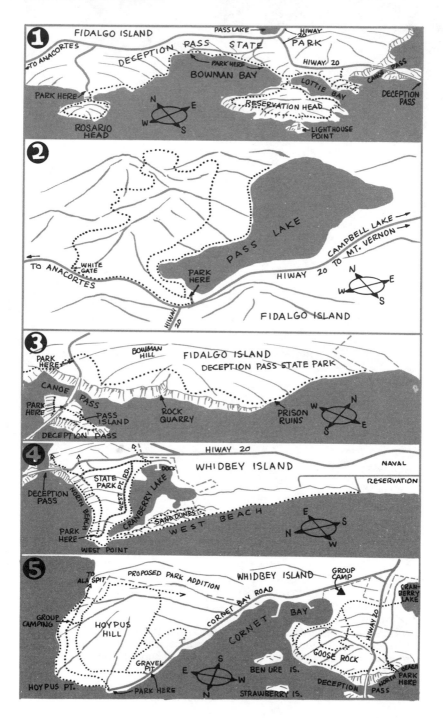

order to help the preservation, please view the dunes, and the sprawling mass of spruce, hemlock, and fir, from the new blacktop paths; indiscriminate walking erodes. See the innermost and highest dune line, standing above the marsh-lake lagoon area, representing a drier climate of the past and now mostly anchored by forest. See the outermost dunes, lightly vegetated, moderately active. From the dunes walk by Cranberry Lake, admiring the unusual sand beach in water of "ocean tea."

Stroll #2, a round trip of 2 miles. Returned to the parking area, walk north to the jutting observation-platform rocks of West Point and take the trail along North Beach, in views over boiling waters of Deception Pass to Fidalgo Island. North Beach consists of four gravel arcs separated by rock points; at moderate tides the route can combine beach and trees, at high it can stay on the forest trail. In 1 long mile North Beach is terminated by up-leaping cliffs.

Stroll #3, 2 miles one way. To complete the melange, from the picnic area short of the cliffs walk the trail in big trees up to the North Beach parking lot (alternative start) and proceed up its access road through an "Avenue of the Giants," huge Douglas firs and Sitka spruces and western hemlocks and western red cedars, and also-huge swordfern, to the park headquarters (alternative start).

Here is a ¼-mile nature trail interpreting the plant community. After walking that, descend by road or trail to the Cranberry Lake picnic area (alternative start), 1 mile from North Beach. Walk out on the dock to survey the lake, in mood and vegetation reminding of Ozette Lake in Olympic National Park. Follow the shore path, tunneling through 8-foot-high salal, to the West Point Road. Soon leave it for trail again and walk by contorted shore pines out on a plank bridge to an islet with a rock point, giving the sensation of being on an alpine lake at 10,000 feet in the High Sierra.

Three-stroll round trip 7½ miles, allow 5 hours
High point 175 feet, elevation gain 250 feet

Cornet Bay-Goose Rock (Map — page 178)

More waterscapes and forestscapes and cliffscapes. But also a miniature mountain, 475 feet high, giving broad views to far horizons. Goose Rock can be conquered from any number of starting points and by several routes. The surveyor's choice is a loop starting from the North Beach parking lot.

Where one big wide trail drops from the road to the beach, find another boulevard contouring east into big firs, then climbing a rock-garden wall to cross under the bridge. The trail goes through woods, gradually dropping near the water, madronas leaning over the beach. Strawberry Island (park) is passed, and then Ben Ure Island (private), as the shore rounds into Cornet Bay, with marina and houses. At a Y of two good-looking forks, take the right uphill (the left deadends on cliffs) to a glorious moss-garden grass-meadow bald high above the boat-dotted bay. The trail then switchbacks down through walls covered with saxifrages and succulents to the beach and a junction 1¼ miles from North Beach.

The path straight ahead leads in ¼ mile to the mudflat head of Cornet Bay and the park's Group Camp, site of one of the CCC work camps (others were

From the trail on Hoypus Point

at Bowman Bay and park headquarters). Two trails lead from the camp back over the highway, for variants on the suggested loop.

However, from the junction reverse-turn right, uphill, and switchback ¾ mile through rhododendrons and big, fire-blackened firs to mossy balds and onto the broad peak. Proceed over the ice-rounded rock domes to the west peak and the best views.

Zounds. See far down Camano and Whidbey Islands and Skagit Bay and Rosario Strait, out to Olympics and Vancouver Island and Lopez and a mess of other San Juans. Especially interesting is the perspective on Cornet Bay, Cranberry Lake, and the dunes. And, on the water, ships and boats, always something going somewhere.

For the looping descent, at the summit note another big obvious trail dropping into the woods. Descend it ½ mile to intersect the North Beach Discovery Trail (starting at the Group Camp). Following a former county road, the trail goes through stunningly-huge fire-blackened firs, crosses under the highway, and in ½ mile from Goose Rock trail hits the North Beach road at ¼ mile uphill from the end at the picnic area.

Loop trip 3½ miles, allow 3 hours
High point 475 feet, elevation gain 900 feet

180

Hoypus Hill-Similk Bay (Map — page 178)

Here is the forest primeval, the park's purest wilderness, most jaw-dropping trees. More sheltered from ocean blasts, the trees grow notably tall and straight — it was here the CCC cut the timbers for park structures. The trails largely overgrown, here too is adventure, and solitude. (For a truly mystic experience, walk these woods on a foggy morning.) And aside from all that, beachwalking. And entirely different views. Plus, probably, eagles.

Drive south past the park headquarters and turn east on Cornet Bay Road. Pass the Group Camp, private land with a marina, and reenter park. Pass the boat-launch parking area and in ¼ mile note a gated woods road climbing the hill to the right — this is the return of the Hoypus Hill loop. Drive on a scant ½ mile more to a gravel pit and park.

This is not a view walk, it's a tree walk. Climb the woods road past the white gate. Soon the eyes bug, the Douglas firs are so incredibly big and tall. In a long ¼ mile a sideroad goes right; this is an alternate return of the loop (see below). The fire-road trail tops out and contours, passing trails down left to group pack-in camps (used by reservation) served by a hand-pumped well. At 1 mile from the start the trail hits private property, steeply climbs the hill, and sets out on a compass course due east on the park south boundary. To the left is a 680-acre property the DNR plans to log; Evergreen Islands, a citizen group, is seeking to stop that and have the land added to the park.

At 1 mile from where private property was hit is a junction. The fire trail goes straight; instead, take the road-trail right. Pass two sideroads right which are alternate, shorter returns (see above). Switchback down to the shore road, reached at the white gate in 1 mile of walking from the park south boundary. Walk the paved road — or the beach — to the gravel pit to complete the loop.

Loop trip 3½ miles, allow 3 hours
High point 350 feet, elevation gain 350 feet

A second Hoypus Hill hike combines monster trees with Similk Bay beach and views, plus a spice of history.

Drive past the gravel pit ⅓ mile to the road-end at Hoypus Point. What's this concrete bulkhead for? The ferry. What ferry? The one that until the bridge was built in 1935 crossed to Dewey Beach on Fidalgo Island.

At low tide the beach can be walked 2 miles south to Ala Spit (which see). Over the waters are Kiket and Skagit Islands in Similk Bay. South are Goat and Ika Islands. Trees lean over the beach, including a grand fir that is horizontal 70 feet, its limbs rising straight up as a row of little trees. Look out for seals. (Or was that an otter swimming in the winter twilight?)

At any tide the forest can be enjoyed. From the road-end scramble up the bank to what was in CCC days a big wide path but now, maintained only by thrusting bodies, is a slow go. But worth it for the gulper firs. In 1 mile are the pack-in campsites and then private property.

At the right tide the correct route is forest one way, beach the other.

Round trip 2 miles, allow 1½ hours

Mount Erie (Map — page 182)

A landmark that orients travelers for miles around, Mount Erie gives panoramas for miles around — over the San Juan island-mountains of which it is so prominent an example, blue seas of saltwaterways and green seas of the Skagit delta, to Cascades and Olympics and British Columbia Coast Range and Vancouver Island Mountains.

Terrific views. How about the walking? At present, crummy — paved roads, route of the Erie Grand Prix, and motorcycle trenches that in years of neglect took over the old hiker/horse paths. However, during the 1980s the walking may gradually come to match the scenery. The City of Anacortes plan developed in 1981 envisions restricting motorcycles somewhat and providing a quiet trail from the bottom of the peak to the top. Until it happens, one does better to drive up Erie for the views and then go to Deception Pass State Park for a walk.

However, if you're set on climbing Erie, choose a weekday morning, well before school lets out. From I-5 drive Highway 20 toward Anacortes. Where 20 splits, take the south fork, signed "Deception Pass." In a scant 2 miles, where 20 turns left along Lake Campbell, go right on the unsigned road. Drive past Lake Campbell 1½ miles to a Y at Lake Erie. Take the right a scant 1½ miles. Watch for a prominent sideroad right, diverging from the highway and shortly rejoining it. Turn in and park, elevation 400 feet.

Narrow, winding, paved Ray Auld Drive climbs 1 steep mile to the saddle between Erie and Sugarloaf, elevation 750 feet.

Two walks start here. For Sugarloaf, just as Auld Drive is reaching the saddle flat, spot the unsigned but obvious, though brush-obscured, trail left. In ⅓ mile the way emerges on mossy balds ringing the forested summit, 1055 feet. For Erie, walk the road, up twisty switchbacks in growing views, 1 mile to the 1270-foot summit parking area. Plan to spend a good long while walking short paths through wind-buffeted forest to cliff brinks for vistas to all points of the compass.

Round trip (from bottom, both peaks) 5 miles, allow 4 hours
High point 1270 feet, elevation gain 1200 feet
All year

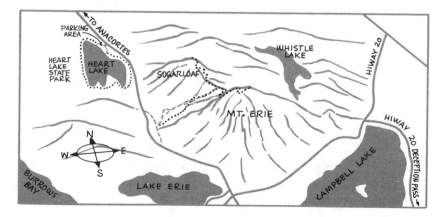

Glacier-scratched rock near top of Sugar Loaf Mountain

When the Anacortes plan is implemented, watch for another star attraction: the Across-Fidalgo Trail that will start in the city at the old ferry dock and extend some dozen miles via Cranberry Lake, Heart Lake, Mt. Erie, Lakes Erie and Campbell, to Deception Pass.

Heart Lake State Park (Map — page 182)

This brand new park was undeveloped and unplanned at survey time (spring 1981). However, existing trails permit fine explorations until State Parks provides better.

From Ray Auld Drive (see Mount Erie) continue north on Heart Lake Road a scant mile to near the north end of the lake and turn west into the large boat-launch/parking area, elevation 310 feet.

The lake is popular with fish, fishermen, birds, and birders. But the unique feature is the old-growth forest of huge Douglas firs, plus goodly hemlocks, spruces, cedars, one of the best big-tree shows in the lowlands.

Walk north from the parking lot and at forks generally choose those that stay nearest the lake. If a path deadends, retreat and try again. Sometimes near the pond lilies and frogs and ducks, sometimes in deep woods, the looping way emerges on Heart Lake Road at the south end of the lake.

Loop trip 2 miles, allow 1½ hours
High point 350 feet, elevation gain minor
All year

Washington Park (Map — page 184)

Better not schedule anything else the day you come to 220-acre Washington Park. Don't be deceived by the shortness of the walk, which any hotfoot could crank out in an hour. The long halts for views over waterways to islands near and far, to examine juniper and madrona groves and granite boulders dropped by the glacier which also polished and scratched the buttresses, and sidetrips on sea-meadow bluffs and down balds to rocks jutting in the waves — well, better bring lunch, because you could be all day at it.

From I-5 drive Highway 20 into Anacortes, turn left, following signs to "Victoria Ferry," and when the highway turns downhill right, to the ferry dock, continue straight on Sunset to the park entrance. At a Y the right, signed "Beach Area," drops to Sunset Beach; go left, signed "Camp Area, Loop Road, Boat Launch." At the next Y take the right, toward the boat-launch, and park, elevation 25 feet.

The basic walk is a big loop around Fidalgo Head on Loop Road, single-lane, blacktop, with speed bumps to enforce slow, quiet driving. All along the way sidepaths lure to unknown wonders, always worth it. And so the whole day just melts away.

Find the Loop Road above the boat-launch. Walk a roadside path in views over Rosario Strait to Cypress, Orcas, Blakely, Decatur, and Lopez Islands. See the ferry from Anacortes to Vancouver Island. In ½ mile round Green

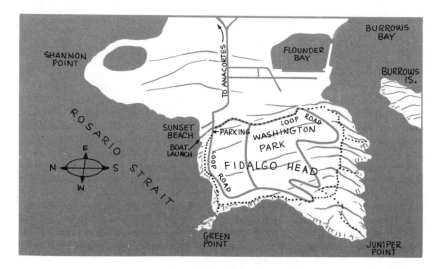

Rosario Strait from Juniper Point

Point and from the green lawns look south to the Olympics. On or beside the road (at low tide, after a sidetrip down to West Beach), climb grassy opens.

After the road switchbacks left into forest, spot a good trail switchbacking right. Follow it away from the road and to the top of Juniper Point, 1 mile from the start. Now sidepaths proliferate, slowing progress, as do carpets of moss and grass and flowers, old, gnarled, wind-sculptured junipers reminding of the Sierra, views across the water to Burrows Island, Mount Erie, fishing boats.

Following this path or that, likely the Loop Road will be touched here and there. And likely as not more trails will beguile, down ravines to secluded coves, out on high meadows. Chances are that after walking about 2 miles, exclusive of sidetrips, one will hit the Loop Road at a view over the Flounder Bay Marina to Erie. If so, the Havekost Monument, commemorating the pioneer of 1871 who gave Anacortes this park, will be passed, as well as concrete footings of the reservoir that served the lumber mill at Flounder Bay until demolished in 1961 (all except the planing mill, now a boatshed). A final scant 1 mile on the Loop Road, through fine cool woods, returns to the parking area.

Loop trip 3 miles, allow 2 hours
High point 250 feet, elevation gain 400 feet
All year

Eagle Harbor from Winslow City Park

NORTH KITSAP AND OLYMPIC PENINSULAS

Whan that Aprille with his shoures soote
The droghte of March hath perced to the roote. . .
Thanne longen folk to go on ferry rides. . . .

Granted, the voyaging, loading-unloading, and waiting, added to the driving, tend to compoundly fracture the Two-Hour Rule. However, vessels must be distinguished from automobiles. Ferries aren't part of the agony, the disease — they're part of the fun, the cure. Even on a pellmell-paced superferry a person can hotfoot around the decks a mile and more during a crossing, soaking up scenery and drinking in salt air like wine.

Ferries are among the better inventions, even though they have sadly declined. How impoverished is the present, how fabulously wealthy were the good old days! Until the Hood Canal Floating Bridge opened in 1961, a ferry connected Lofall to South Point, successor to the earlier Port Gamble-Shine route. Until 1942 the Canal also was served by the toy-cute **Lake Constance** shuttling between Seabeck and Brinnon. Perhaps the most lamented of the lost classics is the old Edmonds-Port Ludlow run, wiped out after World War II; even this was a mere shadow of the Ballard-Ludlow ferry killed before the war. And in the 1930s and 1920s . . . The mosquito fleet . . . Ah well . . .

Bainbridge Island, really only a half-island, having become with the 1949 completion of Agate Pass Bridge an appendage of the Kitsap Peninsula, has the appeals of the voyage through the Seattle harbor, most exciting in the Northwest, and the closeness, beach strolls starting minutes from the dock. As with the entirety of this province, it's costly, being difficult to exploit extensively with leave-the-car-behind, walk-on trips. Someday there'll be a bus.

Whether reached via Seattle-Winslow or Edmonds-Kingston, the north Kitsap Peninsula, except for the walk or two that can be done from the Kingston dock, hits the wallet hard. Consequently only the beaches are surveyed here, the inland forests ignored because there are cheaper woods across the water. Main Street is well-represented, Hood Canal scarcely at all: the Navy is very touchy about trespassers on its Doomsday Headquarters; neighboring residents, edgy about living so near Ground Zero, are private-property extremists; no good put-ins were found south of the bridge. For the view of the Olympics, pause at Kitsap Memorial State Park. For walking, drive on.

Another jolt to the treasury is delivered by the crossing to the Olympic Peninsula, which because of the camel's-back-breaking straw plus the driving time, here getting badly out of joint, is strictly high-graded, nothing included but the cream of the cream, triple-A-plus material. First, the mountains. In the season when a person wants that ferry ride but the High Olympics welcome only snowshoers, or when the rhododendrons are blooming, several high vista points on the mountain front may well be judged worth breaking the Two-Hour Rule and the budget, ferry and flower pleasures the prelude to novel perspectives on Puget Sound-Cascade country.

Second, the Strait of Juan de Fuca, oh my. When a walker yearns for a change from the more intimate beauties of inland-sea beaches, yet hasn't a weekend for wide-sky ocean beaches, the transitional Strait is the place.

Beaches are long and wild and lonesome, the surf often ocean-crashing, seascapes and mountainscapes always enormous, Main Street traffic busy — and here is the mecca to which in dull winter mossy Puget Sounders go on pilgrimage, the rainshadow of the Olympics, the center of that Great Blue Hole around which swirl the eternal grays.

USGS maps: **Duwamish Head, Bremerton East, Shilshole Bay, Suquamish, Poulsbo, Edmonds West, Brinnon, Port Gamble, Lofall, Quilcene, Mt. Walker, Tyler Peak, Hansville, Port Ludlow, Center, Uncas, Nordland, Port Townsend South, Port Townsend North, Gardiner, Sequim, Carlsborg, Dungeness**

Bainbridge Island (Map — page 189, 193)

Aside from the Olympics, what dominates the view from much of Seattle's shoreline is Bainbridge Island, 10 miles north-south long and 4 miles east-west wide. That's a lot of beach. But also, there's a lot of people living there, largely on the beach. Many of the walks thus require toleration, which is quite high on winter Wednesdays, low on summer Sundays. However, the beachwalker's buddies, the glacier-drift bluffs, protect the solitude on some long wild strips, and several bits of tidelands are public. On no day will a visitor ever be completely shut out.

A nice way to do the island is to combine several short walks, in a day sampling all sides, all views. Because of the important propinquity to the masses of boots (and sneakers, and sandals), which can get at their business mere minutes after the Seattle ferry docks at Winslow, the entire shoreline is surveyed here, trips described in a counterclockwise direction starting at Winslow.

Eagle Harbor (Map — page 189)

Site of the island's metropolis, Winslow, its two big industries, a shipyard and creosote plant, and marinas and the ferry dock.

Leave the car in Seattle and walk on the ferry, paying (1978) $1.70 a foot-passenger round trip (cheap).

For a harbor tour, walk up into the neat little village-town, turn left, and left again, down to the little city park, paths through pretty woods, and the beach. Round trip, 1 mile.

For the beach, outside the passenger terminal find a rude path down to the water. A bank fends off houses at first. An old pier can be passed at low tide, at high tide must be gotten around inland on the road. Then the way is open, on a toleration basis, partway to Wing Point. Great ferry-watching. Round trip 2½ miles.

Both round trips 3½ miles, allow 2½ hours

Manitou Beach (Map — page 189)

Views to Main Street ship traffic, West Point sewage plant, Elliott Bay and downtown Seattle towers, Alki Point.

From Winslow drive Highway 305 for 2 miles, turn right on Manitou Beach Road ½ mile, and park on the wide shoulder.

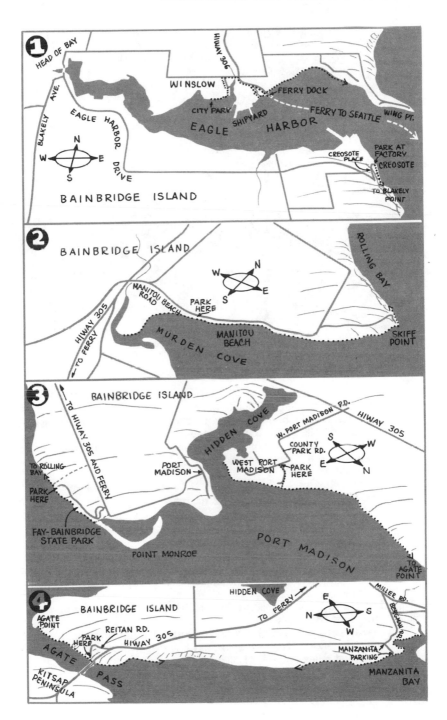

Telephoto of Seattle skyline from Manitou Beach

The walk is open on Sunday, due to the beach-side road. Walk west to the tidal-creek estuary at the head of Murden Cove. Walk east to Skiff Point and views north along Rolling Bay. (On weekdays a person perhaps can pass the ½ mile of beach homes and continue up Rolling Bay nearly 2 bluff-wild miles that otherwise have no public access.)

Round trip (Sunday) 3 miles, allow 2 hours

Fay Bainbridge State Park (Map — page 189)
The 17-acre park has ⅓ mile of public beach wedged between rows of homes. South is downtown Seattle, across the Sound are West Point and Shilshole Bay, and north over Port Madison and the Sound are Richmond Beach, Edmonds, and Glacier Peak.

Drive Highway 305 for 4¼ miles, turn right at the sign for the state park, and follow more signs 3½ miles.

On winter weekdays a person might be tolerated in passing the ½ mile of houses immediately south and then would have open some 2 mostly-wild beneath-the-bluff miles south on Rolling Bay.

Round trip (Sunday) ⅔ mile, allow ½ hour

Port Madison County Park (Map — page 189)

A little walk in big trees of a 13-acre wildland, then a secluded beach with views over Port Madison and fishing boats to Suquamish and Indianola and Three Fingers.

Drive Highway 305 for 6 miles and turn right on West Port Madison Road, which in 1 long mile, at a sharp bend right, becomes County Park Road. At a hundred feet short of Gordon Road, spot a woods road-trail going left into woods. The sign marking the park usually is missing.

Walk the path through nice firs, past dilapidated picnic shelter and fireplaces and privy, and skid down a clay trail to the beach, ¼ mile from the road.

When tolerated, walk east around the corner and peek into charming Hidden Cove. Walk north, few houses near, maybe to Agate Point.

Round trip up to 4 miles, allow up to 3 hours

Agate Pass (Map — page 189)

Boat-watching is notably excellent on beaches of the narrow pass, where at the turn of the tide craft get either an assist or a tussle from the swift current. Partly okay on Sunday.

Drive Highway 305 nearly to Agate Pass Bridge and turn right on Reitan Road. In ⅓ mile, at a powerline tower, are a turnaround and parking area and good trail dropping to the beach.

The walk north 1 mile to Agate Point, views opening over the water to Suquamish and Port Madison and Indianola, is by a row of near-beach houses; avoid on Sunday.

South, though, beyond a couple houses up on the bank that might be passed if done politely, the tanglewood bluff roars up 100 feet and the beach is houseless and wild more than 1 mile and virtually empty the whole 2¾ miles to Manzanita. On the way, Agate Pass widens into Port Orchard. Views open around Point Bolin to the Navy installation at Keyport and south into Manzanita Bay and to Battle Point. On the Kitsap Peninsula rise the peaks of Green and Gold; beyond are Constance and Warrior.

Round trip up to 7 miles, allow up to 5 hours

Manzanita Bay (Map — page 189)

The cozy little bay beguiles. Views are fine over Port Orchard to Keyport, and a wow to the Olympic skyline of Zion to Townsend to Constance to Walker to Turner. Partly okay on Sunday.

Drive Highway 305 for 4¼ miles, turn left at the sign, "Manzanita," and immediately left again on Miller Road. In a scant ½ mile turn right on Bergman Road. In ½ mile it comes to Manzanita Bay and bends right; just beyond, a public street-end stub goes left a few yards to the beach. Very limited parking.

North, with a few houses at the start, requiring toleration, the beach leads to wildness and, in 2¾ miles, Agate Pass Bridge (which see). South, no houses to interfere, it's ½ mile around the bay to the inlet estuary oozing muckily out of secret green forest.

Round trip south 1 mile, allow 1 hour

Battle Point (Map — page 193)

A lagoon-enclosing spit thrusting out in Port Orchard, a light at the tip. Views north to Agate Pass, south to Fletcher Bay and suburbs of Bremerton, and across to Keyport. Heavy water traffic, recreational and Navy. But the beach access is private, via a neighborhood path, so foreigners ought not come except on winter stormdays and must be prepared to turn back at the least frown.

Drive Fletcher Bay Road (see Fletcher Bay) to Island Center. Continue straight on Miller Road ½ mile and turn left on Battle Point Drive. In 1¾ miles turn left on Skinner Road ⅓ mile, down to beachlevel and a farm; at a left bend the road becomes Ollalie Lane. On the right is a wide field grown up in tall grass and scotchbroom. Park on the shoulder and walk the path the several hundred feet to the beach.

Northwest 1 mile is Arrow Point at the mouth of Manzanita Bay. Some near-beach houses require tolerance to pass.

Southwest ½ mile is the tip of the Battle Point sandspit, no houses near the water. The 1½ miles south from there to Fletcher Bay are partly populated.

If you've got to have a battle, this appears a decent spot for it. Who did the fighting?

Round trip to Battle Point 1 mile, allow 1 hour

Fletcher Bay (Map page 193)

Another of the fiordlike coves for which Bainbridge is noted. The harbor is half-plugged with boats, dinghy to million-dollar yacht. Views along Port Orchard to Keyport, and of Olympics from Constance to Jupiter to The Brothers.

Drive Highway 305 for 1 mile and turn left at the stoplight on High School Road. In 2 miles turn right on Fletcher Bay Road ½ mile to Island Center. Turn left on Fletcher Bay Road ⅓ mile and turn left on Foster Road. In a scant ½ mile is a T with Hansen Road. Go right a short bit, then left on the stub Fletcher Landing Road. Parking for two cars at most.

The cormorant-decorated pilings are from the car ferry which into the 1920s ran the 2 miles over Port Orchard to Brownsville. Here in 1923 the Navy petty officer who was to become the surveyor's father, seeking a way to impress the girl who was to become the surveyor's mother, jumped fully clothed from a rowboat and swam the entire ferry route.

Tolerance is required for the short stroll north to the spit at the bay mouth. South, though, beyond one house, residences retreat up the bank into fir forest and the beach is open 1 mile with ease, and, with a bit of tolerance from several houses, another 1 mile to the edge of Crystal Springs (which see).

Round trip 2-4 miles, allow 1½-3 hours

Point White-Crystal Springs (Map — page 193)

Views north up Port Orchard. Views across the narrows of Rich Passage, through which hurtle the Seattle-Bremerton ferry and the U.S. Navy. Okay on Sunday.

Debarking from the ferry at Winslow, at the stoplight in town turn left at the sign, "City Center." Turn right on Madison Avenue, left on Wyatt Way, follow-

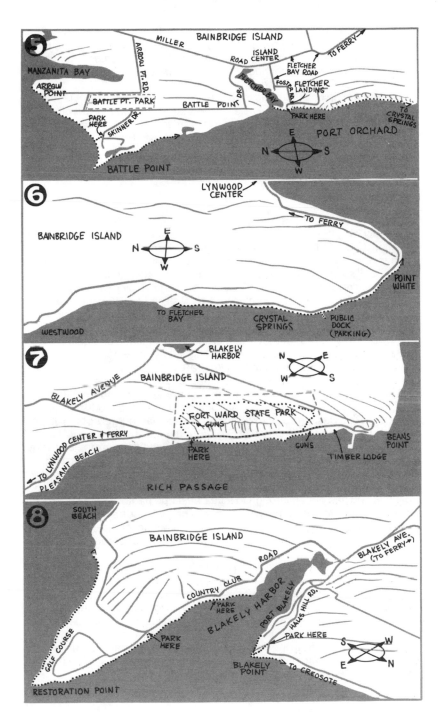

ing signs, "Head of Bay." Bend left on Bucklin Hill Road to a Y; go right on Blakely Avenue, signed "Lynwood Center." Following Lynwood signs, take a right turn, and at a Y go left. At the junction in Lynwood Center turn right 1½ miles to Point White and continue ¾ mile along the shore to a public dock and parking area at Crystal Springs.

Walk out on the dock for the views. Then follow the beach ¾ mile to Point White in one direction, and ¾ mile to the start of houses in the other, the beach-side road preventing objections. (In good trespassing season, the walk can be extended another 2½ miles north to Fletcher Bay.)

Round trip (Sunday) 3 miles, allow 2 hours

Fort Ward State Park (Map — page 193)

A beauty of a forest. A shore that can be walked on the dandy beach or paralleled atop the above-tides wave-cut bench. And mountings of the old gun batteries, strategically located to batter such of the Spaniards as got by the Death (Devil's) Triangle (in rowboats?) and, later, such Japanese as came hurling themselves (in scuba gear?) at the Bremerton Navy Yard. Established in 1891, in 1958 the fort was surplused. Tragically, of the 480 acres only 137 were obtained for park. The remainder, including all the quaint old Army buildings, now are being remodeled into apartment houses and whatnot.

Drive to Lynwood Center (see Point White) and continue straight on Pleasant Beach Road. At the Y in ¾ mile keep right, in ⅔ mile coming to the park gate and in a few yards more the parking area.

The park presently is undeveloped; that, of course, is the best kind for walking. A loop samples the varied entertainments. From the parking area walk the ¾ mile of beach, featuring sandstone outcrops, superferries rocketing through Rich Passage so close you can see the hamburgers being gulped, views of the Kitsap shore and The Brothers, Jupiter, Constance. (Also featured are masses of poison oak, so beware!) At high tide, walk the closed-to-vehicles road. A small gun emplacement is all that's warlike remaining, but here in War II were stretched the anti-sub nets that slowed each ferry trip by a quarter-hour as nets were opened. (After the war it was discovered a Japanese sub had gotten through to take periscope photos of the Navy Yard. Very simple. Just follow the ferry in and out.) The park ends at off-limits Timber Lodge, in previous incarnations an Army recreation center, then Sunset Lodge, then an amusement park; bones of the stripped carousel rust in the grass.

Now for the woods. Backtrack from the park boundary to the gun battery and spot an old road-trail climbing a scant ¼ mile to the bluff top at 150 feet. Hit an old blacktop road and follow it left past two three-storey Army mansions. At blacktop end a woods road-path continues in the woods, first young alder and then splendid big firs, cedars, hemlocks, and maples. Ignore a sidepath that drops left to a deadend at a pump house and proceed straight, at ¾ greenshadow big-tree mile from the blacktop reaching the boundary fence. Here the road-trail descends left, passing an ivy-overgrown gun battery, to hit the park entry road just north of the parking area.

Loop trip 2 miles, allow 1½ hours

Cormorants at Fort Ward

Blakely Harbor (Map — page 193)

Started in the Civil War, what once was the largest lumber mill in the world completely occupied shores of Blakely Harbor; sailing ships carried Washington wood from here around the planet. There actually were three mills in succession; the first two burned, in 1888 and 1907, and the third was closed in 1914 and dismantled in 1923. Lumber schooners remained moored in nearby Eagle Harbor long after; the surveyor attended a birthday party on one. In 1937 the Black Ball Line moved its ferry landing from here to Winslow, previously a stop only for vessels of the mosquito fleet, and Port Blakely was left to quietly marinate in memories.

Debarking from the ferry at Winslow, at the stoplight in town turn left at the sign, "City Center," then right on Madison and left on Wyatt, following "Head of Bay" signs. Bend left on Bucklin Hill Road to a Y. Go right on Blakely Avenue to the head of Blakely Harbor. Turn right on Country Club Road, which in 1 mile touches the beach. Park on the wide shoulder.

Drop off the low bank and walk the beach ¼ mile west. Look out the harbor mouth to Seattle. Look around the harbor to a few old pilings, hulk of a wrecked ship, a couple remodeled houses recognizable as dating from the mill era, remnant pilings of the ferry dock. In mind's eye reconstruct the mill and docks and piles of lumber, the ships filling the harbor, the ferry shuttling in and out, the bustling town.

Round trip ½ mile, allow ½ hour

195

Harbor seals

Restoration Point (Map — page 193)

Named by Vancouver to celebrate restoration of the British monarchy, and at the time of his visit the site of an Indian village, this striking peninsula is the most spectacular natural feature on Bainbridge. However, exploration demands the utmost in courtesy and discretion.

From the parking place for Blakely Harbor (which see) continue on Country Club Road (or better, walk the beach) ½ mile to a Y where Upper Farms Road goes right. Park here if not before.

Walk the bank top on the grownover previous route of Country Club Road. When there's beach, walk that. However, there's not always beach, for this is the center of the only extensive area on shores of Puget Sound proper where hard rock outcrops through glacial drift. From here to Fort Ward, and also across Rich Passage, sandstones, shales, and conglomerates often make buttresses and walls rather than beaches.

All weekends and all summer the walk must end in ¼ mile, at the edge of the country club. Views are fine to Eagle Harbor, the ferry scurrying in and out, and over the Sound to Seattle.

On stormy winter weekdays, a quiet, respectful, humble walker perhaps may proceed to the sanctum of the point. Sandstone-pavement beaches are ribbed and knobbed with protruding strata and nodules of harder rock. Here and there are pockets of dazzling-white shell beach. Above, on the former-island hill are mansions built by some of the oldest money in the Northwest. Around the foot of the forested hill curves a greensward, once a golf course, rolling over an old wave-cut bench to the edge of the sandstone wall that drops a dozen feet to the beach, at low tide providing good cover for a walker who keeps head and voice down.

The views! That way bustles the ferry to Winslow. And that way hustles the ferry to Bremerton. And there's where they come from and go to, Elliott Bay, enclosed by West Seattle and Magnolia Bluff. Far off south, beyond Blake Island, is still another ferry, from Fauntleroy to Vashon Island. Up the Sound is the shore from Alki to Tacoma. Rainier. Down the Sound, past Blakely Rock, is West Point.

On a bleak winter Wednesday the walk can continue past the point 1 mile before encountering the start of beach homes.

Round trip to Point 2 miles, allow 1½ hours

Blakely Point (Map — page 193)

In season when Restoration Point is out of the question, across the mouth of Blakely Harbor is a satisfying consolation prize. As of early 1981, not posted against trespassing, okay on Sunday.

Drive Blakely Avenue to the head of Blakely Harbor (which see) and continue straight. In ⅓ mile, at a confusion of roads, manage to continue east (parallel to the harbor shore) and on Halls Hill Road climb the 100-foot hill to the top, reached in a long ½ mile from the confusion. Park on the turnout.

An undrivable old road skids straight down clay to the beach. A path leads out on the tip of Blakely Point, a fantasy of conglomerate pillars and clefts. The views extend from West Point to Alki Point, over Seattle to the Issaquah Alps and Cascades. Ferries race every which way.

Immediately north of the point are houses; in good trespassing season it's a long 1 mile to Creosote at the mouth of Eagle Harbor.

On the Blakely Harbor side the shore rocks can be clambered from one pocket beach to another. Or, in high tide, a person can stroll the trail along the grade of the ancient shore road, beneath conglomerate walls; madronas and firs lean over the conglomerate bank to the water. In ⅓ mile the old road comes to a house and the walk ends.

Round trip (Sunday) 1 mile, allow 1 hour

Creosote (Map — page 193)

Views to Seattle are fine, but the unique interest of the walk is watching ferries entering and leaving Eagle Harbor, making the long detour south around the buoy-marked sandbar reaching out unseen from Wing Point. (If ferries used the straight-shot route marked on the USGS map they'd run aground — as has happened to merchant ships and in a 1981 fog to a jumbo ferry.)

From the Eagle Harbor "Head of Bay" Y (see Blakely Harbor) take the left, Eagle Harbor Drive. On the hill above the harbor mouth turn left, downhill, on Creosote Place, and park outside the plant.

Watch the ferries. In toleration time, walk 1½ miles south to Blakely Point.

Round trip up to 3 miles, allow 1½ hours

Agate Pass-Suquamish (Map — page 198)

Today cars whiz over Agate Pass high in the air and motorboats churn through from Port Orchard to Port Madison. But just beyond the memory of people still living, the waters were voyaged by dugout cedar canoes of the Suquamish people headquartered here under their leader, Sealth, the white man's friend.

The beach walk comes in two versions, with two put-ins. For the first, drive Highway 305 to the west end of Agate Pass Bridge and park.

A moderately rude path drops to the beach, lonesome-wild under the protective bluff for ¼ mile in either direction, providing good-on-Sunday strolling.

In toleration season, the beach may be walked north past almost solid houses the 1 mile to Old Man House. But the choice trip in such season is south, by widely-scattered clumps of houses, mostly up on a high bank, the 2 miles past Sandy Hook to Point Bolin, at the mouth of Liberty Bay, and perhaps another 2 miles up the bay to a point across from the Navy installation at Keyport.

Round trip 1-8½ miles, allow 1-6 hours

For the history-rich version, just west of the bridge turn north on Suquamish Highway. In 1¼ miles turn right on Division Street, then left on McKinstry, at a scant ½ mile from the highway coming to Old Man House State Historic Site.

On a terrace slightly above high tide was the largest known longhouse, "Old Man House," 500 feet long, up to 60 feet wide. Construction began about 1800 and was completed under Sealth. In 1870, after his death, the U.S. Army burnt the ruins.

Stroll the beach north, looking down Agate Pass, across Port Madison to Agate Point and Point Monroe on Bainbridge Island, across the Sound to Shilshole Bay. North ½ mile is the Suquamish dock, a good viewpoint. Above it in the town, center of the 1375-acre Port Madison Indian Reservation set aside for the Suquamish, Duwamish, and Sekamish Tribes, is a large parking area, an alternate base for the walk. A bit above in Memorial Cemetery is the grave of Chief Sealth (1786-1866), who signed the 1855 Treaty of Mukilteo with Governor Stevens as a representative of the Suquamish and Duwamish peoples, then dominant on central Puget Sound.

Round trip 1½ miles, allow 1 hour

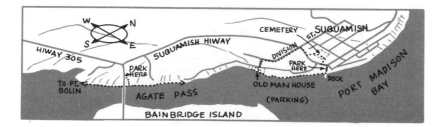

Chief Sealth's grave

Liberty Bay Park (Map — page 199)

A person wouldn't ferry from Seattle for this walk, but in a to-and-fro with a spare hour it's worth a pause — maybe during the Viking Festival held annually in May. The old Scandinavian fishing village of Poulsbo, once site of a large codfish fleet and saltery, has been gussied up very cutely with shoppes. At the same time a charming park has been provided on fiordlike Liberty Bay (nee Dogfish Bay).

From Winslow drive Highway 305 to the stoplight at Poulsbo, turn left on Hostmark Street ½ mile to downtown, and there turn left into the large water-side parking area.

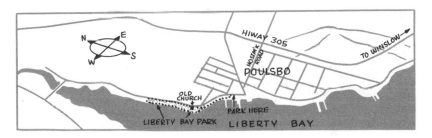

Begin by the marina in green lawns dotted by huge erratics. Northward a unique plank walkway rounds the bluff just above high-tide line. Above is an old church being remodeled; pause to tour the handsomely-timbered auditorium, enjoy the views from a deck over Liberty Bay to boats and uplands of trim houses and kempt pastures, the whole appearing quite Scandinavia-like. Or is it Scotland-like? Beyond the boardwalk a path continues in madronas and firs to the park end. Return, if you wish, via the mudflat beach, distinctly Puget Sound-like.

Round trip 1 mile, allow 1 hour

Indianola To Point Jefferson To President Point (Map — page 200)

A mere 5 miles across the waters is the throbbing (and roaring, banging, rumbling, generally racketing) heart of Puget Sound City, and along Main Street the traffic hurries between points on the inland sea and the Seven Seas. But here one walks in wildness for miles, just waves and gulls for company.

Drive to Indianola. From Winslow ferry the route is via Highway 305 to Agate Pass, then north on Suquamish Highway to the head of Miller Bay, then south on Indianola Road. From Kingston ferry the route is south around Appletree Cove on Indianola Road. Parking space is scanty in the old old summer-cottage settlement. Some room is available by the postoffice and delightful Indianola Country Store. But don't come on summer Sundays to complicate a fine, quiet community that has zero provision for public entertainment. Lonesome winter is the season — there then is also easy toleration of the put-in, the only part of the route that poses the slightest problem.

Walk down to the dock (from mosquito-fleet days) and take the stairs to the beach.

(Note: In toleration season the beach is inviting the 1 mile to the base of the spit reaching nearly across the mouth of Miller Bay. The spit was wanted as a public park but a developer snuck in, providing joy to a dozen families, denying thousands of families a picnic visit.)

The wild walk is east along Port Madison. A couple houses-on-bulkheads

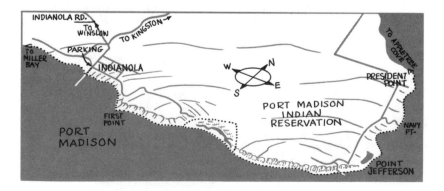

A great blue heron dwarfs a gull at Point Jefferson

are passed and then man retreats to his proper place atop the bank. In a long ½ mile "First Point" is rounded and the bluff rears up a steep, partly-naked 200 feet of till and sand and clay. The view back down Port Madison to Agate Pass is lost, that of Bainbridge Island continues, and beyond Main Street is Seattle.

At ½ mile from First Point is the most unusual feature of the trip. The bluff swings far inland around an ancient bay, long since closed off by a baymouth bar, within which is a lagoon-mudflat, a mass of bleached driftwood, and a broad marsh and great swampy forest. Birds! What a crowd! What secrets lurk here in the heart of the Port Madison Indian Reservation? Marred by a single structure only, the entirety of closed-off bay and surrounding forest hills appear wild. At medium-to-high tides the lagoon-mouth channel must be waded to the knees or detoured around inland on the driftwood; at low tides the channel can be hippety-hopped over, the baymouth bar walked, the impressive ½ mile to a resumption of bluff.

After ¾ mile more of bluff wildness, a dock and road intrude. In ¼ mile more is Point Jefferson, with dune line, lagoon, and a half-dozen modest cottages. Now the view opens north past Carkeek Park to Richmond Beach, oil tanks of Point Wells and Edwards Point, and Edmonds. This may be far enough for many walkers, 3 miles from Indianola.

But onward ½ wild mile is "Navy Point"; atop the bluff is some aged warlike structure, below it another lagoon. And in ¾ bluff-wild (though the bluff top is inhabited) mile more, complicated by a beach-invading stretch of riprap requiring scrambling at medium tides, are the wide flat and lagoon of President Point, sparsely dotted with houses. Now the view is north to Whidbey Island and Mukilteo. Here, 4¼ miles from Indianola, is a good turnaround — though in only 1¼ more (civilized, now) miles, past a beached hulk, is the point at the mouth of Appletree Cove, with close views of the Edmonds ferry arriving at and departing from Kingston.

Round trip to President Point 8½ miles, allow 6 hours

Kingston To Eglon Beach (Map — page 202)

A terrific beach, right on Main Street yet wild much of the way beneath a formidable guardian bluff. What's really sensational about the trip is you don't need to ferry your wheels over the waters, just your boots and attached body, for a low-low round-trip fare.

Drive (or Metro bus) to Edmonds and park in the shopping center near the first (auto) ticket booth or in the Port of Edmonds lot by the ferry dock, where is located the second (foot-passenger) ticket booth. Voyage carfree and liberated over the waves to Kingston. Walk up from the dock, take the first road right, and from it find the broad trail dropping to the beach. And away you go.

The 1½ miles to Appletree Point are beneath a two-step bluff 60-100 feet high, keeping houses distant from the beach except at the halfway mark, where a boulder bulkhead briefly invades, requiring at medium tides a short rock-scramble or wade. The couple dozen modest cottages on the Point are readily passed, no scowls usually, but at the north end is a wicked 100-foot-long bulkhead that is non-detourable via bluff, non-clamberable due to a house, and at middle tides and above requires a kneedeep to nosedeep wade. Face it — to do the whole trip to Eglon you're going to have to get feet and knees wet here, going or coming. The beach then widens. North of the point begins an amusing ½ mile, a half-dozen quirky little cottages-castles, trail-access only, scattered along a slump terrace.

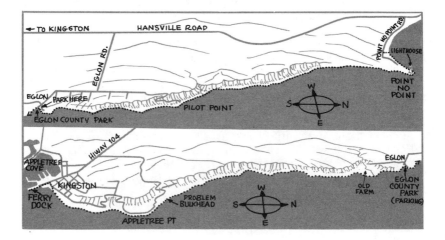

Appletree Cove and Kingston ferry

Now, 2½ miles from the ferry, begin 2½ utterly wild miles, the bluff a steep 300 feet down which chunks of bluff slide onto and across the beach. Fine gullies slice the clay, waterfalls cascade out of greenery, jungle ensures solitude. It's as wild a beach as is to be found anywhere on the inland sea.

Trails and staircases foreshadow the start of civilization, on the flat of a coastal bulge at the mouth of a creek. Oddly, the only development is a couple small farms, several beach houses, and several bleached ruins. Very nice. Wildness resumes, though of a lower order, the bluff a mere 60 feet, the final ¾ mile to Eglon Beach Park.

Sit for lunch. Enjoy views of Main Street traffic, Whidbey Island's imposing bluffs, Edmonds ferry dock whence you came, Pilchuck, Glacier Peak, Rainier. Far across the waters, hear the rumble of trains on the Puget Sound Trail.

Round trip 12 miles, allow 8 hours

Point No Point to Eglon Beach (Map — page 202)

A big-view, lighthouse-tipped point jutting through the rabble of gulls and crows and ducks and fishing boats toward the passing parade of ships on

Lighthouse on Point No Point

Main Street. And a long, bluff-wild beach intruded by civilization only briefly at the middle.

Drive to Hansville. From Winslow ferry the route is Highway 305 to just west of Agate Pass, then north on Suquamish Highway to the Hansville Road. From Kingston ferry the route is west 2½ miles to the Hansville Road. Upon descending to the shore plain, turn right on Point No Point Road ¾ mile to the resort entrance. Park here, if management doesn't object, or if so, on a road shoulder back toward Hansville.

Walk through the resort to the beach, thence to the point; or, where the resort road turns left, walk the road straight ahead to the lighthouse, where very limited parking is available during visiting hours (1-3 p.m. weekdays, 1-4 p.m. Sundays). Dating from 1879, the light is worth a tour.

The view west is past Hansville over Skunk Bay to Foulweather Bluff, and north is across Puget Sound to the gray-white cliffs of Double Bluff and Indian Point and Scatchet Head on Whidbey Island.

South from the spit, jungled cliffs of glacial drift enwilden the beach. Bald eagles may be seen; a pair or two perhaps nest here. The view now is past Possession Point to densely-inhabited slopes of Edmonds, oil tanks of Edwards Point and Point Wells, Richmond Beach, and towers of downtown Seattle. Beyond are Cascades from Rainier to Glacier to Baker. And always ships passing, birds flying and swimming.

Paths indicate unseen residences above. Then, at Pilot Point, 2½ miles from Point No Point, a half-dozen cabins occupy a beach-side flat. Wildness resumes the final 1¼ miles to Eglon Beach Park. To do the walk starting here, from Hansville Road take Eglon Road.

Round trip 8 miles, allow 5 hours

Foulweather Bluff (Map — page 205)

Talk about weather shores! Foulweather Bluff juts out where Hood Canal, Admiralty Inlet, and Puget Sound meet, and the weather comes at it every which way. The skinny beach at the base of the vertical jungle is a terrific viewpoint, resounding finale to a walk by two great spits and a marvelous nature sanctuary.

Drive to Hansville (see Point No Point) and keep going. Upon reaching the beach, Hansville Road turns west as Twin Spits Road. At 3 miles from the bend watch for a wide marsh to the left; summer vegetation can make it hard to see. A bit beyond, spot an obvious path into the woods, signed only by demure "Nature Conservancy" tags and a little plaque identifying this as a Nature Sanctuary. (Let's hear it for the Conservancy!) If you come to Skunk Bay Road, you've gone 800 feet too far. Alternatively, drive on ¾ mile to the road-end and a public beach access beside Twin Spits Resort.

However, the Sanctuary is the special treat. Walk the footpath through dense-salal woods past the marsh, then the broad lagoon, ⅓ mile to the beach. To appreciate how glorious a spot this is, and how fortunate we are that the Conservancy saved it, walk 1¼ miles southeast, first along the baymouth bar that encloses lagoon and marsh, then under an 80-foot-high naked bluff, to the monster development newly decorating the spits of Coon Bay.

But the main show (other than the Sanctuary, which a birdwatcher just may not want to leave) is the other way, on what was, when sealevel was 20 feet higher, Foulweather Island. Houses are safely atop the 60-foot till wall the 1 wild mile to the southern of the Twin Spits, where are located Last Resort, Twin Spits Resort, and the public beach access. Proceed by several beach-near houses ¼ mile to the northern spit and a resumption of wildness. At low tide walk across the lagoon outlet onto the spit and stick with the beach; otherwise follow the foot of the bluff until saltgrass and driftwood can be walked around the lagoon to the beach. Views are superb south along Hood Canal to Hood Head, the once-and-future temporarily floating bridge, Port Gamble, the mouth of Port Ludlow directly across the Canal, and Zion, Townsend, Walker, and Constance.

The spit beach is ¾ mile long, a lonesome splendor of grass-anchored sand dunes, driftwood, and waves on the Canal side and birds on the lagoon side. Two modest summer cottages at the spit base only briefly break the solitude, which resumes under the bluff leaping to 100 feet, then 220 feet, and too steep and clay-slidey-mean to permit trails from the top (which, oh the pity of it, soon

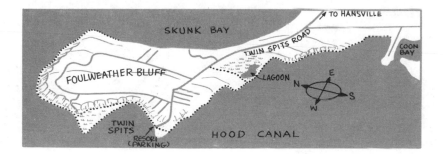

Madrona tree near Foulweather Bluff

will be subdivided). The shore rounds from northerly to east, the view extending to Marrowstone Island and Fort Flagler State Park, to the distant San Juans. Directly across Main Street is Double Bluff, between Mutiny Bay and Useless Bay on Whidbey Island. Ocean steamers race by, making wonderful crashing waves, ocean-size, to delight the beachwalker. Fishing boats work and sailboats play. Ah, but what's missing from the scene? The Edmonds-Ludlow ferry, scuttled soon after War II. Foulweather Bluff was a famous landmark, in those distant days, to voyagers en route to the high Olympics, Trapper Nelsons lashed to fenders of the Model A.

At 1 mile from the northern Twin Spit the bluff shore turns sharp south into Skunk Bay. About ½ wild mile more and the bluff dwindles to naught (where once the water cut off Foulweather Island) and houses begin, time to turn around.

Round trip 7 miles, allow 5 hours

Port Gamble (Map — page 207)

No museum specimen under glass is this, no artist colony or row of shoppes, but a lived-in, working mill town, with the oldest operating sawmill in North America. The place seems too old for this raw young corner of the country, looks like it belongs in New England. Indeed, when A.J. Pope, Captain William Talbot, and Cyrus Walker founded the town in 1853, they built it to resemble their native East Machias, Maine. Take away the cars and TV antennae, fill the bay with square-rigged ships, and the scene would be straight out of the 19th century.

Parking areas in town permit walking tours from a number of starts. A nice way to grasp the geographical setting is to approach via beach from Salsbury Point County Park. Drive Highway 104 from Kingston, or, from Winslow, Highways 305, 3, and 104, to ½ mile east of Hood Canal Floating Bridge, and turn onto the road signed "County Park" a scant ½ mile to the beach.

The little park is hedged by homes but in toleration season one can walk the beach by them to the shelter of Teekalet Bluff, in views south on Hood Canal to the Olympics, north to Port Ludlow and Foulweather Bluff. In 1 mile is the millyard, from which a road-path climbs to the town and the parking area across from the postoffice (Land Office) and the Port Gamble General Store (1853). Here too is the Pope and Talbot Office; the company restored and maintains the town and runs the mill on timber from lands it has been logging all this while, in some cases now milling a third crop as the fourth grows.

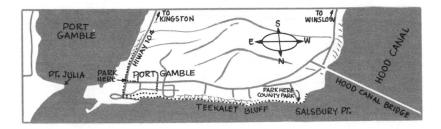

Salsbury Point County Park, the floating bridge that stopped doing so in 1979 and Olympic Mountains

In the basement of the General Store is the Historical Museum, the basic introduction when open and providing a walking-tour pamphlet-guide. But there's plenty of history out in the open. Stroll the sidewalks along tree-shaded streets, by workers' by-no-means-humble homes and capitalists' mansions, in views down to the mill, rafted logs, and over Port Gamble Bay to where the Indians lived, watching all this with mixed emotions.

Ascend the bluff-rim lawn westward to the hilltop cemetery, where headstones bear such legends as "died at Teekalet W. T. 1860." Note the memorial to "Gustav Englebrecht — Germany — Cox US Navy — Indian War — November 21, 1856." When the Haida attack came, the millworkers called for help from the **Massachusetts.** During the desultory skirmish known to history as the Battle of Port Gamble, the coxswain poked his head over a bulwark for a better view of the action and became the first U.S. Navy man to be killed in a Pacific Ocean war.

Admire the view to Hood Canal Floating (?) Bridge, Olympics, Marrowstone Island, the plume of the pulpmill at Port Townsend, Foulweather Bluff. In mind's eye see the tall ships spreading sail to carry Washington lumber the world around.

Round trip 3 miles, allow 3 hours

Hood Head (Map — page 209)

Stroll shores of a secluded little bay, poke around amid ducks and herons thronging a lagoon half-ringed by saltmarsh and forest, explore spits, venture

208

out on a former island and from its tip look up and down Hood Canal. All this in an undeveloped state park on public beaches with no hassle except from tides.

Drive to the west end of the Hood Canal Floating Bridge and turn right on Bywater Bay Road.

The state park has two parking areas and thus two trip starts. For the longest walk, immediately after turning onto Bywater Bay Road turn right again, steeply down to the beach, and drive past a Puget Power station and a lagoon to parking on Termination Point. Walk 1 mile along the quiet beach of Bywater Bay to the second trip start.

For the latter, drive Bywater Bay Road ⅔ mile, up to a plateau crest and down, and turn right on an unsigned (except "Dead End") gravel road that leads through forest, by a few houses, ½ mile to the large beach-side parking area.

The 131-acre state park contains a forest of sizable firs and cedars crisscrossed with paths that someday will be formalized in a beauty of a nature trail; you can find your own way now. Aside from that, the nearly 4 miles of public tidelands offer exercises short and long. Two may serve as samples.

Short Tour: South Spit

From the north parking area walk the beach north along Bywater Bay, by a log-filled lagoon, onto South Spit, which thrusts into the bay and nearly cuts off its head, forming a large inner bay-lagoon, a mudflat at low tide, a duck pond at high, surrounded by spits, saltmarsh, and woods. At ½ mile from the parking area the South Spit ends. At quite low tides the channel can be waded to North Spit, providing a shortcut to Hood Head. But don't count on it.

For the return, at the log-filled lagoon find a path in the woods and to beach gray add forest green.

Round trip 1 mile, allow 1 hour

Long Tour: North Spit and Hood Head

Where the entry road to the north parking area bends right, toward the beach, at the start of the parking space look left under limbs of a cedar and spot an old road-become-trail. Walk it, frequently to the ankles in black muck, through fine mixed forest to ruins of a house by the inner lagoon of Bywater

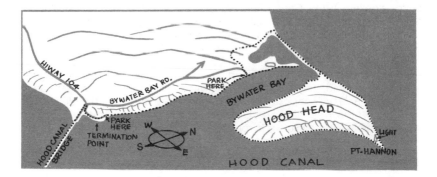

Bywater Bay and Hood Head

Bay. Continue along the shore in noble big trees and skunk cabbage to the base of North Spit, ¾ mile from the parking area.

The spit beach (swept over by storm tides, let it be noted) leads ¾ mile to Hood Head, once an island, now a tombolo. Walk the north shore beneath a high bluff of tree-tangled glacial drift the 1 mile to Point Hannon, a superlative viewpoint thrust out in Hood Canal. Look north to the entrance portals, Tala Point and Foulweather Bluff, and beyond to Marrowstone Island. Look across to the mill and town of Port Gamble, Rainier rising above. The first edition of this book, delivered to the stores in February of 1979, said "Look south to the bridge floating in the Canal (floating, that is, until the next approximately twice-in-a-century event, the last coming in the 1930s, a northerly gale on a bull tide, a combination for which the bridge was not engineered, and thus the fittingness of the location near Port Gamble)." On February 13, 1979 the bridge sank.

Though the uplands of Hood Head, rising to a near-mountainous 220 feet, were not surveyed, they are an intriguing wildwood, 1 mile long and averaging ½ mile wide. The shore, too, is perfectly wild except for the dozen-odd cottages on the west side. Though this stretch depends on toleration, the logical completion of the trip is to round the island, in a scant 2 miles from Point Hannon returning to North Spit.

Round trip from north parking area 6 miles, allow 4 hours

210

Indian Island-Marrowstone Island-Fort Flagler State Park (Map — page 211)

Good gracious, what an embarrassment of riches! Miles and miles of grand beaches with views of Main Street traffic and of mountains from Olympics to Baker to Glacier Peak to Rainier. And absolutely the bulliest of the three forts of the Death (Devil's) Triangle that once protected cities of Puget Sound from naval bombardment. A pity the Spanish (or whoever) battle fleet never attempted to force a passage through Admiralty Inlet. See the ships of the gallant, foolish hidalgos, staggering and burning, riddled with shells! What a shooting match! Absolutely a bully show!

Drive Highway 104 west a scant 4 miles from Hood Canal Bridge and turn north at the first of the signs, "Fort Flagler State Park," which lead infallibly to the goal.

But before the chief goal are others. Beyond Hadlock 1 mile is a Y. The left is signed "Fort Flagler," but first go right on Oak Bay Road ½ mile and turn left on the second of two side-by-side roads and drop a scant ¼ mile to the sandspit of Oak Bay (Jefferson) County Park. A birdy lagoon, ½ mile long, and a spit beach, 1 mile long. Terrific. Back in the car, return to the Y, take the "Flagler" road ¾ mile, crossing Portage Canal onto Indian Island. Just beyond, park at Hadlock Lions Public Park, or continue a long ½ mile to a sign, "Jefferson County Park," and drop on a sideroad ¼ mile to more of Oak Bay Park. Here are 2 miles of public beach, in views from Port Townsend to Rainier.

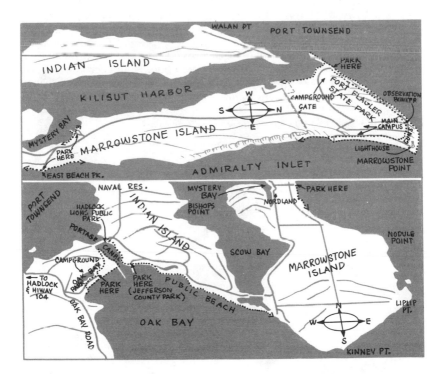

Moreover, the beach continues over a sand isthmus to Marrowstone Island, making possible a beach walk, in toleration season, the 7 more miles to Fort Flagler State Park. Wow.

Oak Bay-Indian Island round trips 6 miles, allow 4 hours

Now, onward. Drive from Indian Island over the Scow Bay causeway onto Marrowstone Island. In 3 miles, at Mystery Bay, a sideroad leads ½ mile east to East Beach (Jefferson) County Park, a good put-in for walking the beach between Flagler and Oak Bay. North of this sideroad ¼ mile is an isolated section of state park, Mystery Bay Recreation Area, a cozy boat harbor worth a pause. Continue 2 miles to Fort Gate, the park entrance, and ½ mile more to a Y. The right fork leads to the main campus of the fort, the headquarters, the Marrowstone Point Lighthouse, and several good starts for walks. However, for the suggested introductory loop take the left fork, in 1½ miles (it's a huge park — 804 acres, with 4 miles of public beach!) dropping to the beach at the northwest tip of the island. Park in the campground on the broad sandspit.

For openers, walk west ⅓ mile to the tip of the spit pushing across the mouth of Kilisut Harbor. Look over Port Townsend Bay to the pulpmill and town and Fort Worden, to Olympics from Constance to Zion to Blue to Angeles.

Returned from this sidetrip, head east, leaving the spit flat for the base of the 120-foot vertical bluffs of what Captain Vancouver called "marrow stone" — what we call glacial drift, here represented by concrete-like till and some of the finest sand cliffs around. Ships, tugs and barges, sailboats, waves, birds, the Keystone-Townsend ferry. Across Admiralty Inlet, the Ebey's Landing section of Whidbey Island, Baker, Shuksan, Woolley Lyman, Cultus, Chuckanut, San Juans. In a scant 2 miles are the flats of Marrowstone Point, the lighthouse on the tip, and views south to Whitehorse, Glacier, Rainier, and Foulweather Bluff at the mouth of Hood Canal. The parking area here is an alternate start (in case high tide bars the beach walk). Continue south down the beach ¾ mile to

Gull dropping clam to break shell at Oak Bay County Park

the old dock. The fine beach continues (to Indian Island, should you so desire).

For the introductory tour, however, leave the beach and follow the old road-trail up the hill to the main campus (more parking) and its handsome 1900-era frame buildings. Proceed on the bluff-edge road ½ mile, past the road down to Marrowstone Point, onto an old, barricaded road-become-trail. The route from here the 2 miles back to the campground is partly on this or that old road, partly on trails; the rule is, stick with the easy going as near the bluff edge as feasible and safe. The way is in forest (miles of trails, not surveyed, go inland to green solitude) and sky-open, wide-horizon sea meadow, passing (explore with care!) concrete emplacements of the 10- and 12-inch disappearing guns and 12-inch mortars, and underground fire-control posts. Set aside as a military reservation in 1866, the fort was developed from 1897-1900 and declared surplus in 1954. Three wars lurk in the memories here. Stand in the wind on the brink of the meadow-top precipice and look over the waters to the other forts of the Death Triangle and visualize the climax, here, of a fourth war that never was; only in phantom history books is there, to rank with Trafalgar and Midway, a Battle of Admiralty Inlet.

Introductory loop trip 6 miles, allow 4 hours

Quimper Peninsula-Fort Worden State Park (Map — page 213, 216)

How impoverished our park systems would be without wars — and foolish fears of implausible wars. Forest wildlands are preserved, and miles of lonesome beaches, all wonderfully haunted. Even if a person lacks a taste for ancient bloodshed the Quimper Peninsula has plenty to enchant — history that is not military, ocean-like beaches, and unsurpassed water-and-mountain views.

Drive a scant 4 miles west from Hood Canal Bridge and turn north on the highway signed "Port Townsend." At all junctions pursue this destination.

But first, turn in to clearly-signed Old Fort Townsend State Park. Unlike neighbors, this was an Indian War fort, established in 1856, abandoned in 1895, the 377 acres deeded to the state in 1953. The beach is a dandy, extending north under guardian bluffs 1 mile to Glen Cove, nearly to the steam-spewing pulpmill, and south 1¾ miles to Kuhn Spit and Kala Point, all in broad views. The park is almost entirely a lonesome woodland full of paths; a

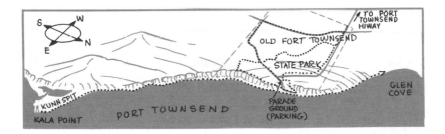

loop trip of some 3 miles can be readily figured out and is especially attractive in May when the rhododendrons are in bloom.

Now, onward. Enter Port Townsend on Highway 20 and before entering downtown turn left at the sign, "Fort Worden State Park," and turn right and left and right and left (always signed) and voila, the park entrance. The car can be parked and the walk begun at any number of places. Three sample tours are suggested.

History Tour (War) (Map page — 216)

Had Spain tried to storm the entrance to Puget Sound, the guns of this corner of the Death (Devil's) Triangle would've fired the first shells, perhaps leaving Flagler and Casey little to do but finish off cripples. Work on gun emplacements began in 1897 and in 1904 this became headquarters of the Harbor Defense of Puget Sound. (Against Germany? Surely not Britain? Japan wasn't known to be a naval power until it sank Russia the next year.) In 1911 the 12-inchers of Battery Kinzie were at last in place. In 1920 aerial warfare arrived with the construction of balloon hangars. On December 8, 1941, the fort briefly revived. In 1953 it was closed, to become a 339-acre park.

To absorb all this, first drive around the parade ground to the flagpole and park office to obtain a copy of the park map and chronology. A methodical way to do the history is with a periphery tour. From the chapel at the entrance walk by the guardhouse, turn left to the balloon hangar and cemetery, turn right up the boundary to bluff-edge views over the Strait of Juan de Fuca, turn right and prowl gun batteries, return right to the neatly-white buildings of the old barracks, now the Conference Center, and stroll the parade ground to the mansions of Officers' Row, now leased as vacation homes.

Loop trip 2½ miles, allow 2 hours

On the Beach From Lighthouse to Old City (Map — page 216)

Drive by the parade ground, down to the beach, and north to the parking area at Battery Kinzie, just short of the Point Wilson Lighthouse.

First, of course, tour the lighthouse (visiting hours, weekdays 1-3, weekends 1-4) on the tip of the superb spit poking into Main Street, the Strait of Juan de Fuca on one side, Admiralty Inlet on the other, great ships often passing close to make the turn, sloshing giant waves on the beach. Views are overwhelming across to Victoria on Vancouver Island, the full east-west width of the San Juans, the high sand bluffs of Whidbey Island, the shuttling Keystone-Townsend ferry, Cascades from Baker and Shuksan to Glacier to Whitehorse and Three Fingers. Gasp.

Walk south along the spit beach (wide, sandy, all-tides-walkable) by the driftwood line, the grass-grown dunes, the (filled) lagoon. South ¾ mile from Point Wilson is the pier, providing out-in-the-water perspectives. Leave the spit for the foot of a wild bluff, pass under Chetzemoka Park (alternative in-town start), and at 2¼ miles from Point Wilson come to the end of beach, start of port facilities, at Point Hudson (parking, alternative start).

Port Townsend is one of the few towns this nature-oriented guide deigns to push. Turn onto Water Street, main drag of the lower, below-bluff city, visit the ferry dock, and tour the scene. A thriving seaport when Seattle was only a

City Hall at Port Townsend

highly improbable real-estate promotion, Port Townsend lost out. That's our good luck, because the long languishing in limbo preserved much of a 19th-century metropolis. The 1891 City Hall at Water and Madison houses an historical museum; the basement, when a jail, offered hospitality to Jack London. The Bartlett Building, when a tavern, specialized in shanghaiing seamen. The 1874 Leader Building is claimed to be the oldest remaining all-stone structure in the state. The upper town has many well-kept Victorian homes.

Beach round trip 4½ miles, city tour 2 miles, for both allow 4 hours

Long Wild Beach (Map — page 216)

If it's a good leg-stretching you seek, a good lung-filling with salt winds, a good eye-filling with ocean-like marine vistas, the north shore of Quimper Peninsula is for you. What do you want? A few-minutes' stroll? Or a long day's journey into night?

Park at Battery Kinzie and hit the north beach, walkable at all but the highest tides. Views are east by the Point Wilson Lighthouse to Whidbey Island bluffs and the white tower of Baker, north by ships to Vancouver Island. When a freighter rushes past, the surf turns ocean-size, sort of scary there under the tall bluff of old glacial drift, hard and steep. Cormorants perch atop erratics. Grebes dive, oystercatchers squeal, gulls soar, crows caw, plovers scurry, peep run over the sands. After 1 mile of splendid isolation is the park boundary and a dropping-away of the bluff to a flat. Here are fields and homes and North Beach (Jefferson) County Park, an alternative start (from Fort Worden entrance drive west, then north).

After ½ mile the bluff rises, with homes atop. But at 2¾ miles from Point Wilson the houses end, the bluff rears up to a frightful precipice, loess topped by vertical till, the brink 280 feet from the water, the tallest naked vertical wall encountered in **Footsore** surveys. A long 1 mile Champion Cliff continues, then diminishes somewhat to McCurdy (Middle) Point, 4 miles from Point Wilson and a logical turnaround.

But the wildness, the splendid isolation continue under a more-than-ordinarily-vertical bluff rising to as much as a daunting 200 feet of clays and gravels and tills. Watch those tides, folks! Escape routes are few and cruel and mostly dangerous, not a single deep-slicing ravine to breach the wall. Spice is added by the fact that at high tides there is no beach much of the way, just clay walls battered by breakers and clawed by fingernails. Yes, a wilderness to sing in, and no fear that any developer will invade the combat zone where waves buffet the clay cliffs, great chunks of which slide down to counterattack.

At 3¼ miles from McCurdy Point (atop which is an abandoned military reservation of some sort) is Cape George at the mouth of Port Discovery, with views to Olympic foothills, Miller Peninsula, and Protection Island. Time to turn around, because soon start houses of Cape George Colony, and after all these wild miles who needs that?

Round trip (Point Wilson to Cape George) 14½ miles, allow 9 hours

Port Discovery-Miller Peninsula-Sequim Bay-Dungeness Bay (Map — page 218)

If such short shrift is going to be given these beaches, why give any shrift at all? Because they offer excellent wild miles of sands and waves, lonesome alternatives to more famous trips nearby. The shortness is due to a recogni-

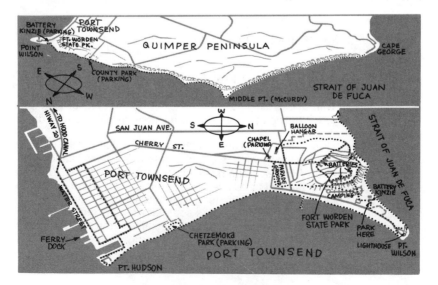

tion that the famous trips will nevertheless attract most pedestrians from Puget Sound City.

Drive Highway 101 westward from Hood Canal Bridge to Port Discovery and commence pondering alternatives.

Gardiner Boat Ramp

Port Discovery waters are calmer, beaches tamer, than those of the Strait. But near the bay mouth they are quite entertaining, with fine views over to Quimper Peninsula.

West ½ mile from the KOA Kampground above Port Discovery, turn right ½ mile to the public Gardiner Boat Ramp.

The best walk is north, the beach open and wild (with only a couple beachside houses) beneath a green-tangled 200-foot bluff the 3 miles to Diamond Point at the bay mouth.

Round trip 6 miles, allow 4 hours

Diamond Point

Terrific. Views over the Strait to close, magical Protection Island and beyond to San Juans and Cascades. A good-surf Strait beach and wild 200-foot bluff similar to the north shore of Quimper Peninsula.

Drive Highway 101 west from Gardiner 1½ miles and turn north on a road signed "Diamond Point." Proceed through proliferating "sunshine belt" subdivisions, by the airport designed to bring refugees from California, and down among spiffy new homes on Diamond Point.

As of 1978 there are enough unbuilt-on lots to provide easy parking and inconspicuous beach access. But when gaps are filled the toleration of trespassing probably will cease. This being the only ready access to beaches found by the surveyor, it means the whole blessed Miller Peninsula will be lost. Unless Clallam County or State Parks have something in mind.

Not surveyed except by eyeball, the way west is alluring, the 200-280-foot bluff guarding close approach to the water even when presently-wildwooded blufftops become Californicated; the putting in of public feet will be the problem. The map shows nice things like Thompson Spit, Rocky Point, nameless creeks with ravine valleys, and at the far west end of wildness, jutting into Sequim Bay, Travis Spit, the tip 6 miles from Diamond Point. Heavenly days, what a walk.

Round trip 12 miles, allow 8 hours

Sequim Bay State Park

Its mouth nearly closed off by two nearly-joining spits, Sequim Bay is rather tame for hikers jaded by big waves. Still, in wild weather a walker may rather enjoy a touch of tameness.

From Highway 101 west of Blyn enter 92-acre Sequim Bay State Park. The public beach is a meager ⅓ mile but in the off-season the mostly-empty beach might be walked ½ mile to Schoolhouse Point and 2 miles to Pitship Point.

Round trip 5 miles, allow 3 hours

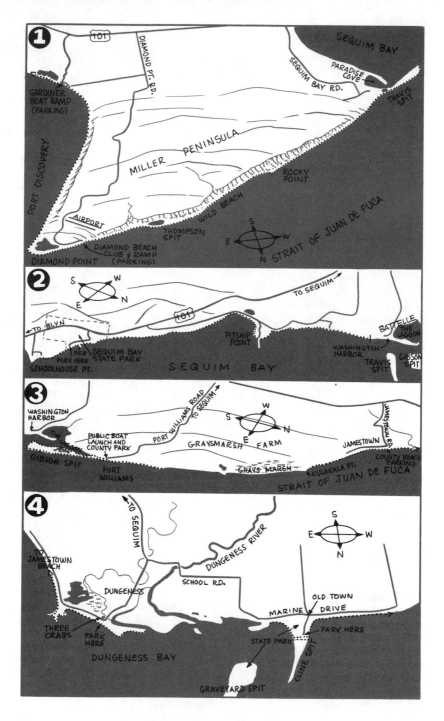

Pitship Point and Sequim Bay

Pitship Point

Here near the mouth of Sequim Bay the view of opits intrigues. Beach access is public, but in 1983 the Port of Port Angeles got permission to build a $6 million, 524-boat marina on 23 acres donated in 1975 by John Wayne, so scratch the walk. In fact, in view of the limited water circulation, scratch Sequim Bay.

West on Highway 101 at ½ mile from Sequim Bay State Park turn right at the sign, "West Sequim Bay Recreation Area." In 1½ miles park at the Pitship Point boat-launch.

The interesting direction is north to the shoals of Middle Ground, close across the waters from Klapot Point on Travis Spit. But do not continue to Washington Harbor, where Battelle Institute has research in progress — research that entails never-ending construction. The Port Gamble Klallams are very upset.

Round trip 2 miles, allow 1½ hours

Port Williams County Park

A miniature version of Dungeness Spit, Gibson Spit is one of the two that make Sequim Bay essentially a lagoon.

At the town-center stoplight in Sequim turn north on Sequim Avenue. In 1 mile turn east on Port Williams Road, signed "boat launch." In 3 more miles, in a gully mouth at the site of the old dock, is Port Williams County Park, at the base of Gibson Spit.

Walk the spit 1 mile south on the Strait side. Round the tip and return on the calm side, by The Lagoon, not black but full of creatures. Then walk beneath the bluff ½ mile northward, halting at the boundary of the enormous private shooting preserve, Graysmarsh Farm.

Round trip 3 miles, allow 1½ hours

Jamestown County Beach

Now for something completely different. No more bluff, because this is the delta of the Dungeness River. And now no more waves to speak of, because this is Dungeness Bay, sheltered by Dungeness Spit. But there's mud, at low tide a vastness of it.

At the town-center stoplight in Sequim turn north on Sequim Avenue 3¼ miles and turn right on Jamestown Road 1 mile to the beach. Where the road turns right to parallel the water is a lonesome stretch where parking is possible.

East along the beach ½ mile is the road-end and the start of enormous Graysmarsh Farm, private, but public entry permitted by the owner at times announced on the boundary signboard. In ½ mile is Kulakala Point, where public feet must stop.

In the other direction, if trespassing is tolerated, it's 2¼ miles to The Three Crabs restaurant. That's a lot of mud. With views over the calm bay to Dungeness Spit. Just beyond is the mouth of the Dungeness River.

Round trip 5½ miles, allow 4 hours

Dungeness Spit (Map — page 220)

The longest natural sandspit in the United States thrusts 5 miles out from Olympic Peninsula bluffs into the Strait of Juan de Fuca, so far that on a stormy

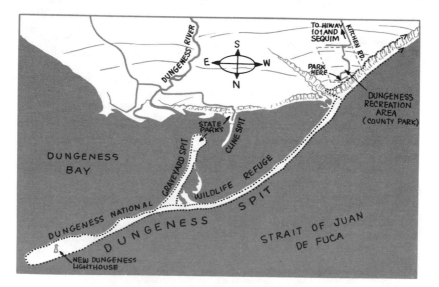

Sandpipers searching for food on Dungeness Spit

day a walker feels wave-tossed and seasick, and on a foggy day wonders if he's passed over to another and totally watery planet. Birds run the sands and swim the waters and fly the air. Seals pop heads out of breakers to marvel what you're at.

Drive Highway 101 west from Sequim's town-center stoplight 4½ miles and turn north on Kitchen Road, signed "Dungeness Recreation Area." In 3¼ miles the road makes a right-angle turn east and just beyond is the entrance road to the recreation area, a 240-acre Clallam County park. Drive 1 long mile, passing the head of the horse trail, going by the picnic area and through the campground, to the road-end parking area and restrooms and trailhead, elevation 120 feet.

As a prefatory note, there's more great walking here than just the spit. Southwest are at least 4 miles of open-to-boots big-surf Strait beach, totally wild below naked, vertical, 100-foot bluffs of glacial drift. In the same direction, an unsurveyed distance, runs a bluff-top path through grass and wind-tortured scrub trees and broad views.

However, the spit calls. The trail ("no camping, no fires, dogs on leash, no guns, no wheels") enters forest, then emerges to a viewpoint of spit and Strait, joins the horse trail coming from the right, and drops to the mouth of a nice little creek valley, in a scant ½ mile reaching the beach and the base of the spit.

So, there you are. Go. Via the outside route or the inside, separated by the driftwood jumble along the spit spine. The outside is the surf side, with views to the Panamanian merchant marine sailing to and from the seven seas, to Vancouver Island, San Juan Islands, Whidbey Island, and Baker-dominated Cascades. The inside is the bay side, the first half a lagoon, often glassy calm and often floating thousands of waterfowl come to enjoy amenities of Dungeness National Wildlife Refuge; the view is to mainland bluffs, delta of the Dungeness River, and the Olympics. The best plan is to alternate routes.

Mt. Townsend from Mt. Zion

Both end in the standard pretty government-issue lighthouse, the foghorn, and the tip of the spit ⅓ mile beyond. A light has been on this site since 1857, earliest in the state. Note that the precise name is New Dungeness Lighthouse; when Captain Vancouver gave the name in 1792 he was observing the resemblance to Dungeness "in the British channel" of Olde England. Note, too, that the beach is wheel-traveled; when the Coast Guard had the lighthouse keeper maintain contact with shore by boat, we were denied the pleasure of the company of his jeep.

There's a sidetrip. Graveyard Spit, commemorating the day in 1868 when 17 Tsimshians were massacred by the Clallams, branches off, extending 1½ miles south, nearly touching Cline Spit reaching from the mainland, the two enclosing the inner lagoon.

Round trip 11 miles, allow 8 hours

Mount Zion (Map — page 223)

From a fragrant garden of rhododendron blossoms on a bald-rock knob, see the Strait of Juan de Fuca and mountains on Vancouver Island, waterways of the inland sea far south on Puget Sound and north to the Strait of Georgia, islands and towns and cities of the plain, and Cascades from Rainier to Baker, and — but why go on? Especially since all the surveyor saw on a first assault was the white insides of a cloud enwrapping a snow-white ridge. Returning next day he found the cloud broken up a bit, revealing to the west, over the valleys of Gold Creek and the Dungeness River, snowy peaks of Graywolf Ridge, and, over Bon Jon Pass and the head of the Little Quilcene River, the great white alpine barrens of Mt. Townsend. But in the other direction the cloud remained, thinning just enough to reveal Port Discovery close enough below to see the fish jumping. Nevertheless, usually reliable sources declare Zion verily is the promised land for fans of the big picture.

From Highway 101 at 2 miles north of Quilcene, take the paved Lords Lake Loop Road. In 3½ miles, just below the (Port Townsend) reservoir dam, go left on gravel road 2909. In 4 more miles is a triple fork; koop right on 2909, with views down the Little Quilcene valley to the head of Quilcene Bay. In 1¼ miles, at Bon Jon Pass, 2900 feet, take the right, contouring the northeast side of Gold Creek valley. At 2 miles from the pass, 11¼ miles from Highway 101, is the trailhead, elevation 2900 feet.

In a corner of the Olympics with roads for fun-loving squirrelers everywhere, why the Forest Service should permit wheels on this last surviving scrap of trail is a mystery. Why these scant 2 miles cannot be reserved for feet is a question every hiker should ask the ranger.

The summit ridge of Zion seems secure from logging; regrowth since the 1916 forest fire is so scrawny that not for generations will a logger salivate here. The trail quickly switchbacks to the first windows out on Gold Creek

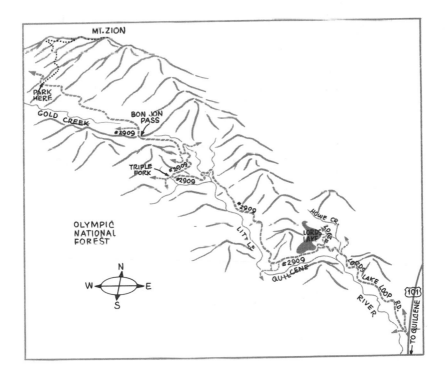

valley and its clearcuts. Cliffs outcrop of rubbly basalt, then conglomerate, providing scenic rest-stop perches.

The summit is pleasantly open, all trees diminutive if only a few are alpine-seeming, and in early summer the flower show brilliantly culminates in the rhododendrons. Sit on the site of the long-gone lookout cabin and enjoy the views. An "island mountain" cut off from the main range by deep valleys, Zion is a very high peak to be so far out. There's absolutely nothing to block the view from Seattle to Bellingham to Vancouver to Victoria. Unless, maybe, a cloud.

Round trip 4 miles, allow 3 hours
High point 4273 feet, elevation gain 1400 feet
May-November

Big Quilcene Lookout (Map — page 224)

Mt. Constance is so close you can see the mountain goats begging cookies from the mountain climbers, and Quilcene pastures are just a long moo below, and if a Navy torpedo ever went astray on the Dabob Bay practice range you'd have to dodge splinters of the fishing boats. All this and more from a scalped summit at the edge of the Olympics.

Drive Highway 101 southerly 1 mile from the Quilcene Ranger Station. Just past milepost 296, where the highway curves left, go straight ahead right on an unsigned blacktop road pointed at a small quarry. Stay on this road, eventually revealed by signs to be road 2812, through a batch of junctions. Climbing steadily, the way bends around the end of the Quilcene Range ridge, following the valley of the Quilcene River far below. At a creek crossing 7 miles from the highway, 2812 continues up the valley and road 2752, the summit route, switchbacks right. Park here, elevation 2200 feet.

Yes, but 2752 all too often is readily drivable. The ascent must be finished afoot because the views are perilously attractive. But because of sporting

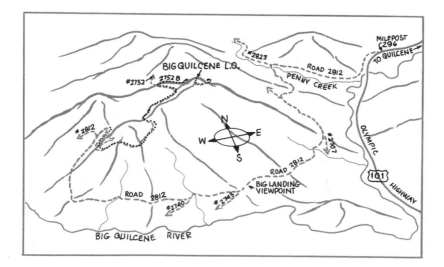

Mt. Constance from Big Quilcene Lookout

wheels the walk is best done as a snowline-prober in winter.

Road 2752 passes a deadend spur left and rounds the south end of the ridge, curving north through a saddle to the east side of the ridge. Clearcuts of the 1950s-70s open wide windows on the view, alternating with virgin forest of hemlocks and cedars hung with yellow-green lichen. All the way are rhododendron — an argument for walking the road in early summer to sniff the blossoms. In 2 miles, at 2900 feet, is a Y, 2752 going straight; switchback right on 2752B the final long ½ mile to the summit, 3450 feet.

All the horizons have been seen on the ascent; now they all are seen at once. (But from no lookout tower — that's gone.) The ridge juts into the Big U Turn of the Quilcene River. East across its gorge is Mt. Walker, blocking much of the world in that direction, but big windows open southeast through Walker Pass and northeast down the Quil valley to Hood Canal and its arms, notably Quilcene Bay and Dabob Bay, the village of Quilcene, cows and boats, and cars on the highway. If Walker gives the broader view east, this summit is much more intimately involved with snowfields and crags of Constance, and Warrior, Buckhorn, Townsend, plus looks straight down to the Quilcene River, Townsend Creek, Tunnel Creek.

Round trip 5 miles, allow 4 hours
High point 3450 feet, elevation gain 1300 feet
February-December

Mount Walker (Map — page 226)

The absolute easternmost summit of the Olympics, zapping straight up from Hood Canal, sitting out by its lonesome cut off from neighbors by a deep glacier trough, Walker is, apart from skyline peaks, the most prominent point in the range as seen from Seattle. It follows that from Walker one can readily see Seattle. And so one can. And all the other neighborhoods of Puget Sound City and everything in between.

The only thing wrong is a road to the top. The best time for the trip is winter (October through April), when the road is a trail, gated at the highway; the survey was made in utter solitude on a crisp February Wednesday in 4 inches of overnight snow, plenty for animal tracks and pretty tree decorations but not enough to hinder feet. In other seasons, such as early summer during the great big rhododendron show, a person may wish to drive to Wow Window.

Note: At the time of the survey in 1978, the old trail, 2 miles in length, was overgrown and unusable. It has been reopened but not surveyed as of 1983. Look for it.

Drive Highway 101 to the Mt. Walker Viewpoint road at Walker Pass, 5 miles south of Quilcene. Park here, elevation 727 feet.

The narrow, steep road actually is safe, but intimidates folks unaccustomed to driving tilted terrain; they'll be happier walking in any season, and never mind the dummies who throw the beauty away by rolling swiftly past on wheels. Pleasures include the virgin forest, flowers in season, basalt walls, and windows opening this way and that. In 1½ miles, at 1300 feet, are a half-bridge across a cliff, one of the road's only two practical parking places for shorter hikes, and the first exclamation-point view, east over the Big U Turn Gorge of the Big Quilcene River to Constance. The way circles the peak, passing small windows north; at 4 miles, 2300 feet, are Wow Window, east over Hood Canal to Seattle, and the second practical parking place, suggested for a short Sunday rhododendron stroll in June. In a scant 1 mile more the road tops the forested summit ridge at 2960 feet and divides.

Left a scant ¼ mile, at 2804 feet, is North Point Lookout, the tower gone but the basalt garden of rhododendrons and other shrubs intact and the views enormous over Walker Pass, up the Big Quilcene valley to Constance, Warrior, Buckhorn, Townsend, and their supporting cast of green ridges proposed

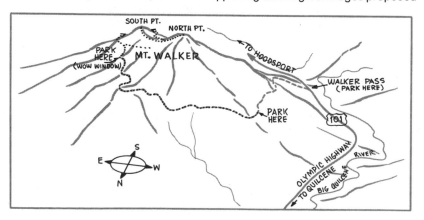

Canada jays (gray jays) scavenging bread crumbs on Mt. Walker. Mt. Constance in distance.

for inclusion in a new Olympic Skyline Wilderness. Closer are clearcuts on Turner, Buck, and Crag. The Quilcene Range, with Big Quilcene Lookout at the tip of the ridge, runs north toward Zion and Big Skidder Hill, and San Juan Islands and Canada.

Right a scant ½ mile, at 2750 feet, is South Point Observation, with another garden and a panorama that'll open your eyes wide and shut your mouth. The foreground is saltwater at the foot of the mountain — Quilcene Bay off Dabob Bay off Hood Canal. The middleground is the Kitsap Peninsula. The background: Cascades from Baker to Glacier to Rainier to St. Helens; cities and towns from Everett to Seattle to Bremerton to Tacoma. Look at a map of Puget Sound country — whatever is on the map you probably can see from Walker. (Alternatively, as on the day of the survey, the east may be a shining cloudsea from horizon to horizon, only volcanoes poking above. But that's not bad either, on a winter day when the Olympics are carved from white ice and the forests are sugar candy.)

Round trip 11 miles, allow 8 hours
High point 2960 feet, elevation gain 2600 feet
February-December

Jupiter Ridge (Map — page 228)

Jupiter is a fraud. Sitting between The Brothers and Constance, as viewed from Seattle it pretends to be nearly their equal, the central high point of the

227

Olympic skyline. But it's really a much lesser peak, enabled to deceive by being thrust out from the range, close to Hood Canal. All the better for the views.

The summit is beyond ambitions of this book (see **102 Hikes**). Anyhow, the best panoramas of lowland waterways and cities are from the ridge, and the trail that far, on a south slope, melts free of snow early in spring — or, often, in the middle of winter. The trip thus is a prime snowline-prober. Yet it's also, from late May to early July, a prime rhododendron-blossom walk.

Drive Highway 101 to ¾ mile north of the Duckabush River bridge. A couple hundred feet south from where the Black Point (signed) road goes east, take the unsigned road turning off west, paralleling the highway a bit before veering inland (at the turn a private driveway goes straight).

The road — a logging railroad grade from the 1920s — is signed "Not maintained for public travel" and the narrow, rough start is discouraging. However, the track is maintained and never gets much worse than at the beginning. At 1¾ miles is a broad powerline swath with views south to the Duckabush valley and Hood Canal. In another 1¼ miles, after a switchback, after a Y (go left), the powerline is recrossed and then paralleled for ¾ mile, to views north to the Dosewallips valley and Hood Canal. At 1170 feet, where the right is to the Dose, the left (perhaps signed "Heliport 3") is to Jupiter. Here is a logical spot to park for a snowline-probing road-walk; from here on the forest is deliciously green-mossy, the way is a lovely footroad. At a fork ¼ mile from the 1170 Y, switchback left. With no further distracting sideroads, switchback upward a final 2 miles to the road-end, 6½ miles from the highway. Elevation, 2050 feet.

Ignore the jeep track climbing higher and take the pleasant trail, in nice though scrubby forest dating from a 1920s fire. (From the looks of the struggling trees, there'll be no crop here to interest loggers until about the year 2130.) Switchbacking steeply, in ¼ mile, at 2350 feet, the trail switchbacks right

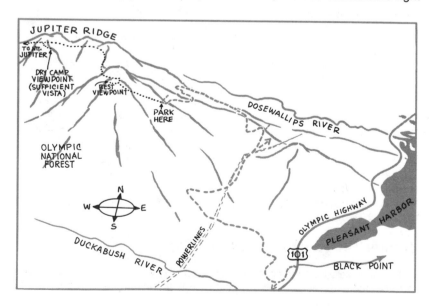

The Brothers from Jupiter Ridge

again; an obvious, meager path leads off the end to a mossy bald and the best views of the trip. Look down down to the Duckabush River and out to its delta thrust into Hood Canal. See cars on the highway, boats on the water. Hear dogs barking. North and south sweeps the waterway and beyond is the Kitsap Peninsula, bumpy with Green and Gold Mountains, beyond which lies Bremerton. More saltwater, beyond which lies Seattle. Is that Tacoma down there in the murk? Beyond all are the Cascades and Rainier.

After this there is no single goshamighty panorama, but as the trail switchbacks higher in little trees and rhododendrons and salal and beargrass more windows open. At about 2750 feet the path gentles and becomes an airy, open stroll. At 2 miles, 3200 feet, the way rounds a spur and passes a dry camp. A couple hundred feet out on the spur is a superb picnic spot, mossy rock slabs to spread food and bodies on while admiring the Duckabush and The Brothers. This Sufficient Vista is suggested as the turnaround because not for miles are there new views and the summit is still 2500 feet higher and 5 more miles, a real trudge.

Round trip to Sufficient Vista 4 miles, allow 3 hours
High point 3200 feet, elevation gain 1200 feet
March-December

INDEX

INDEX

Dungeness Spit